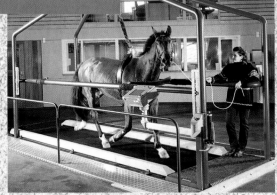

Advertisements

Impressum

Editor

Dr. Arno Lindner, Science Consult
Laurahöhe 14
D–45289 Essen, Germany
Tel: +49 - 2 01 - 57 18 873
Fax: +49 - 2 01 - 57 18 874
E-mail: ArnoLindner@t-online.de

Copyright

Dr. Arno Lindner, Essen

Layout

GESTALTmanufaktur GmbH, Dortmund
Frank Allery

Print

Lensing Druck, Dortmund

ISBN – 3 – 00 – 006051 – 0

Table of contents

Author's Index

Foreword

It has worked again: CESMAS! Thanks to all those who have contributed to making it work: committee members and friends, sponsors, exhibitors, participants.

Show-jumping is by far the most widespread equine sports discipline. Thus it is amazing to see how little scientific information is available on it, and on the horses bred, fed, trained, conditioned and treated to compete in the discipline. This book contains a good overview of state-of-the-art information on the Show Jumper. In addition, it contains selected papers on all aspects of sport horses presented at the Conference on Equine Sports Medicine and Science in Messina and Taormina, Italy between May 14th and 16th 2000. We would like to wish readers pleasure in reading the book.

Adriana Ferlazzo and Arno Lindner

Scientific Committee

Warwick M. Bayly, USA
Giovani Caola, Italy
Hilary Clayton, USA
Anne Couroucé, France
Jean-Marie Denoix, France

Sue Dyson, UK
Arne Holm, Norway
Arne Lindholm, Sweden
José Luis López Rivero, Spain
Marianne Sloet van Oldruitenborgh-Oosterbaan, Netherlands

Local and organizing committee

Daniela Alberghina
Vincenzo Aronica
Ester Fazio
Mario Graber, Switzerland
Pietro Medica

Sponsors

CORTEX Biophysik GmbH, Germany:
MetaVet®, Portable mask for measurement of respiratory parameters
KAGRA AG, Switzerland:
Mustang 2000®, highspeed treadmill
HMT AG, Switzerland:
EquiTron®, Shock-wave therapy machine

1 SPORTS SCIENCE

1.1 Overview articles

How to breed for elite show jumper?

Take home message

An overview of the methods applied for breeding elite show jumpers is given. Two main sources of information are available: competition results and evaluation of the sporting ability of the 3-year-old horses by the means of free jumping tests performed in breeding shows.

The use of the competition results for genetic evaluation is performed using a Best Linear Unbiased Predictor (BLUP) procedure on two performance criteria: the annual earning and ranking criteria. A new jumping test is proposed to measure the jumping ability of young horses using a gait analysis system. It is applied in breeding shows.

Introduction

Show jumping is the main equestrian sport practised in France. About 36,100 horses compete in 11,800 events each year. There are two types of show jumping: one type is a breeding event reserved for young horses of 4, 5 and 6 years of age, and the other type is sporting events for experienced horses. The breeding events are included in the breeding plan to test the jumping ability of the males and females. Each year, the best young horses compete in these events and do the final in Fontainebleau in early September. The mares and stallions are better evaluated by their offsprings and relatives which have performed in all events.

The jumping ability is a complex trait which requires a set of physiological, behavioural and mechanical characteristics that give the horse reactivity, muscular power and jumping skill. These factors are both genetically and non-genetically determined. Many genes are involved to explain the genetic component of jumping ability which should be considered as a continuous quantitative trait. The polygenic mode of inheritance allows to calculate the heritability for measuring the percentage of the trait that could be transmitted genetically from the parents to the offspring. The higher the heritability of the trait, the more efficient the selection on that trait will be.

In order to improve a trait or a small number of traits by genetic selection the following steps should be considered to have good results:

1. Define the breeding objective as precisely as possible
2. Measure the traits included in the breeding objective easily and acurately
3. Estimate the heritability and genetic correlations of the traits
4. Apply a rigourous selection plan on the traits for a population as large as possible

The purpose of this review is to present the main strategies that have been applied for breeding good show jumpers.

I Define the objective of selection: performance in show jumping

In order to improve the characteristics of a breed by genetic selection a clear objective of selection has to be defined and measured. Two strategies have been applied successfully to select good jumpers: a single trait selection on performance obtained in competitions and a multiple traits selection on young horses evaluated before competitions.

- The selection of the French Saddle horses (Selle Français) is based on a single trait: annual performance in competition. The breeding objective is the annual performance in show jumping which is measured by a phenotypic performance index (ISO). A genetic index is also calculated each year on the basis of the performance records. The first step of selection can take place at the age of 4 years after the final of the national championship in Fontainebleau.

- The selection of the Hanovrian and other German horses is based on multi traits measured during a stallion performance test at the age of 3 years for the stallions and at 3 and 4 years for the mares during a one day test. The selection is based on several traits: ridibility, free jumping, jumping course, walk, trot, gallop, cross country. The weight given to each trait for the genetic evaluation is different for dressage and jumping. After the performance test, the stallion can be licenced, and a genetic evaluation based on performance records in competitions is performed.

The selection for show jumping should be conducted independently of the selection for dressage because it has been shown that there is a negative genetic correlation or no correlation at all between the two disciplines. However, it is possible to reach a compromise to breed a horse with mixed ability.

II Information available for breeding show jumpers

In order to breed a good show jumper, objective information is required to select the mares and stallions for maximizing the chance to obtain an offspring with a good jumping ability (Figure 1).

Figure ❶   Information on jumping ability available for breeding elite show jumpers

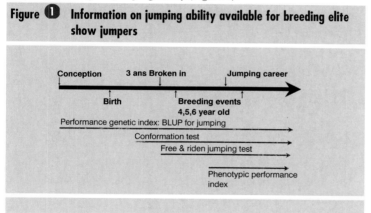

The genetic indexes could be used to select the parents and simulate the jumping potential of the offspring before conception. Between the day of birth and the age of 4 years, jumping tests and other measurements such as conformation and muscular characteristics could be used but the information is not sufficiently specific to predict the performance in show jumping. With horses that are older than 4 years, the jumping performances in competition are recorded and will be used to estimate the sporting and genetic value of the horse which could become a good sire. The genetic values of the mares and stallions are better estimated when their offsprings compete with success in breeding events.

II-1 Performance index

The performance records of all the show jumping events are collected by the French Equestrian Federation. These data are used to calculate a phenotypic and genetic index of jumping performance.

The performance level is measured by the annual performance index (ISO=Indice de Saut d'Obstacles). This criterion is computed and published annually for all the French jumping horses. The average national ISO is considerd to be equal 100 (1 Standard deviation = 20) and this index is normally distributed in order to supply a linear scale for comparing jumping ability (Figure 2) (Langlois 1975).

Figure ❷   Distribution of variables in jumping in 1981 in France

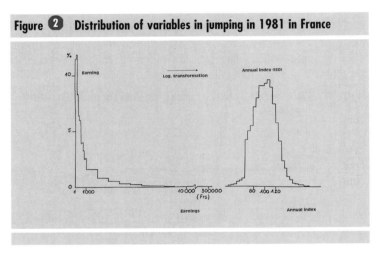

It is calculated by taking into account both the annual earnings logarithm and the ranks of the horse in all the events.

The heritability of jumping performance has been estimated for both criteria (Table 1): These performance criteria are moderately heritable and the accuracy of these values is good. A high pressure of selection should be applied on these criteria to choose the stallions and mares for improving the performance of the offsprings.

Table ❶   Heritability of show jumping criteria

Performance measurement	Heritability	Repeatability
Log(annual earnings)	0.20	0.45
Ranking records	0.15	0.29

Explanations
(Langlois 1975; Tavernier 1990)

Genetic index

A genetic index is calculated using a best linear unbiased predictor (BLUP) under animal model which takes into account all the performance records available on all the relatives. The national mean is 0, and a good mare or stallion should have a positive value up to +10. The best mares and stallions can be characterized by their genetic indexes calculated on the basis of the jumping performance obtained firstly by all their relatives, secondly by the horse himself and thirdly by their offsprings. The genetic index becomes more acurate when the horse itself performed in competition and then when its own offspring also performed in competitions. The measure of accuracy is given by the coefficient of determination (CD). The greater it is (<1) the more accurate the BLUP index will be.

Performance tests

Direct evaluation of jumping ability can be a good strategy to select the young horses which have more potential. Free or ridden jumping tests are used in several countries during the "performance test" or breeding events. The judges evaluate the approach strides, jumping style and muscular power at take-off.

In Germany, the jumping ability of the stallions and mares are evaluated at the ages of 2.5, 3 and 4 years. The heritabilities of these criteria were estimated in Germany and were rather high (Table 2).

In France, the 3-year-old horses can compete in breeding shows organised all over the country. There are final events in each region and then a national show in September in Fontainebleau. The horses are judged at walk and trot in hand and perform a free jumping test. However, the results of these breeding events are not used in the breeding plan. They are only used as a marketing tool. Some improvement of the early selection is necessary, and the use of gait analysis is currently tested in breeding shows.

Table 2   **Heritability of the jumping ability evaluated during performance tests.**

Criteria	Heritability
Free jumping test	0.56-0.76
Jumping parcours test	0.70

Explanations
(Bruns et al 1985)

III Early evaluation of jumping ability using gait analysis

It is known that the measurement of a trait could improve the efficiency of the genetic selection. A trait which is evaluated qualitatively or semi quantitatively by an expert is always less heritable than the same trait measured by a device. Consequently, the use of physiological and/or gait measurements could improve early evaluation of jumping ability. Gait variables provide a quantitative measurement which gives more details than traditional judgement. However, gait analysis cannot test all the components of the sporting ability. For example, ridibility and behaviour should still be evaluated by an expert.

Exercise physiology and biomechanics of jumping

The jumping exercise requires a set of physiological and gait characteristics that contribute to the jumping skill:

- a high muscular power in the back and hind limbs;
- a good coordination of the limbs at take-off.

Cardiac, hematological and biochemical variables have been studied in horses competing in show jumping events of 4 levels in order to compare their physiological response (Barrey and Valette 1993). Heart rate during the jumping course rose to peak values ranging from 183 to 206 beats/min; the packed cell volume reached extreme values ranging from 42 to 60 %; the blood lactate reached maximal values ranging from 3.25 mmol/l to 5.3 mmol/l. These results indicated that horses cantered aerobically and an anaerobic contribution was required for jumping. The great differences of the horse performance levels were poorly correlated to the variation observed in cardiac, hematological and lactate variables. Consequently, a show jumper should be trained for aerobic exercise but no prediction of the jumping ability could be done on the basis of cardiac, hematological and lactate variables.

The percentages of each muscle fibre type influence the muscular power which is necessary at take-off phase. Horses with a good performance in show jumping competition had a higher percentage of fast myosin heavy chains in the gluteus muscle than poor performers: good jumpers = 74.1 % > poor jumpers = 67.8 % of fast myosin heavy chains.

The average performance index obtained in show jumping was more correlated with the fast myosin heavy chain percentage in the gluteus medius (0.47) than in the biceps femoris muscle (0.34) (Barrey et al 1999).

The gallop and jump characteristics are more related to jumping performance than the other physiological traits. However, the biomechanic of jumping is a complex phenomenon because the horse should be considered as a set of articulated body segments which is much more complicated than a rigid body system like a bullet. Theoretically, the Newtonian laws should be applied to each segment in translation and rotation. There are two complementary approaches to study the body in motion:

- Kinetics or dynamics is the study of cause of the motion, which can be explained by the force applied to the body, its mass distribution and its dimensions. Kinetics is concerned with forces, accelerations, energy, and work which are also in relation to kinematic variables such as acceleration and velocity.
- Kinematics is the study of changes in the position of the body segments in space during a specified time. The motions are described quantitatively by linear and angular variables that relate time, displacement,

velocity and acceleration. No reference is made in kinematics to the cause of motion.

The shape, height and width of the obstacle dictate the characteristics of the ballistic flight of the horse's centre of gravity (CG) and the trajectories of its hooves. These have to be well positioned relative to the location of the poles in space. The jump involves the three main mechanical factors (Figure 3):

Figure ❸   Mechanics of the jumping phase

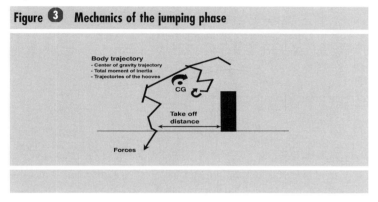

- the distance of the hindlimb hooves from the base of the obstacle at take-off (Leach et al 1984; Deuel and Park 1990; Barrey et al 1993);
- the external force impulses developed by the fore and hindlimbs at take-off (Merkens et al 1991, Schamhardt et al 1993);
- and the rotation characteristics of the body around the CG in the sagittal plane (Galloux and Barrey 1996).

The impulse of the external forces applied by the hooves on the ground at take-off determines the ballistic flight of the CG by setting the magnitude and direction of the initial velocity at the beginning of the airborne phase. The value and influence of the velocity components at take-off has been demonstrated in high and broad jumps (Clayton et al 1995). Moreover, the external forces exerted by the hindlimbs at take-off also determine the total kinetic moment during the airborne phase and thus influence the characteristics of the body rotation over the obstacle. From a theoretical point of view, the external forces on the jumping horse appear to be important factors for clearing obstacles. The range of these forces has been explored under experimental conditions both directly by using force plates (Merkens et al 1991, Schamhardt et al 1993) and indirectly using accelerometers placed near to the presumed centre of gravity of the body (Preuschoft 1989). It is assumed that individual variations in jumping techniques and abilities should be related to differences in the external forces developed by the fore and hindlimbs at take-off. Thus, the acceleration recordings located near to the CG should be able to detect the differences between the techniques of good and poor jumpers. We developed a gait analysis system (Equimetrix) to measure the dorsoventral accelerations of horses competing in show jumping in order to study the relationships of these values with their actual jumping technique.

Kinematic studies of elite show jumping horses were undertaken during Olympic and World Equestrian Games. They allowed a description of some characteristics to distinguish a good jumping technique. However, in order to know better the relation between the jumping technique and the jumping performance, a more heterogeneous and larger population of horses has to be studied to have a greater variability of jumping abilities. This could be done when a test procedure is available to rapidly collect the more interesting locomotor variables.

During the 1988 Seoul Olympic Games, the kinematics of 29 horses jumping oxer was analysed (Deuel and Park 1990). Fewer total penalities were associated with lower velocities during the jump strides, closer take-off hindlimb placements and closer landing forelimbs placements. Another study on elite horses jumping a high vertical fence demonstrated that the push-off produced by the hind limbs at take off explained most of the energy required for clearing the fence (van den Bogert et al 1993). The action of the forelimbs should be limited to putting the body of the horse into a good orientation before the final push-off of the hind limbs.

A more vertical component of the initial velocity was observed in the horses that successfully cleared a 4.5 m wide water jump (Clayton et al 1995). The angle of the velocity relative to the horizontal was 15% in the sucessful jumps as compared to 12% in unsuccessful jumps, and the vertical components of the velocity were about 0.5 m/s greater in the sucessfully completed jumps than in the unsuccessfully completed jumps. This initial velocity was generated by the impulse of the hind limbs and determined the ballistic flight characteristics of the body.

The previous kinematic data agree with our first kinetic study which showed that poor jumpers produced a high acceleration peak with the frontlimbs and a low acceleration peak with the hind limbs (Barrey and Galloux 1997). This result means that the hind limbs of a poor jumper produce a weaker force to push-off than the ones of good jumpers. This force determines the ballistic flight of the centre of gravity and also the characteristics of the body rotation over the obstacle during the airborne phase.

A fault was significantly associated with the production of a lower acceleration peak by the hind limbs at take-off, and a high forelimbs / hind limbs ratio between acceleration peaks at take-off. The final push-off by the hindlimbs was considered to be the major factor contributing to the success of the jump (Van den Bogert et al 1993). In this case, a fault could be explained by a weakness in the hindlimb acceleration impulse resulting from inadequate or poor coordination of the hindlimb motions. The group of "poor jumpers" exhibited some constant characteristics that were observed even if they jumped without fault (Table 3):

Table ❸ Means of the gait variables measured during the approach and at take-off phase.

Variables	Fault		Faultless	
	Good jumper	Poor jumper	Good jumper	Poor jumper
Stride frequency (str./s)	1.81 a	1.73 b	1.81 a	1.76 b
Vertical activity (g^2)	0.65 a	0.85 b	0.65 a	0.73 ab
Forelimbs acc. Peak (g)	2,50 a	2.92 a	2.41 b	2.76 a
Hind limbs acc. Peak (g)	1.24 a	1.15 a	1.55 b	1.32 a
F/H acc. Ratio	2.21 a	3.43 b	1.82 c	2.52 d

Explantions
means followed by the same letter on a line are not significantely differnt at $p<0.05$

- a higher forelimb/hind limb acceleration ratio at take-off (>2);
- more penalities were recorded with horses that cantered at a low stride frequency (lower or equal to 1.76 stride/s) and suddenly reduced their stride frequency at take-off.

The stride frequency and thus the velocity of the approach strides were probably too low to produce enough kinetic energy for a good jump. At take-off, the acceleration peak of the forelimbs was higher and the peak of the hind limbs was lower than in good jumpers. This phenomenon could be explained by too much braking by the forelimbs at the end of the last approach stride, followed by a weak acceleration impulse of the hind limbs.

Variations in individual jumping ability were mainly related to differences in stride frequency values as well as the changes during the end of the approach, and the acceleration impulses produced by the fore and hind limbs at take-off. A good balance between these two successive acceleration impulses and a specific range of frequency values were required for an adequate jumping technique.

A jumping test applied in routine in breeding events

After this first kinetic study on experienced show jumpers, a jumping test was designed for 3-year-old horses for early selection. About 200 young horses were tested during breeding events before competing in show jumping. The horse is equiped with a gait analysis system (Equimétrix, TM). This device measures the dorsoventral and longitudinal accelerations during the test in order to analyse the approach strides, take-off, jumping and landing phase. The accelerometers are fixed in the sagittal plane between the muscle pectoralis ascendens by means of an elastic girth fastened onto the horse. This anatomical location was chosen in order to provide the good stability for transducer and for its closeness to the horse's CG. The transducers are connected to a mini recorder which is placed on top of the girth. The horse performs a free jumping test in an arena of 17 x 40 m with semicircular curves. After 5 min warming up, it jumps a vertical fence of 1.10 m high (5 trials) and then an oxer fence 1.10 x 1.10 m (5 trials). After the end of the test, the recorder is removed from the horse and the data are transferred to a computer.

Temporal and kinetic variables are calculated with a specific software to analyse the approach strides, take-off, jump and landing phase (Figure 4). For each jump, 15 variables are calculated on the acceleration-time curve using a specific signal processing software. The mean values of the 5 trials are calculated for each type of fence. The main temporal and peaks of acceleration variables measured on the acceleration curves are:

- Approach phase: The mean stride frequency and the dorsoventral activity are computed for 3-15 approach strides to single obstacles.
- Take-off phase: The acceleration peak produced at take-off initially by the forelimbs and secondly by the hind limbs were measured. The sum and the ratio of these acceleration peaks are calculated. The maximum longitudinal acceleration at take-off is measured. The maximal dorsoventral speed reached immediatly after take-off is estimated.
- Landing phase: The acceleration peak produced at landing of the forelimbs is also measured.

According to the ranking in the breeding events, a good jumping ability is characterized by the following jumping characteristics:

- The horse approaches the fence with a stride frequency at least equal to 1.86 strides/s and a high vertical activity (>29 Hz.g^2).
- The balance between the acceleration peaks of the forelimbs and hind limbs should be low for indicating a high push off of the hind limbs (< 1.93)
- The sum of the peaks of dorsoventral accelerations of the forelimbs and hind limbs should be high ($>2.37g$). The maximum velocity at take-off should be high (>1.98 m/s).

The data collected in breeding events for show jumping started in 1997. The horses that have been tested at the age of 3 years start to compete at

4 years. The number of values of performance and of the variables measured during the tests entered in the correlation analysis increases each year, and will possibly allow to improve the prediction of performance.

Conclusion

According to the international results in show jumping over the last 20 years, two strategies of genetic selection have proveed successful for breeding elite show jumpers :
- one single trait model based on performance records obtained after 3 years of age;
- one multi traits model based on performance tests obtained at 3 years of age.

Both breeding plans have advantages and drawbacks but they should be combined for increasing the genetic progress. The pressure of selection could be applied earlier and could be higher at each step. Because of the earlier step of selection of young horses, it should be possible to reduce the time between generations which is very long in horses (about 10 years). The use of gait measurements could improve the efficiency of the performance test by increasing the accuracy of the scores. However, the testing procedure should be applied on the largest possible population to detect the best horses among genetic variability of the population.

Figure ❹   Example of a dorso-ventral acceleration recording of the approach, jump and move of strides

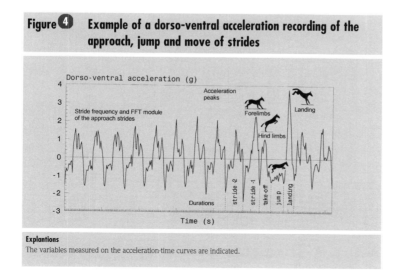

Explantions
The variables measured on the acceleration-time curves are indicated.

Biotin
A missing element in horse health

Roche Vitamins Europe Ltd
CH–4002 Basel · Fax: ++41 61/688 11 53

Feeding the Show Jumper

Since the horse was first domesticated around 5000 BC its role in society has varied according to man's requirements but has been based on its ability to run and jump, pull and carry. This century has seen the horse change from having important roles in the military, agriculture and transportation to becoming part of the expanding leisure industry. A large variety of competitions (show-jumping, gymkana, vaulting, racing, eventing, polo, showing, dressage etc.) have developed to provide a competitive angle. These sporting activities vary, not only in the intensity and duration of the exercise undertaken, but also in the degree of skill and aptitude needed by horse and rider.

At first glance these different competitions have very different demands. Flat racing could be considered to be at one end of the duration/intensity spectrum, with American Quarter horses racing at speeds up to 20 m/s over 400m. In contrast an endurance ride may take place over several days at speeds around 5-6 m/s (on average). The show jumper may only have 3 minute competition bouts, but this may include a number of fences, each of which could be 5ft or more in height and spread. Many believe the 3-day-event competition to be one of the most demanding equestrian activities as it involves a number of phases including dressage, steeplechasing, "endurance", showjumping and cross-country jumping within a relatively short time period.

For the show jumper ideally the horse has to have the strength, agility and ability to produce a clear show jumping round and then the controllable speed as well as suppleness, agility and ability to compete against the clock. For the 3 day eventer, at the event it means that "ideally" or "hopefully" one has a horse with sufficient sparkle, presence and yet controllable power to undertake and succeed in the dressage phase. With the speed, endurance , jumping stamina and skill to complete the "X-country" phase with no jumping or time faults and still have on the "3rd" day the stamina, agility and ability to finish up with a clear show jumping round.

But for all types of competition the horse also has to have sufficient reserves to go on to compete successfully on other occasions. For the show jumper this may mean later that day or the next and the next. In addition, a horse cannot make it to the 3DE or Show jumping competition without having been healthy and active during its training. This is true for all performance horses regardless of their use and so really we should be feeding the performance horse for health and activity be it a show jumper or a 3DE or whatever.

Show jumpers ideally need to be well-conditioned, responsive horses without excess energy or excitable behaviour when in the ring and yet with sufficient stamina and explosive energy to be able to clear the jumps. The effect of any diet on their behaviour is therefore an important consideration and the majority are fed relative to their own temperament, how they are kept, and the nature of the training as well as the type of ride preferred by the rider.

This means that, as for other disciplines, there is no single correct way to feed "a show jumper" and therefore only general principles can be discussed.

What role can nutrition play?

The horse naturally is a social animal, which lives in groups and spends the majority of its time foraging in a diverse and seasonally variable environment. Today, our horses tend to be kept in stables and/or on managed pastures and we are now responsible for their nutrition.

- Good nutrition will only help a horse to be able to compete optimally; it will not improve the intrinsic ability of the horse (or rider).
- Poor or inappropriate nutrition on the other hand may impose limits on an animal's ability to perform.

Critical to feeding any performance horse for health and vitality is the appropriate and adequate supply of energy, especially during the training phases.

Why is energy supply and utilisation so important?

The supply of energy is crucial for life and movement. If a horse is fed too little energy for its needs it will tend to become dull and lethargic and/or lose weight and/or become clinically ill. If a horse is fed too much energy or inappropriate energy it may become hyperactive and/or gain weight and/or become ill.

Horses are fundamentally non-ruminant herbivores, which means that they are suited to eating high fibre diets due to continual microbial fermentation within the caecum and colon. Domestication, and an increasing demand for horses to perform at levels that require energy intakes above those able to be provided by their more "natural" diet of fresh forage, has resulted in the inclusion, in particular, of cereal grains and their by-products as well as supplemental fat in many horse diets.

Energy is supplied to the horse via its diet but fundamentally energy is not a nutrient. The chemical energy or gross energy contained within feeds needs to be converted into a form of energy that the cells can use for work or movement (useable or net energy). Ultimately the "currency" used to fuel this movement is Adenosine Triphosphate (ATP).

Dietary energy is provided to the horse by four dietary energy sources:

- Hydrolysable carbohydrates e.g. sugars & starch
- Non starch polysaccharides: component of dietary fibre e.g., Cellulose, pectins, hemicelluloses etc.
- Fats
- Proteins (not a preferred source- see below)

In general, a high proportion of the starch ingested is degraded to glucose before absorption. However, a proportion of the starch and, depending on the extent of lignification, a varying proportion of the dietary fibre will be subjected to microbial fermentation, primarily in the large intestine, producing predominantly short chain or volatile fatty acids. The extent to which cereal starch provides glucose or volatile fatty acids as the end result of digestion will depend on its precaecal and even its pre-ileal digestibility which, in turn, will vary according to the feedstuff under consideration and the extent and nature of the processing to which it has been subjected (Frape 1986, Frape 1994, Kienzle et al 1992). See figure 1.

Exercise requires the expenditure of metabolically derived energy in the form of ATP. At certain speeds, under steady state conditions, the ATP used can be regenerated by oxidative phosphorylation or aerobic metabolism of fats and glucose. For short periods of non steady-state work at high exercise intensities ATP can be regenerated by net anaerobic metabolism of glucose with accumulation of lactate in muscle and blood (Harris et al 1995). The efficiency of the conversion of chemical energy (derived ultimately from the diet) to mechanical work is only about 20-25%. Most of the energy released appears as heat (Kronfeld 1996, Harris 1997).

Different feeds and feedstuffs contain differing amount of the raw chemical energy and the efficiency of their conversion to usable or net energy also differs widely (Harris 1998). It is well known from practical experience that it is very difficult if not impossible to feed a successful 3DE or SJ or racehorse on grass alone and especially not on grass hay alone. We therefore tend to feed concentrates or sweet feeds/coarse mixes to such animals. Recently there has been increasing use of supplemental vegetable oil in horse diets. Initially this was only common in the endurance discipline but it is being increasingly recommended for many performance horses including the show jumpers and eventers.

Figure ❶ **Schematic picture of where the three main energy sources are digested and how the end products of digestion are utilized**

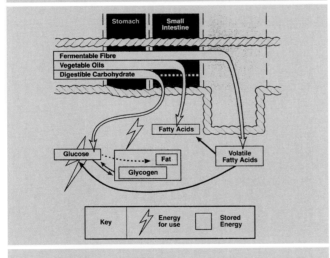

Cereals have more net energy than does hay which in turn contains more than twice the net or useable energy than straw. Hay produces much more spare "lost" heat than do cereals so is much more "internally heating" and is therefore especially useful in Winter. Vegetable oils contain proportionally more net energy than the cereals.

Figure ❷　Comparative Net Energy values UFC/kg DM:

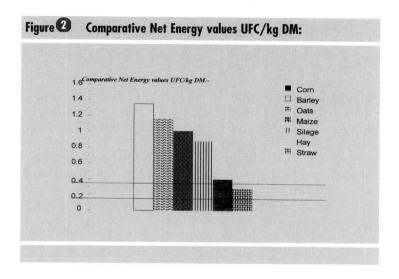

How does this relate to the performance horse?

Take the example of a (~ 500 kg) horse in hard work which needs approximately 60 MJ of Net energy to live and compete. If it is assumed that all this energy is to be supplied by its daily ration and it was fed only hay it would need to eat around 25 kg of hay! – which it could not possibly manage. If cereals (which provide more than twice the net or useable energy weight for weight than hay) were substituted as part of the diet then the ration would be more realistic. If in addition to the cereals, very energy dense oil was added to the diet then it would easily be possible to match such an energy intake requirement with appetite (Kronfeld 1996, Harris 1997). This explains that even though animals vary in their energy efficiency it would be difficult if not impossible to maintain weight and energy output in regularly competing show jumpers only fed hay.

What are the possible benefits of oil supplementation?

Feeding fat supplemented diets to horse has resulted in a range of effects on a variety of physiological, metabolic parameters as well as on performance. These variations may result from the variances in the study protocols and horses used in these trials; but because of the variable results, a untied view of the benefits on performance is not yet available.

Long term fat supplementation in combination with appropriate training, however, has been proposed to result in the following adaptations which could result in improved performance (see also Harris 1997; Potter et al 1992):-

* increased mobilisation of free fatty acids (FFA)
* increased speed of uptake of FFA into muscle (Orme et al 1997) – often considered to be rate limiting
* a glycogen sparing effect so that fatigue is delayed and performance improved – could be especially important in endurance activities
* increased high intensity exercise capacity (Eaton et al 1995)
* increased pre-exercise muscle glycogen levels (Meyers et al 1989; Scott et al 1992; Hughes et al 1995).

In order to obtain metabolic benefits from the feeding of oil or oil supplemented diets, in addition to those associated with its high energy density and lack of starch content, the oil needs to be fed for several months.

The increase in the energy density of the feed (vegetable oils have about 2.5 times as much digestible energy as maize/corn and 3 times as much as oats) effectively means that the horse may take in more energy even if its appetite decreases (which happens in some show jumpers when in hard work and regularly competed). Replacing forage with cereals and/or fat may help not only by decreasing the amount of feed the animal has to eat to obtain the required amount of energy (important as horses have a finite appetite) but it is believed that it reduces the amount of gut ballast/fill, so making the horse less heavy (Kronfeld and Harris 1997) – but it should be noted that this should not be taken to extremes as an adequate fibre intake (normally recommended to provide forage at levels equivalent to more than 1% of the bodyweight/day) is needed to relieve boredom, assist with fluid dynamics and maintain a healthy hind-gut. In fact one of the other advantages of feeding fat is that it means more fibre can often be fed and less cereals or hydrolysable starch needs to be fed whilst still maintaining the desired energy intake. This in turn helps to maintain the microfloral population in the hind-gut and prevent over production, in particular, of lactic acid which could lead to digestive and other metabolic disturbances (Kronfeld and Harris 1997).

A fat supplemented diet may also have behavioural advantages over high cereal starch diets which may possibly be an added advantage for the show jumping rider (Holland et al 1996). As fat in the diet is more efficiently converted to useable energy than feeds such as hay and cereals this may reduce the heat load on the horse, which may be particularly useful when competing under hot and humid conditions – it also reduces the water requirement. The relative heat production ratios illustrate this clearly: if one takes the heat production at rest (Heat lost/net or useable energy produces) for long chain fatty acids (from oil) as being 100% it would be 145% for glucose (from cereal starches and sugars), 350% for amino acids (from protein) but 410% for the short chain fatty acids (from fermentable fibre) (Kronfeld & Harris 1997).

Feeding a low starch, high fibre diet, (which is supplemented if necessary with oil) is recommended for the feeding of horses that are prone to suffering from Tying up (Harris 1999).

Practical Hints

- Supplemental fat or oil diets can be supplied in four main ways
  a. As an oil supplemented, manufactured diet – the advantage here is that such diets should come ready balanced with respect to the protein, vitamins and minerals intake that they provide when fed with forage (and as required salt). Can be a simple, practical and convenient way to feed high fat diets.
  b. High fat supplemental feedstuffs – (such as rice bran), which are also high in fibre and usually low in starch. However, many of the rice brans available have the same disadvantages of wheat bran in that they have a very imbalanced Calcium to Phosphorus content
  c. Supplemental animal fat – many horses find most animal fats to be unpalatable and they seem often to be more likely to cause digestive upsets. Their use is not to be recommended.
  d. Supplemental vegetable oils – such as corn oil or soya oil.
- Any supplemental oil or oil supplemented feed should be introduced slowly. Dietary fats are usually hydrolysed in the small intestine and the capacity to hydrolyse lipids seems to adapt in herbivores over a week or two. Horses have been shown to be able to digest and utilise up to 20% of the diet as fat although around 10% of the daily intake has been suggested in the literature to provide the maximal beneficial metabolic effects (Kronfeld 1996, Kronfeld and Harris 1997). Levels of 5 – 8 % (~ 0.5 – 0.8kg in a 500 kg horse in work) in the total diet are more common in some high performing horses and many performance horses (~ 500 kg BW) can be fed up to 400 mls (~ 370 g) daily in divided doses without any problems – provided that it has been introduced gradually and is not rancid.
- It is very important to note that supplemental oil does not provide any additional protein, vitamins or minerals. If the horse is not receiving

sufficient, for its work load, from its basal diet, then an appropriate additional mix may be needed (usually it is helpful to contact the Nutritional Helpline of the feed being fed and inform them of the diet and workload, and get direct advice appropriate for their supplement) or consider a manufactured, balanced, high oil feed.

- It is recommended that additional Vitamin E be fed in combination with any supplemental Vegetable oil. Exact recommendations are not known but an additional (above requirements) 100 iu Vitamin E per 100 mls of added supplemental oil is the author's current recommendation.

What is the right type and amount of energy to feed your show jumper?

Horses are individuals and vary in many of the areas which influence what they need to be fed, in order to provide us with the nature and type of ride we would like – (accepting that this is not always possible to achieve nutritionally – some horses seem to be "extremely lively" whatever you do or feed – others remain stoical)! However, what might make one horse fat or excitable may be ideal for its stable mate. Breed differences also need to be taken into consideration Kohnke (1998) suggests that the daily energy requirements for a show jumper of around 500-600 kg will be around 130 –145MJ DE although many will not require as much. Horses are like us: – HARD WORK does not necessarily mean high-energy requirements; LIGHT/MEDIUM work does not necessarily mean low energy requirements : and what we each mean by hard and light work will vary.

If the amount that needs to be fed to enable the horse's desired body condition to be maintained and the rider to have the type of ride they prefer, is less than the manufacturers recommend for that work load, then an appropriate vitamin and mineral supplement may need to be provided (usually it is helpful to contact the Nutritional Helpline of the complementary feed being fed and inform them of the diet, workload and get direct advice appropriate for their feed) or it may be beneficial to change to a diet which is less energy dense so that sufficient can be fed to provide the appropriate amount of vitamins and minerals required.

Kohnke (1998) recommends that approximately 45-50 % of the ration is grain when show jumpers are in hard training with the total amount of feed restricted to a maximum of 12.5 –14kg relative to type and stress of exercise, body frame and temperament.

Which cereal is best?

In general, processing has relatively little effect on the small intestinal dige-stion of oat starch (which is around 80-90%) but it has a significant effect on the small intestinal starch digestibility of barley and in particular corn, increasing it from around 30 to 50 to 90% for whole, ground and popped corn respectively (Meyer et al 1993). So unless the horse has poor dentiti-on there is little advantage in processing oats (& therefore increasing the risk of them going "off" more quickly). Popping, flaking, or micronising of corn/maize, however, may be very advantageous to maximise the useable energy obtained from the feed.

The use of processed corn can be advantageous especially in the smal-ler framed horses where you wish to reduce the bulk of the feed being fed as the relationship between weight and volume, as shown below, varies, e.g. Oats weigh less for a given volume than corn so if measured in volu-mes you, will effectively, be feeding less weight of oats and far less actual energy. Ideally we should always feed by weight and not volume.

Table ❶   Comparison of cereals

Feed	kg/L i.e. Vol.	Digestible Energy – MJ/kg	Relative feeding value to corn by weight	Relative feeding value to corn by volume
Corn	0.8	14.2	100	100
Oats – regular	0.4	11.7	85	45
Oats- naked	0.7	15.9	110	95
Barley	0.7	13.8	95	85

Practical Hints

Feed smaller , more frequent concentrate/cereal based meals (ideally aro-und 2 kgs/meal for a 500 kg horse). Divide the feed into 3-4 meals a day rather than 2 large cereal based feeds. (Harris 1999)

*   The horse is naturally a "trickle feeder" (i.e. horses evolved to bite, chew thoroughly and then swallow small amounts of highly fibrous diets almost continuously for up to 18 hrs/day)
*   The horse has a small, relatively inelastic, stomach – limited capacity.
*   The smaller the meal the slower the stomach empties (as the rate of empty-ing is proportional to the square root of the volume).
*   The smaller the meal size, the slower the transit time through the gut which means more chance for digestion of starches in the small intestine.
*   Small cereal based meals don't overwhelm the ability of the small intestine to digest starch.

- This means less of the more easily and quickly fermentable carbohydrate (especially starch) reaching the hind-gut, so reducing the fluctuations in microbial populations and the possibility of adverse consequences such as colic and laminitis.

Why add chaff?

The jaw sweeps 60,000 times a day when grazing. The duration of feed intake depends on the type of feed and the size of the animal. The jaw movements in horses at grass are relatively wide and long but when eating hay and in particular cereals or pelleted feeds the movement is confined which increases the chances of developing lateral and medial hooks as well as speeding up the time of ingestion.

The nature of the feeds fed to horses will dramatically influence the chewing rate and speed of ingestion. The average 500 kg horse will chew 3400 times/kg of hay consumed taking about 40 minutes or just 850 times/kg oats and take just about 10 minutes (Meyer et al 1975, Harris et al 1995) – leaving more time to get "bored" on a low forage diet. Regular dental care is essential to maintain optimal mastication and steps should be taken to prevent horses from bolting their food, such as adding short chopped fibre or chaff.

Figure ❷ Comparison of hay with oats

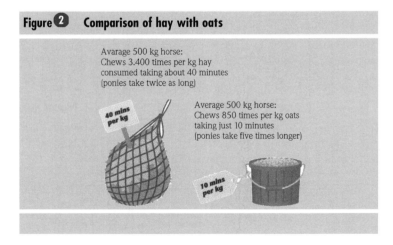

Average 500 kg horse:
Chews 3.400 times per kg hay
consumed taking about 40 minutes
(ponies take twice as long)

40 mins per kg

Average 500 kg horse:
Chews 850 times per kg oats
taking just 10 minutes
(ponies take five times longer)

10 mins per kg

Practical Hints

Consider adding chaff (short chopped fibre) to your feeds (especially for those greedy eaters and those that are only fed a small amount of feed/meal) as this can help to:-

- Increase the chewing time of meal (see Cuddeford 1996)
- Decrease boredom.
- Decrease the rate of feed intake which may consequently have positive effects on the plasma volume changes usually associated with intake of large cereal based meals.
- Decrease the dry matter content of the material swallowed, and therefore the stomach contents, which may help increase digestive efficiency.

The length of the chaff may be important. It has been recommended that the chaff should not be less than 2 cms long and that around 4 cms may be preferable for horses. Finally depending on the chaff used, other benefits may be obtained: Alfalfa chaff for example can be a good source of calcium.

When should you exercise in relation to a meal?

There has been considerable debate across the years about when and what should be fed horses before they are exercised and/or at a competition. Should they be fed or fasted and when should the hay be fed in relation to the grain and/or exercise? Several studies have shown that a pre-exercise concentrate meal suppresses free fatty acid (FFA) availability and increases blood glucose disappearance during exercise (Rodiek et al 1991, Lawrence et al 1993, 1995, Duren et al 1999) but these did not look at the influence of forage on these responses.

In a series of studies carried out recently (Pagan and Harris 1999) some of these questions were evaluated in thoroughbred horses at rest and during a simulated competition exercise test (CET) on a high speed treadmill. In the first study horses were fed hay at different times relative to a grain meal and it was shown that the time of feeding did affect the glycaemic and plasma protein response, as well as the water intake post grain feeding. Feeding hay either before or with grain significantly reduced the glycaemic response and it was suggested that this was probably a result of an increased rate of passage of grain through the gastrointestinal tract. This in turn could mean reduced digestion of the grain in the small intestine.

The next study investigated whether feeding grain with or without hay prior to a Competition exercise test would affect substrate utilisation and exercise responses. As with the previous studies, feeding grain with or without hay reduced FFA availability and increased blood glucose disappearance during the exercise which may not be beneficial in competition horses. Feeding hay either along with the grain or ad libitum (when not accustomed to ad lib hay) the night before exercise resulted in reduced plasma volume as well as higher lactate concentrations and heart rates during exercise. Although hay fed horses had a lower glycaemic and insulin response following a grain meal this did not guard against the large drop in blood glucose during exercise.

The final study looked at whether feeding forage but no grain prior to CET would affect substrate utilisation and performance on the treadmill. Feeding only forage had a smaller effect on the glycaemic and insulin response to exercise than a grain meal and did not affect FFA availability; however, in the ad lib fed horses the plasma total protein was elevated before and during exercise and the heart rate was elevated during the gallop. The horses that had been grazing before the CET tended to be heavier but did not show the same changes in plasma volume or heart rate.

These studies concluded that feeding large amounts of hay along with grain may result in a lowered plasma volume and an increase in body weight which may be detrimental to performance; grain should be withheld from horses for at least 3 hrs before exercise but small quantities of hay should be fed to ensure proper gastrointestinal tract function. However these conclusions can only be taken as a guide for performance horses in general as they did not evaluate the effects of such feeding practices on specific groups of animals such as show jumpers.

In conclusion at this moment in time the recommendation appears to be : Try not to start to exercise close to feeding a large concentrate/grain rich meal , which is based on the following

- Glucose peaks around 1-3 hrs past a meal which is associated with a rise in Insulin. If you exercise at this point one may see a drop in blood glucose during the first stages of exercise which may not be desirable (the brain can only use glucose as a fuel) and may retard the release of free fatty acids into the circulation (so the horse has to rely even more on stored glycogen – potentially resulting in a quicker onset of fatigue).
- A large amount of fluid, which comes effectively from the circulating blood, is secreted into the gut during digestion. With large concentrate meals, especially in quick or greedy feeders, there can be up to 24% loss in plasma volume within the first hour following feeding (Clarke et al 1990) Exercising under these conditions would effectively be like working a dehydrated horse.
- A large full gastrointestinal tract may restrict the space available for lung expansion.
- Following a meal blood flow is diverted to the gut to enable the products of digestion to be efficiently utilised – this may reduce the blood flow to working muscles and other organs where it may be better employed.

What about protein requirements?

The precise protein requirements for exercise are unknown and the current NRC recommendations are 9, 10.4 and 11% crude protein in the total ration for horses in light, moderate and intense exercise respectively (NRC 1989). Surveys in the past have suggested that Thoroughbred and Standardbred performance horses are often fed around 14% CP in their diets which is in excess of the NRC recommendations (Gallagher et al 1992 a, b) Although no specific detrimental effects of moderately high protein have been reported in the horse (Graham Thiers et al 1999) it is thought that an excess protein intake is undesirable, as protein is an inefficient energy source and produces a lot of waste heat (thermogenic); excess protein intake increases water requirements and may result in raised urea levels in blood/urea in urine/ammonia in stables (ureogenic), plus it may lead to acid-base disturbances (acidogenic) during exercise (Meyer 1987 , Kronfeld and Harris 1997). Meyer in 1987 recommended that exercising horses should not be fed more that 2 g DCP/kg BW/day. Despite protein being thermogenic, acidogenic and ureogenic, additional protein over maintenance may be needed with exercise and training because of the accompanying muscular development, the need for muscle repair and to replenish the nitrogen lost in sweat. An increase in nitrogen retention with conditioning suggests that increased protein is needed for exercise (Freeman et al 1988).

A recent study suggested that at least over the short term (9 weeks) feeding a low protein, high fat diet supplemented with lysine and threonine (which have been shown to be limiting for muscle growth) moderated several of the acidogenic effects of sprint exercise on blood plasma without any apparent adverse effects and therefore could be beneficial for the performance horse (Graham Thiers et al 1999).

Quality and nature of the protein fed is important especially in growing horses and those in hard or repetitive work. The lysine and possibly threonine content of the diet of competition/actively exercising horses should be considered – soya bean meal/flakes are, for example, a good source of lysine. The amount of additional lysine needed will depend on the hay and pasture being fed as for example alfalfa and other legumes are higher in lysine than many meadow hays and grasses. NRC currently recommends lysine in g/day at 0.035 x Crude Protein requirements (g/day) for horses in work whose protein requirements are given as 40 g/Mcal Digestible energy/day.

Can diet help my horse jump higher and faster?

An ergogenic aid can be considered to be any factor which can increase or improve work production. This could result in an increase in speed, or endurance or strength and therefore could potentially improve performance. Possible ways that ergogenic aids, apart from equipment etc., could improve performance in the horse could include (see also Harris 1994):

* Psychological effects
* Improved co-ordination or recruitment of muscle fibres
* Provision of a supplementary fuel source or the feeding of a feed with a higher energy content
* Increased levels of available stored energy
* Improved efficiency of conversion of the chemical energy of the feed, or stored energy, to mechanical energy for work
* Improved ATP/ADP homeostasis in contracting muscle fibres
* Decreased substrate depletion
* Decreased end product accumulation including improved intra-cellular acid base regulation.

These could result in increased mechanical energy for work and/or a delayed onset of fatigue or improved neuromuscular co-ordination. Many substances have theoretical ergogenic properties (see previous CESMAS paper: Harris and Harris 1998). Here we will briefly look at one potential agent, Creatine, as its use may have particular relevance to the show jumper.

Creatine

The power (force per unit time) generated by muscle contraction is a function of the rate of generation of ATP. If we take 1 as being the rate for fatty acid oxidation then it would be around 2 for glucose oxidation about 4 for the anaerobic conversion of glucose or glycogen to lactic acid and about 8 for the transfer of the high energy containing phosphate bond from Creatine-P to ATP (Kronfeld and Harris 1997). Creatine phosphate or phosphocreatine (PCr) facilitates the rapid production of ATP from ADP, therefore meeting sudden increases in energy requirement. Jumping or supra-maximal work therefore tends to use Creatine phosphate as its energy source whenever possible. Various estimates as to the amount of "fuel" (excluding proteins) stored by a horse have been made for example, a 500 kg horse has about 640,000 KJ of available energy stored as triglyceride, 75.300 KJ stored as glycogen, 188 KJ stored as PCr and 38 KJ as endogenous muscle ATP (McMiken 1983). The amount of stored PCr is not sufficient to support more than a few seconds of effort and therefore has to be replenished. Creatine is also important in helping to transfer energy across the cell, as Creatine phosphate is resynthesised using energy derived from the oxidation of carbohydrates, fat and protein within the mitochondria and reforms ATP in the cytoplasm. If this resynthesis becomes limiting then there will be a build up of ADP and a reduced power output.

The theory is that if there are greater initial stores of this Creatine Phosphate with greater circulating levels of Creatine, this may result in

- Increased capacity to resynthesise ATP so the muscle fibre would be more effective in maintaining a high ATP content and a low ADP content.
- Increased total Creatine pool so increased shuttling of energy from the mitochondria to the cytoplasm where it is used, leading to increased stamina and faster recovery.
- Increased protection against acidosis from the production of lactic acid during strenuous exercise.
- Decreased loss of ATP to uric acid with a concurrent decrease in the production of free radicals and therefore a potential decrease in the incidence of muscle soreness.

In the horse, Creatine is synthesised from Arginine and Glycine within the liver, released into the blood and transported to the muscle. In man this biosynthesis is augmented by a natural dietary supply. Even among meat eating individuals the muscle creatine levels vary from around 90 to 160 mmol/kg dry muscle reflecting possible differences in the capacity of individuals to synthesise creatine or their ability to concentrate it in the tissues. Creatine in man is rapidly absorbed and especially in those with initial levels at the lower end of the range the muscle concentrations may increase – but only up to a limit. There are no known obvious side effects in healthy man of supplementation and it has been shown to improve muscle function and physical performance in general over a relatively short period of time to a level which could be advantageous to athletes engaged in sustained or intermittent intensive exercise, such as weight lifting. Creatine supplementation in such cases may delay the development of fatigue, enable individuals to recover more quickly from intensive exercise and increase ability to perform more work during repeated bouts of intense exercise. (see Balsom et al 1993a, Birch et al 1994, Earnest et al 1995, Greenhaff et al 1993, Greenhaff et al 1994 Harris et al 1992, Harris et al 1993, Vandenberghe et al 1997)

The potential is great for Creatine use in the horse and for the show jumper in particular where there are periods of intensive explosive exercise. However, the horse in general does not seem to absorb Creatine very well from the gastrointestinal tract. In studies intubation of 50 mg/kg bwt resulted in an increased plasma concentration from 40 to 100 μmol/l after

4-6 h and in other species uptake of creatine into muscle only occurs when blood levels exceed 500 umol/l; the same dose resulted in an increase to 800-1000 μmol/l in the human (Sewell and Harris 1995).

At the moment for the horse we do not seem to have a way to increase blood levels of creatine in all horses practically – we do not know whether in fact we can increase the muscle levels of creatine in the horse and what effects, if any, would be achieved on performance by such increases in concentration.

What about salt ?

The sodium requirements for a horse at rest have been estimated at 20 mg/kg/day (assuming that the sodium sources are 90% available) It has been suggested that the sodium requirements for exercise should take into consideration the sodium content of sweat (~3.2 g/L) and the amount of sweat produced i.e. for light, moderate, hard and very heavy exercise around 0.5 -1, 1-2 , 2-5 & 7-8 L/100 kg bodyweight (Meyer 1987, Harris et al 1995, Pagan 1999).

As an example: a 500 kg show jumper which is in competition work, does not sweat excessively and is working in temperate conditions is estimated as losing 8 l of sweat on a work day or competition day (including travelling), its estimated requirements would be:

Maintenance	= 10 g
+ For the Sweat	= 8 X 3.2 = 25.6
Total	= 35.6 g of Sodium
	(equivalent to just over 3 oz of salt).

It should however be noted that this method of determining sodium requirements most likely overestimates daily requirements of horses, especially those that are sweating considerably, as the content of the gastrointestinal tract may provide an important reservoir for sodium during hard work and therefore the electrolyte losses that occur with heavy sweating may not need to be restored all at once. We also do need to understand more about the availability of sodium from different sources when horses are in work.

If this show jumper was fed 6 kg of hay and 4 kg of oats, such a diet would provide around 12g of sodium a day, meaning that the horse would require a further ~24 grams or just over 2 oz of salt. Even if fed 4 kg of a well fortified manufactured horse feed the daily intake without any supplementation would be around 26 g per day, meaning that around 1oz of additional salt may be required. Most complementary feeds, and home mixed rations, therefore do not provide sufficient sodium and chloride intake for horses that are significantly losing these electrolytes in sweat. Salt should be provided, therefore, to many horses in work. For those horses in little or no work the provision of a salt block may be adequate (but ensure that it is sited so that its use by that individual horse can be monitored). Where complementary feed or a vitamin mineral supplement is being fed, any block should be a pure salt rather than a mineralised one. It is not advised that owners use blocks formulated for other species.

For those horses in more work or who sweat noticeably the recommendation is that additional salt should be added to the feed. Advice on how much salt should be needed for a particular horse and diet may be obtained from a nutritionist but as a very practical guide : for a 500 kg horse the amount should start at about 1/2 oz – ~ 14 g/day and build up to around 2 oz -~ 56 g/day depending on the time of year, work load, and sweating rate. If, when the additional salt is fed, the horse either will not eat the feed (& providing it is not a fussy feeder!) or obviously urinates more than normal it may be helpful to reduce the amount by 1/2 oz, leave it at this level for a few days, monitor and reassess.

It is important to note that in various references within the literature, slightly different amounts of sodium may be recommended for the various work loads. This may in part occur because each of these references allow for slightly different amounts of sodium in sweat, estimate different amounts of sweat that each level workload will produce as well vary in the level of availability of sodium that they use.

Practical Hint

An estimate of the amount of sweat an individual horse has lost can be made by accurately weighing the horse before and after exercise (and before the horse drinks). Approximately 0.9 L of fluid has been lost for every 1 kg loss in bodyweight.

What about vitamin E and selenium?

Free radical reactions are responsible for many key biochemical events and under controlled circumstances they are essential for life but when uncontrolled they can cause the irreversible denaturation of essential cellular components and can result in a number of degenerative disease processes. Free radical induced damage has been associated with processes including ageing, as well as joint, muscle and respiratory disease. A system of natural antioxidant defences is present in the body to help counteract such free radical induced damage , including the selenium containing enzyme, glutathione peroxidase and Vitamin E. GSHPx for example acts to reduce the production of hydroxyl radicals. Vitamin E acts as a scavenger of free radicals and Vitamin C may assist by reducing the tocopheroxyl radicals formed by this scavenging. In addition, Vitamin E helps to block lipid peroxidation and may also form an important part of membrane structure. During exercise there is a marked increase in free radical production in the horse due in particular to the increased activity of xanthine oxidase during anaerobic degradation of purine nucleotides and the partial reduction of oxygen during oxidative phosphorylation within the mitochondria. It is thought that free radical production may play a role in muscle damage and fatigue of exercise if the production exceeds the capacity of the cells, natural defence mechanisms. Vitamin E and selenium are needed by all horses but especially those in work such as the show jumper.

The NRC (1989) recommends as a minimum for horses in work: Vitamin E : 80 iu/kg DM intake/day. The author's recommendation is at least double this figure at 160 iu/kg DM intake plus additional Vitamin E to support any supplemental oil (see above). For Selenium the NRC recommends as a minimum for horses in work: 0.1 mg/kg DM intake/day. The author's recommendation again is twice this at 0.2 mg/kg DM intake.

What about Stress, Mobility, Nutrition and the Show Jumper?

There have been relatively few scientific studies that have looked specifically at the show jumper. Interestingly it has been reported that acute jumping exercise and the environment associated with show jumping competition does not cause the classic stress response in experienced show jumping horses. In one study 26 horses with various levels of show jumping experience were blood sampled at rest, upon reaching the schooling area and after completing the jump course. The stress response was primarily assessed through changes in plasma cortisol concentrations (which does have its own limitations). Schooling jumpers had higher baseline cortisol concentrations when compared with the intemediate and most experienced jumpers. Overall, the plasma cortisol concentration in all horses was not elevated after jumping the course of fences regardless of experience, although lactates and heart rates were raised (Covalesky et al 1992).

It has been suggested that a horse that is under the stress of a rigorous competition schedule will have a need for extra B Vitamins and possibly ascorbic acid as well as Vitamin E (Malinowski 1997). Others have suggested that the chromium status of performance horses may be adversely affected by the physiological and psychological stresses of training and competition (Pagan 1998). However there is limited work that has been undertaken on the advantages of chromium supplementation especially in horses on a balanced and appropriate diet. It has been suggested that horses in hard work, especially when being fed a high grain feed, may have an increased loss of chromium in the urine and therefore have an increased requirement (Pagan 1999).

The repetitive stress on joints can lead to wear and tear with some degree of pain and often a decrease in performance. Nutritional strategies in such cases include keeping the horse at an appropriate weight and most definitely avoiding obesity. Ensuring an adequate protein intake so that tissue repair is not compromised and certainly ensuring that the diet provides an adequate amounts of lysine, methionine and cysteine will be beneficial. However, there is currently little scientific evidence to support the need for feeding increased intakes of these and other core nutrients beyond those recommended for horses in work (see Harris et al 1995, Kronfeld and Harris 1997, Pagan 1999) or indeed any evidence for an advantage in joint health resulting from such an increased intake. However, certain nutraceuticals marketed to improve joint health and mobility are becoming increasingly fashionable. Chondroitin sulphate consists of repeating units of the disaccharide galactosamine and glucuronic acid but unlike the poly-sulphated glycosaminoglycans which have 3- 4 sulphate groups per disaccharide molecule there is only one. Whilst in-vitro studies have shown some anti-inflammatory effects of chondroitin sulphate (Bassleer et al 1992) it appears that absorption by the oral route is very poor in the horse and it has been suggested that, as in man, the use of this compound as an oral supplement for horses with joint disease will become less popular in the future (personal comments Wright 1999).

Glucosamine is a precursor of the disaccharide units of articular cartilage glycosaminoglycans. Work has suggested that the compound is absorbed in other species and can be incorporated into newly synthesised glycosaminoglycan. It has been suggested that glucosamine may be more likely to be of value in the horse (personal comments Wright 1999). In vitro studies in other species have suggested that glucosamine may produce increased glycosaminoglycan, proteoglycan and collagen synthesis and stimulate production of hyaluronan. Several studies in man suggest that oral supplementation may improve physical performance in people with joint pain (see Fassbender et al 1994, Theodosakis et al 1997). There have been very few studies that have been carried out in the horse In one study in the horse, articular cartilage was obtained from the carpal joint of horses that had been euthanised for reasons other than joint problems. Explants were maintained and the effect of lipopolysaccharide addition with and without glucosamine was evaluated. Glucosamine significantly inhibited the nitric oxide production caused by the LPS and also inhibited prostaglandin release. This effect was significant with the highest dose of glucosamine. All doses of glucosamine tested, significantly decreased the gelatinase/collagenase activity. The authors suggest that this work provided support to anecdotal in vivo observations of the benefits of glucosamine in horses and suggested a biochemical mechanism through which glucosamine might possess chondroprotective properties (Fenton et al 1999a) but this is unproven. In another study in yearling quarter horses, no effect of either longeing or glucosamine supplementation on serum concentrations of keratan sulphate or osteocalcin were seen (Fenton et al 1999b). A few studies have evaluated a product containing both chondroitin sulphate and glucosamine (see Hanson et al 1997). There were no apparent benefits in the study which evaluated the effect on experimentally induced joint disease. In another, some non-specific benefits of reduced lameness and improved flexion were reported.

All of the studies reported to date have their limitations and one of the world's leading equine orthopaedic surgeons has in fact stated that "there is no controlled work that has been completed with these products in the horse" (McIlwraith 1999). Further studies, for example, are needed to confirm that glucosamine is absorbed in the horse and that it may have a role to play not only in the prevention of joint disease but also in the recovery or recuperation from joint injury.

How do we recognize elite Show Jumpers?

Introduction

Probably as long as the horse has been used by man, conformation has been one important indicator of performance and soundness. Due to different use of the horses, many different types of horses have developed over time, ranging from heavy draught horses to light, refined and fast thoroughbreds. The result has been a huge number of breeds, all with their own specific conformational characteristics, not always related to performance and soundness.

In the selection of elite show-jumpers conformation must be considered together with all other properties characterizing an elite horse. Temperament, movements and jumping ability are of course the most important ones, but the significance of the conformation must not be neglected. Besides the fact that dressage riders seek "good looking" horses, the conformation, of both show-jumpers and dressage horses, must facilitate good movements, jumping ability, soundness, and above all, the collection of the horse. The competition results of Grand Prix horses are certainly dependent on the skill of their riders and trainers, but the conformation and movements must have the basic qualities that create the necessary conditions for a successful training of the horse. A horse´s resistance is often interpreted as bad temperament but might just as well be due to pain or lack of ability to carry weight on the hind limbs, caused by inappropriate conformation or/and movements.

Much has been written in books about the conformation of the horse over the past 200 years, but very little is based on research. This doesn't mean that the contents of these books are of less interest. It is thought-provoking that a lot of the relationships between conformation and performance described by Bourgelat as early as 1750 shows great accordance with the results from recent research. He stressed the importance of the hindquarter conformation. Horses with well camped under hind limbs were found suitable for dressage work, whereas those with hind limbs camped behind were likely to be fast. Another early author, J Hörman, wrote in 1837 that a long and forwardly sloping femur facilitates lifting of the hind limb and the horse's ability to step under itself. CA Ehrengranat, director of the Swedish National Stud at Flyinge between 1814 and 1837 maintained that a sloping shoulder, long radius, short fore cannon and a flat croup are desirable for good movements. A great deal of these horsemen's knowledge is still in practice but parts of it seem to have been forgotten in the meantime. In Sweden, the results from research based on both subjective evaluation and quantitative methods have confirmed some of these old relationships and rejected others. Some of the "forgotten" relationships have also been rediscovered. For the further interpretation of these studies, it is important to keep in mind that there are aspects of the conformation and gaits that can't be measured by objective methods. For instance, the type of the horse and the conformation of head, neck and body must be judged subjectively. Consequently, subjective evaluation can never be totally replaced by objective measurements.

Presumptive world class Grand Prix dressage horses and show-jumpers are difficult to find. Many promising young dressage horses with excellent gaits fail to learn passage, piaffe and other collected movements, resulting in years of wasted training. Finding the young horses that will subsequently be able to clear an Olympic or World Cup course is also very difficult. Accordingly, riders, trainers and breeders would benefit from better precision in the selection.

Up to now, evaluation of the conformation, gaits and jumping ability has mostly been subjective. Even though the judging standards of today are based on long experience they could be questioned partly due to limitations in the human eye and its ability to register fast movements and subtle variation in movements and conformation. However, new methods for measuring the conformation objectively have made it possible to improve the accuracy of the conformation evaluation, and computerized analyses of high speed film or video will most certainly contribute to a better understanding of the gaits and the jumping technique in relation to subsequent performance. In the very near future, faster and smaller computers together with deeper knowledge of the biomechanical properties of the elite horse will make it possible to combine traditional evaluation with objective analyses of conformation and gaits in young horses.

This article will focus on conformational characteristics that, subjectively or objectively evaluated, are important for the performance and soundness of the jumping and dressage horse. It is a summary of two articles by Holmström et al (1990 and 1993), and it also presents the preliminary results from a recently finished unpublished study on correlations between conformation and soundness. As you will see, with regard to the conformation, there are many common factors between elite show-jumpers and elite dressage horses. In fact there are very few differences between them. This is due to the fact that most conformational determinants, characterizing elite performance, are really determinants for good balance. Something that is essential for all sport horses.

Material and methods

Horses

The horse material consisted of 412 Swedish riding horses distributed on 195 4-year olds measured at the Quality Events 1984, 217 4-year olds measured at the Quality Events 1996, 40 international Grand Prix dressage horses and 51 international elite show-jumpers. Furthermore, the conformation of 52 horses treated for back problems or recurrent lameness problems at two major horse clinics in Sweden was analyzed objectively, and during 1998 the insurance statistics for the horses analyzed 1984 and 1996 were examined.

Objective analysis

The objective method used for the conformation analysis is based on reference points marked on the horse with small paper dots glued to the skin. It was originally developed by Magnusson (1985) for a study on standardbred trotters. The reference points used are described in detail by Holmström et al (1990). In the beginning all measurements were registered "by hand" from a picture projected on a wall using a simple measuring band and a protractor. The measurements were transferred to the computer via punch cards. Nowadays, the whole procedure is computerized. A picture of the horse is digitized, from a regular camcorder or a digital camera, into a laptop computer. The measurements are registered by clicking with the mouse on the white markers. Then the computer calculates all length and angle measurements (Figure1). The procedure takes 5-10 minutes.

Subjective evaluation

In the conformation studies of 4-year olds at the Quality Events in 1984 and 1996, the official judges recorded scores for conformation, gaits and jumping ability. The

Figure ❶

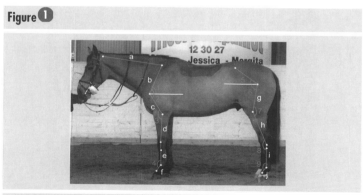

Explanations
Length measurements: a) neck b) shoulder c) humerus d) radius e) fore cannon f)fore pastern g) femur h) tiba i) hind cannon j) hind pastern
Angle measurements: 1) shoulder inclination 2) shoulder joint 3) elbow joint 4) fore fetlock joint 5) pelvis inclination 6) femur inclination 7) stifle joint 8) hock joint 9) hind fetlock joint

conformation was judged according to the traditional Swedish procedure with five sub-scores ranging from 1 to 10 for: type; head, neck and body; correctness of extremities; locomotion in walk; locomotion in trot.

The main purpose of the study in 1984 was to investigate correlations between conformation and gaits under saddle; a reference judge scored the gaits for all the 195 horses. In that way the effect of different judges could be eliminated. The gaits were also scored according to a more detailed protocol than normally used at the Quality Events. Subjective scores from 1 to 10 were given for seven characteristics of each gait:

Walk: regularity, footfalls, forelimb movements, engagements of the quarters, engagement of the back, covering of ground and elasticity.

Trot and canter: regularity and balance, cadence, lightness of the forehand, activity from the quarters, engagement of the back, covering of ground and elasticity/suppleness.

The horses were given two scores (ranging from 1 to 10) for jumping ability, one for ability and technique and one for temperament. Regularity, footfalls and elasticity in walk and regularity and balance, cadence and elasticity/suppleness are considered to be of great importance for the riding horse and were assigned a coefficient of 2.

It is important to emphasize, that irrespective of the judge, the results must be interpreted in relation to the fact that the performance traits in these studies were gait under saddle and loose jumping over 1.20 m fences, not elite performance.

Results

Conformational differences between elite horses and "normal" horses.

There were no significant differences in the frequencies of limb- and toe-axis deviations between "normal" horses and elite dressage and jumping horses.

The results from analysis of differences in conformational measurements between international elite horses, "normal" horses (4-year old horses measured at Quality Events) and horses with recurrent lameness problems are shown in table 1. Adjustment was made for the effect of sex. Significant differences between the elite horses and the "normal" horses were found for most measurements except for the hock joint and the hind fetlock joint. Both the dressage and jumping horses had a smaller pelvis inclination and a more forwardly sloping femur compared to the "normal" horses. Comparing the elite horse groups, the jumping horses had significantly longer necks and a somewhat smaller stifle angle than the dressage horses. For the rest of the measurements, no significant differences were found between the dressage and jumping horses.

Table ① **Comparison of adjusted means for length and angle measurements between elite dressage horses (n=40), elite show jumpers (n = 51), 4- year olds tested at Quality Events (n = 217) and horses with back problems or recurrent lameness problems (n = 52). Differences in sex, and for the stifle angle differences in femur inclination, have been taken into consideration.**

Variable	Q. Event 1996	Dressage	Jumping	Injured
Length measurements (cm)				
Neck	70.51a	71.55ab	74.02c	72.87bc
Scapula	40.07a	42.00c	40.51a	41.00ab
Humerus	32.10a	33.07b	32.14a	32.01a
Radius	37.15a	37.64b	37.69b	37.58ab
Fore cannon	20.92a	21.56b	21.37b	21.14ab
Fore pastern	9.12a	9.52b	9.51b	9.16a
Femur	40.24a	41.20b	40.36a	40.09a
Tibia	48.52a	49.14ab	49.74b	49.40ab
Hind cannon	26.83a	27.36b	26.68a	26.55a
Hind pastern	8.74a	9.01ab	9.34b	9.07ab
Angle measurements (degrees)				
Shoulder inclination	64.5a	66.3b	67.0b	66.5b
Shoulder joint	126.3a	124.5b	126.2a	126.0a
Elbow joint	152.4a	148.5b	151.1a	150.7a
Fore fetlock joint	148.7a	149.9ab	151.3b	148.2a
Pelvis inclination	31.0a	27.5b	28.2b	31.0a
Femur inclination	85.4a	84.7b	84.5b	87.8c
Stifle joint	154.1a	155.6b	154.0a	153.4a
Hock joint	159.4a	160.4a	159.2a	157.0b
Hind fetlock joint	154.6a	153.4a	155.7a	156.1a

Explanations
Values with different superscrips differ significantly from each other.

Correlation between conformation and performance in 4-year olds at Quality Events

The results from studies of relationships between conformation, gaits under rider and jumping ability in 4-year olds at the Quality Events are shown in table 2.

Table ❷ Results from multiple regression analysis of the effects of conformation measurements and scores on gaits under saddle and jumping ability 1984 and 1996. Partial regression coefficients for variables that showed either significant correlation to the performance traits or significant diffrences between elite horses and "normal" horses. Effects of sex and event (site) were included in the model

Variable	Gaits under saddle 1984		1996		Jumping ability 1984	1996
Objektive measurements (cm)						
Humerus length	0.16***	0.12**	0.12**	0.10**	-0.12	0.13
Pelvis inclination	-0.04*	-0.02	-0.005	-0.005	0.05	0.03
Femur inclination	-0.21***	-0.15***	-0.13***	-0.08**	-0.06	0
Stifle angle	0.04*	0.01	-0.006	-0.01	0.09	-0.04
Hock angle					0.01	0.11*
Subjektive scores						
Type		0.11		-0.04	0.40	0.02
Head. neck and body		0.12		0.11	-0.13	0.18
Extremeties		-0.08		0.02	0.18	-0.28
Walk		0.38***		0.25***	0.08	0.05
Trot		0.19**		0.45***	0.16	0.11
Coeff. of determination. R2 (%)						
Conformation score		26.12		25.13	3.86	0
Objektive measurements	24.76	24.76	13.32	13.32	1.85	1.31
Score + measurements		42.24		42.61	3.84	0.42

Explanations
Levels of significance: *=p< 0.05; **=p< 0.01; ***=p< 0.001

The objective measurements and conformation scores in the table had either shown significant correlation to performance in the 4-year olds or had shown significant differences between the elite horses and "normal" horses.

In both studies significant correlations were found between gaits under saddle and objective measurements as well as conformation scores. Horses with high scores for the gaits had a longer humerus and smaller inclination of the pelvis and femur to the horizontal plane compared to those with low scores. Strong correlations between walk and trot in hand and the gait score under rider could be found in both materials. However, the correlation between the scores given for trot in hand and under rider was much stronger in 1996 compared to 1984. The coefficient of determination for the subjective conformation score was approximately the same in 1996 and 1984 (25-26%), but it decreased from 25% to 13% for the objective measurements. When both objective measurements and subjective scores were included in the same model, 42% of the variation in gaits under saddle could be explained by the variation in conformation.

No more than 0-4% of the variation in jumping ability could be explained by the variation in conformation. In the horses measured in 1996, a straight hock had a significant positive influence on the scores for jumping.

An objective conformation index was constructed from the results summarized in this article. The index was transformed so that the scale would be from 1-10. In table 3, differences in the objective index between the groups of horses are shown together with the most important conformational details. There was an improvement in the conformational details as well as in the index from 1984 to 1996.

Table ❸ Adjusted means for the conformational measurements that are included in the objektive conformation index. Differences in sex between the groups have been taken into consideration.

Group	Femur incl. (degr.)	Pelvis incl. (degr.)	Stifle angle (degr.)	Humerus length (cm)	Index
Dressage	84.7	27.5	155.6	33.1	8.37a
Jumping	84.5	28.2	154.0	32.1	7.97b
Q. Event 1996	85.4	31.0	154.1	32.1	7.39c
Q. Event 1984	87.1	33.5	154.1	31.5	6.28d
Injured horses	87.8	31.0	153.4	31.9	6.48d

Different superscripts at the index indicate significant differences

In the new horse materials, there was a considerable difference between the 4-year olds and the elite horses. The elite dressage horses showed the highest (8.37) and the lame horses the lowest index (6.48).

Conformation and soundness

In 1998, the conformation of 52 horses treated for back problems or recurrent lameness problems at two major horse clinics in Sweden was analyzed subjectively. The results are shown in table 1. The femur inclination was significantly larger and the hock joint angle smaller in the injured horses compared to both the elite horse groups and the 4-year olds. The stifle angle was somewhat smaller in the injured horses than in the dressage horses.

In 1998, the conformation measurements of the 217 horses measured at the Quality Events 1996 were compared to the veterinary records at the four major insurance companies in Sweden. 146 horses had been insured during the period. 71 horses were not found in the records or were not identified. No significant conformational differences were found between the insured and not insured horses. Out of the 146 insured horses, the insurance companies had recompensed 42 horses (29%) for veterinary costs. Six horses (4%) had been put down. Twenty-five horses (17%) had been recompensed for treatment of recurrent lameness problems.

The conformation of these 25 horses was compared to the rest of the insured horses.

The horses treated for recurrent lameness problems had a larger femur inclination and hind fetlock joint angle compared to the "sound" horses. The injured horses were also somewhat taller and had a significantly lower objective conformation index (Table 4).

Table ❹ Significant conformational differences between horses treated for recurrent lameness and other insured horses.

Variable	Lame horses Mean (s.d.)	Sound horses Mean (s.d.)	Significance
Height at the withers	165.4 (4.2)	163.5 (3.6)	*
Femur inclination	86.7 (1.7)	85.4 (2.3)	**
Hind fetlock joint angle	156.6 (6.2)	153.8 (6.4)	*
Objektive conformation index	6.86 (0.74)	7.41 (0.94)	**

Levels of significance: *= $p < 0.05$. **= $p < 0.01$. ***= $p < 0.001$

When the insured horses were divided into three equally large groups according to their objective conformation index, 2 of the 25 lame horses were found in the best group (index > 7.80). In the worst group (index < 6.80) 13 lame horses were found. Expressed as percentage of the number of horses in each group, 4% of the horses with high indexes had been treated for recurrent lameness while the corresponding percentage in the group with the lowest indexes was 26%. Dividing the horses into two groups according to the conformation index (higher or lower than the average index: 7.40), 10% of the horses with high indexes and 24% of the horses with low indexes had been treated. 76% of the treated horses had a femur inclination larger than the mean for all the 4-year olds.

Discussion

Correlations between conformation and performance in 4-year olds

Both studies on 4-year olds at Quality Events showed similar results with significant correlations between both subjective conformation scores and objective measurements, and gaits under saddle. Horses with high scores for gaits had a longer humerus and smaller inclinations of the pelvis and femur. In 1984 there was a positive correlation, not found in the 1996 study, between gait scores and a large stifle angle.

In both 1984 and 1996 the subjective conformation scores explained about 25% of the variation in gaits under saddle. In 1984 the objective measurements also explained approximately 25% of the variation. When combined the subjective scores and the objective measurements explained 42%. At the Quality Events 1996, the total coefficient of determination was the same as in 1984, but the objective measurements explained just 13%. There might be several explanations. A change, or less accuracy, in the measuring procedure can most probably be excluded because reference points and photo procedure were the same. Furthermore, with new computer technology the analysis procedure has been improved in a way that has decreased the error in the angle and length measurements. A possible explanation might be that the changes in the horse material between 1984 and 1996 has to a major degree involved the objective measurements that best explain the differences in gaits under saddle. It is also possible that the differences can be explained by shortcomings in gait evaluation. The coefficient of determination for the objective measurements was lower in 1996, which probably can be explained to a large extent by the fact that the scores from the original gait judges were used in 1996. In 1984 a more skilled and experienced judge and dressage trainer judged all the horses. The variation in the subjective conformation and gait scores was lower in the material from 1996. It indicates that the judges did not use the available scale properly. If the judges lack experience they often are uncertain as to how to judge the horses' balance and ability to collect, and the scale will be squeezed together around the average. Thus, the quality of the gait scores 1996, and their relationship to dressage performance, might not have been as good as in 1984. However, the decreased variation in the subjective conformation score might just as well be real.

By combining subjective scores and objective measurements, a considerably greater share of the variation in gaits under saddle could be explained than when the methods were used separately. Thus, much can be gained by including objective measurements in the conformation evaluation, especially in young horses that cannot be judged under rider. The results also show that a skilled judge can never be replaced by an objective method. Different parts of the conformation are evaluated, and subjective and objective methods complement each other.

In contrast to the gaits under saddle, only very weak correlations were found between conformation variables and jumping ability. Obviously, both subjective conformation scores and objective measurements are poor instruments for prediction of jumping ability at Quality Events.

Differences between elite horses and "normal" horses

Studies of relationships between conformation and gaits in young horses have the disadvantage that the correlation between the performance trait, i.e. gaits under rider and loose jumping, and elite performance can be questioned. By comparing elite horses and "normal" horses, information about conformational characteristics of the elite horses can be obtained. Together with the results from the 4-year olds, this will give a more complete picture of what should be considered in the selection of horses for elite performance and breeding purposes.

For the time being, the conformation of 40 dressage horses on Swedish and international Grand Prix level has been objectively analyzed together with 51 elite show-jumpers. The conformational differences found between the elite horses and "normal" horses are very much in accordance with the results from the studies of the 4-year olds. The elite dressage horses had a longer humerus, a smaller inclination of the pelvis and femur to the horizontal and a larger stifle angle compared to the 4-year olds measured in 1996. The show-jumpers had a hind limb conformation similar to the dressage horses but were also characterized by a longer neck and a more sloping shoulder.

The most important conformational detail that has shown correlation to gaits under saddle in young horses as well as elite performance in dressage and show jumping is the femur inclination. It is however not correct to assess just one detail in the hind limb conformation, because other angle measurements can, to some extent, compensate for a poor femur inclination. That is the reason why it is impossible to make an accurate evaluation of the hind limb conformation without an objective method. To see the horses moving, as in all subjective evaluations, is of course a very important help in evaluating the performance potential, but does not give enough accurate information about the horses' potential as Grand Prix horses. There are a lot of horses with excellent gaits and good jumping technique that fail to perform well at the highest level of dressage and jumping because of lack of ability to maintain balance and increase the collection. Many of these horses have a poor hind limb conformation resulting in weak hind limbs that cannot carry enough weight. Consequently, objective measurements are a necessary complement for an accurate selection on elite performance.

It might be surprising that there are no vital differences in the hind limb conformation between elite dressage and jumping horses. From a biomechanical point of view, it is however quite logical. The conformation that characterizes the elite horses facilitates the horses' balance and ability to carry weight on the hind limbs. Both dressage and jumping horses benefit from good balance. Also riders competing at a lower level will enjoy a well-balanced horse because it is more comfortable to ride.

It is interesting to notice that the elite show jumpers had significantly longer necks than both the dressage horses and the 4-year olds. A long neck might improve the jumping horse's balance over the fence, but does not seem to have any effect on the dressage performance.

The objective conformation index showed significant differences between 4-year olds, dressage and jumping horses. The highest average index was found in the dressage horses, which is not surprising since the index is mainly based on gait scores and dressage performance. At the same time it is obvious that, in spite of the fact that there was no significant correlation to jumping ability in the 4-year olds, there was a correlation between the index and elite jumping performance as well. The explanation is probably that elite show jumpers benefit from good balance while other factors are more important in young horses evaluated at relatively small fences.

Some of the differences found between elite horses and the 4-year olds might be an effect of age. Some effect of training must also be considered, but is probably limited in the conformational measurements of interest as determinants for performance.

Limb- and toe-axis

The correctness of the extremities is of less importance for the performance of the dressage and jumping horse than most people think, at least as long as the deviations are mild to moderate. The frequencies of faulty limb conformation were the same in all the investigated groups of horses. If mild or moderate deviations of the limb and toe axis had negative effects on performance and soundness, it should have shown in lower frequencies in the elite horses. Almost 90 % of the elite dressage and jumping horses had outwardly rotated hind limbs, i.e. with strait limb and toe axis the hind limb is rotated in the hip joint resulting in a "toe-out-looking" conformation. Boldt (1978) states in "Das Dressurpferd" that rotated hind limbs are necessary for the dressage horse ability to perform half pass and traverse because this hind limb conformation results in more space between the stifle and the trunk of the horse.

Conformation and soundness

The results from this study are preliminary but very interesting. The general conclusion that can be made is that there does not seem to be any contradiction between a conformation that is good for performance and one that has a positive effect on soundness. Thus, breeding for performance will also mean breeding for soundness.

Among the insured horses investigated in this study, there were far more horses with recurrent lameness problems in the group with poor hind limb conformation than in the group with good conformation. This is not surprising since horses with poor hind limb conformation are unbalanced in most cases. The risk of injuries due to overloading must be higher reasonably in unbalanced horses that are unable to carry the rider correctly.

Conclusions

By way of introduction it was mentioned that objective methods for measuring the conformation will improve the accuracy of the horse evaluation. The results from the conformational studies can be summarized in some major points.

- Subjective conformation evaluation cannot be replaced by objective measurements. The two methods work as complements to each other.
- Inclusion of selected conformational measurements (the inclinations of femur, pelvis and scapula, lengths of humerus and neck and the stifle and hock angles) would improve the traditional judging of conformation as a means to predict performance. It is particularly interesting in young horses not yet ridden.
- Avoid horses with small hock angles.
- Mild to moderate deviations of the limb and toe axis have no negative effect on performance and soundness.

Skeletal muscle profile of show jumpers: Physiological and pathological considerations

Introduction

Jumping is a highly specialised sport. The show jumper is an adaptable and versatile athlete that must perform different kinds of exercises during competition. During a round the horse usually canters aerobically between fences, with anaerobic bursts of power at each takeoff (Clayton 1990). The majority of show-jumping competitions lasts from half a minute to two minutes and requires a minimum speed in the range of 300 to 400 m/min. Show jumping is associated with a marked elevation in blood lactate (Covalesky et al 1992), indicating that anaerobic metabolism makes a significant contribution to the energy supply (Clayton 1994). Overall, the physiological demands of show jumping are that the relatively slow average speed must be combined with intense efforts required to jump fences every 5 seconds or so.

One of the most limiting factors involving successful jumping is the external force impulses developed by the fore- and hindlimbs at take-off (Merkens et al 1991). The pushoff generated by the hindlimbs at takeoff explains most of the energy required for clearing the fence (van den Bogert et al 1994). The action of the forelimbs is limited to putting the body of the horse into a good orientation before the final pushoff of the hindlimbs (Barrey 1997). The results from some kinematic (Clayton et al 1995) and kinetic (Barrey and Galloux 1997) studies suggest that the hindlimbs of poor jumpers produce a weaker force for pushoff than the ones of good jumpers. This means that the optimal conditioning of good show jumpers should develop explosive power in the muscle groups that provide the force needed to elevate the horse's body mass into the air at takeoff. Elevation of the body centre of gravity is minimal over fences less than 1 m high, but muscular strength becomes progressively important over higher fences (Clayton 1994).

The great diversity of physical activities that are needed for jumping is mainly possible because the working muscles adapt to the different demands placed upon the horses in connection with training and competition. All alterations during exercise are related to movement and therefore are either directly or indirectly related to the requirements of the involved skeletal musculature. Furthemore, an understanding of the demands of various types of exercise requires a knowledge of the specific changes that occur within working muscles and the modifications that result from training. During locomotion coordination of activation and relaxation of large groups of muscles is necessary.

On the other hand, jumping is an activity with a very high incidence of injuries of components of the locomotor system. Soft tissues, like skeletal muscles, are exposed to injuries because of the high physiological demands of this sport activity and/or inappropriate training schedules. Thus, each strength training workout causes some minor muscular damage which is repaired on the days between workouts (Clayton 1994). Nevertheless, if this kind of work is repeated too frequently, damage accumulates, predisposing to injury or breakdown. In contrast to the situation in human athletes, strength training is not continued to exhaustion in horses because of the risk of injury. Instead, the workout is terminated when signs of peripheral (muscular) fatigue occur (Clayton 1994). In addition to this local muscle strain, one option in the evaluation of muscular disorders in jumpers is muscle biopsying. Lumbar and gluteal muscles are the most frequently injured ones in jumpers (Snow and Valberg 1994). Muscle biopsy is, however, not a routine procedure for evaluation of muscular problems in show jumpers and is best used when physical examination and imaging methods do not reveal a diagnosis or when conventional treatments are unsuccessful.

With the aid of the muscle biopsy technique it has been possible to study skeletal muscle characteristics of different types of horses over the past 25 years. In an exhaustive review, Snow and Valberg (1994) summarised the relationships between anatomical and biochemical properties of skeletal muscle and physiological performance, and described in lucid detail many of the changes in these characteristics that are modulated by exercise, training and pathological conditions. This paper brings a complementary perspective of this subject by focusing explicitly on show jumpers, with particular attention to the following aspects: 1) muscle fibre type profile of inactive young jumpers, including a comparative study with other types of horses; 2) muscular adaptation to a conventional training programme for jumping considering the molecular basis by which these adaptations occur and the functional significance; and 3) histopathological features of muscle biopsies from horses with different myopathies. We will begin with some preliminary considerations about the equine skeletal muscle fibre types in order to provide a structure for subsequent discussions of experimental results and criteria for diagnosis of muscle problems.

Muscle fibre types

Locomotor muscles in the horse are strategically located proximally on the skeleton, creating a pendulum-like effect that decreases the energy necessary to swing the limb. Over 90 % of muscle consists of the muscle cells, with the rest comprising nerves, blood vessels and extracellular connective tissue. Muscle fibres contain rod-like contractile structures, myofibrils, which are about 1 mm in diameter. They are made up of protein filaments arranged in units called sarcomeres. Each sarcomere consists of one set of thick (myosin) filaments and two sets of thin (actin) filaments, and during the contraction of muscle the thin filaments are pulled in over the thick filaments so that each sarcomere shortens and generates force (Huxley 1969). The myosin molecule consists of two heavy chains and four light chains. All these chains occur as several distinct isoforms coded by different genes, the expression of which determines the speed of contraction, force production and fatigability of each muscle fibre.

Equine skeletal muscles are composed of clusters of muscle fibres (Fig. 1).

Each fibre is a multinucleated cell. In mature horses, at least four basic fibre types can be histochemically and immunohistochemically distinguished upon the basis of the myosin heavy chain (MHC) isoform they express (Rivero et al 1996a). One type is adapted for a high power output over a short period (fast, glycolytic or type

Figure 2

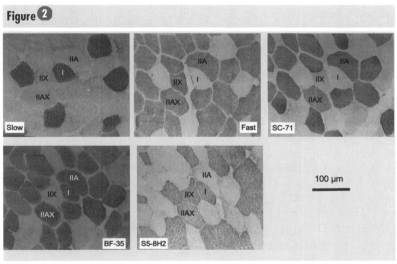

Explantions

Figure 1: Immunocytochemical identification of equine gluteus medius muscle fibres according to the myosin heavy chain (MHC) isoform they express. Serial sections were stained with five monoclonal antibodies against specific MHC isoforms: Slow, anti-MHC I; Fast, anti-MHCs IIA and IIX; SC-71, anti-MHC IIA; BF-35, anti-MHCs I and IIA; and S5-8H2, anti-MHCs I and IIX. The three pure MHC fibres types I, IIA and IIX and the hybrid co-expressing MHC isoforms IIA and IIX are identified. In addition, horse skeletal muscle has a fifth muscle fibre type co-expressing MHCs types I plus IIA (not shown).

IIX), and another is adapted for a high power output over a longer period (fast, oxidative, glycolytic or type IIA). Both of these type II fibres possess types of MHCs and other contractile proteins that produce a fast contraction and develop force rapidly. However, the type IIX fibres have a type of MHC with a higher speed of contraction than the MHC isoform expressed in IIA fibres (Rivero et al 1999). Moreover, type IIX fibres are usually larger than type IIA, so that they can develop more strength and power per unit of area. However, the type IIA fibres have more mitochondria, more capillaries surrounding them and a more oxidative metabolism, so that they are capable of sustaining a high power output over a reasonably long period. A third major type of fibre found in horse muscle is the hybrid type IIAX fibres that coexpress the two MHC isoforms of type IIX and type IIA fibres, so they have intermediate properties. The fourth major type of fibre of horses is the slow oxidative or type I fibre, which has a MHC isoform that hydrolyses ATP only slowly, resulting in a slow velocity of contraction. This makes these fibres more efficient and more economical for producing slow repetitive movements and sustaining isometric force, but not for generating power (work done per unit time).

Multiple factors in both developing and adult muscles regulate the expression of the amounts and types of protein. These factors include myogenic (genetic linkage) as well as nonmyogenic (e.g. neural and hormonal) signals. The combination and interaction of these factors seems to regulate the percentages of the given fibre types that are found in a muscle. During the majority of physical exercises it seems that the slow type I fibres are recruited first, and only when the force requirements increase are the fast type II fibres recruited to provide the necessary speed and power. Thus, the general order of recruitment of muscle fibres during most types of exercise is type I, type IIA, type IIAX and type IIX. This sequential muscle fibre type pattern is directly associated with the nature, intensity and duration of exercise carried out.

Muscle fibre types and areas of untrained young jumpers

The gluteus medius is the most frequently sampled when studying the effects of training, growth and pathology in the equine athlete because it is a major propulsive muscle active in all fast gaits and it is easily accessible (Lindholm and Piehl 1974). This muscle is composed of three major fibre types (I, IIA and IIX), which vary in their relative frequency, fibre size, capillary supply and metabolic profile, particularly as a function of sampling depth (Kline and Bechtel 1988; López-Rivero et al 1992; Rivero et al 1993b). The pattern of variation in muscle fibre properties between different depths of the muscle probably reflects different functional demands on the muscle. In addition, a single biopsy taken from this muscle is a poor representative of the whole muscle and care should be exercised in sampling and interpreting data obtained from limited biopsy of this muscle. We have routinely examined more than one biopsy from the gluteus medius muscle removed at different sampling depths.

Tables 1 and 2 show the proportion and size of the three main fibre types in two different sampling sites (superficial and deep region) of the gluteus medius muscle of show jumping horses compared to horses used in other disciplines. These data were obtained from young horses at the beginning of their respective training programmes. Jumpers were all 4-year old crossbred Thoroughbred x Hackney with very low experience in jumping. These animals were selected for starting a specific training programme for this sport activity. The remaining groups of horses were all animals of national or international competiti-

Table ① Mean values (±sd) are shown for fibre type composition (%) in the superficial (2-3 cm) and deep (6-7 cm) sampling depths of the M. gluteus medius of different types of horses used for various sportive disciplines *

| Activity | Breed | N | Superficial region of the muscle | | | Deep region of the muscle | | |
			I	IIA	IIX**	I	IIA	IIX**
Jumpers1	Cross thoroughbred	10	16 ± 4	37 ± 3	47 ± 5	27 ± 8	36 ± 6	37 ± 11
Endurance2	Arab and cross Arab	18	22 ± 5	41 ± 6	37 ± 8	51 ± 9	46 ±8	3 ± 6
Racetrack3	Thoroughbred	7	12 ± 2	29 ± 3	59 ± 3	16 ± 1	34 ± 6	50 ± 6
Carriage4	Andalusian	7	19 ± 2	33 ± 1	48 ± 2	39 ± 5	32 ± 2	29 ± 4
Dressage5	Andalusian	30	20 ± 6	37 ± 6	43 ± 6	33 ± 11	41 ± 6	26 ± 11
Saddle6	Haflinger	6	15 ± 3	42 ± 6	43 ± 6	29 ± 6	45 ± 8	26 ± 3
Draugth7	Chilean cross- breed	16	30 ± 9	24 ± 4	46 ± 21	62 ± 10	24 ± 4	15 ± 9

* All these animal were horses without training and experience at the beginning of their sportive lives (ranging from 2 to 4 years old)
** This fibre group also includes the hybrid IIAX fibres.
1 From Islas et al (1997); 2 from Rivero et al (1993a); 3 from Martí-Korff, Lindner and Rivero (unpublished data); 4 from Rivero and Serrano (1999); 5 from Serrano et al (1996a); 6 from Kissenbeck, Lindner and Rivero (unpublished data); 7 from Rivero et al (1996b).

Table ② Mean values (±sd) are shown for the mean cross-sectional areas (μm^2) in the superficial (2-3 cm) and deep (6-7 cm) sampling depths of the M. gluteus medius of different types of horses used for various sportive disciplines*

| Activity | Breed | N | Superficial region of the muscle | | | Deep region of the muscle | | |
			I	IIA	IIX**	I	IIA	IIX**
Jumpers1	Cross thoroughbred	10	2335 ± 1000	3466 ± 840	5578 ± 1439	2455 ± 701	3929 ± 1061	5558 ± 1477
Endurance2	Arab and cross Arab	18	2451 ± 510	3412 ± 545	4609 ± 912	3454 ± 699	3929 ± 730	4239 ± 497
Racetrack3	Thoroughbred	7	1507 ± 326	1873 ± 351	3176 ± 675	1624 ± 374	1932 ± 643	2999 ± 101
Carriage4	Andalusian	7	2499 ± 206	3493 ± 312	5633 ± 420	2748 ± 168	3339 ± 221	5265 ± 391
Saddle6	Haflinger	6	1976 ± 766	3254 ± 1664	5465 ± 1807	1976 ± 426	2590 ± 454	4698 ± 1221
Draugth7	Chilean cross- breed	16	2800 ± 700	4100 ± 900	6200 ± 1500	3800 ± 800	4800 ± 800	5800 ± 1600

* All these animal were horses without training and experience at the beginning of their sportive lives (ranging from 2 to 4 years old)
** This fibre group also includes the hybrid IIAX fibres.
1 From Islas et al (1997); 2 from Rivero et al (1993a); 3 from Martí-Korff, Lindner and Rivero (unpublished data); 4 from Rivero and Serrano (1999); 5 from Serrano et al (1996a); 6 from S Kissenbeck, Lindner and Rivero (unpublished data); 7 from Rivero et al (1996b).

ve level, which were biopsed before they completed their respective training and conditioning programmes.

The most remarkable muscle characteristic of jumpers was the balanced percentage between the three major fibre types and the relatively high homogeneity of muscle fibre composition and fibre size between the two sampling sites of the muscle. While elite endurance horses were characterised by a high percentage of type I and IIA fibres, particularly in the deep region of the muscle, active thoroughbred racehorses had a very high percentage of fast-twitch fibres, particularly type IIX, as well as muscle fibres with a very small fibre size (Table II). The balanced proportion among the three main fibre types found in jumpers is in agreement with the versatility of movements and exercises that these animals must perform during competition. Another remarkable muscular feature of show jumping horses is the relatively high size of type II fibres. This property is also in line with the functional demands on these horses, since the explosive nature of the acceleration required for certain activities (e.g. show jumping and sprinting) demands the recruitment of larger (type II) fibres (López-Rivero et al 1990). We have found that in the gluteus medius muscles of several types of horses, type I and IIA fibres are larger in deep regions than in superficial ones, while the opposite patterns were found for type IIX fibres (Table II). However, in both thoroughbred racehorses (Serrano et al 1996b) and show jumpers (Islas et al 1997) no significant differences in fibre sizes were detected between different sampling sites of the muscle. This disagreement could be related to the fact that Thoroughbred related breeds are selected for high speed races, and thus homogeneity of fibres sizes across the muscle might well be a breed characteristic.

Muscular adaptations with show jumping training

Skeletal muscles of horses exhibit a remarkable capacity for stable, long-term adaptation to changing work demands. Depending on the nature, frequency, intensity and duration of the inducing stimulus (physiological exercise), the adaptive response can take the form of hypertrophy, in which muscle fibres increase in size but otherwise retain their initial ultrastructural and biochemical properties, or remodelling without hypertrophy, in which myofibres do not enlarge but acquire markedly different enzymatic and structural characteristics, often accompanied by changes in the microvasculature. No adaptation can occur in the muscle fibres unless they are recruited during exercise.

Hypertrophic growth, as an adaptive response of skeletal muscle to changing work demands, is stimulated by short bursts of muscle activity against high resistance or by prolonged stretch beyond normal resting length (strength training). Myofibre hypertrophy is characterised by a generally co-ordinated increase in abundance, per cell, of most protein constituents of the muscle fibres. The hypertrophic process includes, to a limited degree, selective activation of specific genes, in a transient manner in the period immediately following the onset of work overload, and in a sustained manner as the hypertrophic process proceeds and reaches equilibrium. The major events, however, that underlie muscle hypertrophy involve a general and non-specific augmentation of protein synthesis within the cells. The major physiological consequence of this response is to produce a muscle with a greater capacity for peak force generation.

Remodelling of skeletal muscles, without hypertrophy, a second adaptive response of muscle to changing work demands, is induced by extended periods of tonic contractile activity either sustained continuously or repeated on a regular basis over the course of several weeks or months (training). Myofibre are not enlarged, but undergo a striking reorganisation, with selective activation or repression of many genes. These long-term responses require changes in gene expression, mediated by changes in the rate of transcription of specific genes and in the rate of synthesis of specific proteins (William and Neufer 1996). Mitochondria proliferate and occupy a larger fractional volume within the myofibres. Profiles of expression of many enzymes, cytosolic proteins and membrane receptors are regulated, and switching among different isoforms of myofibrillar proteins may occur. From a physiological standpoint, this form of adaptation (commonly termed the endurance training response) produces a muscle that is resistant to fatigue during extended periods of repetitive contractions.

Over the past 25 years, many studies have examined the effect of several training programmes on equine skeletal muscle (see Snow and Valberg 1994 for a review). Most of these papers have been designed with Thoroughbred racehorses, Standardbred trotters and Endurance horses, but our current knowledge about the adaptive muscular response to training in horses is still scarce. Although there is a great deal of controversy between the results from all these studies, the most common muscular adaptation to training seems to be an increase in oxidative enzymes and capillarisation, as well as a fibre transition between the subtypes of fast fibres (IIX>IIA). Others among these previous studies have also reported different kinds of muscle hypertrophies associated with training, as well as a fast to slow muscle fibre transition associated with long-term endurance (Rivero et al 1995) and draught training programmes (Rivero and Serrano 1999). Overall, the physiological demands of show jumping should be reflected with specific skeletal muscle adaptations to specific training programmes commonly used in horses for this activity.

Skeletal muscle adaptations of muscle fibre sizes and types to a 6 month show jumping training programme are summarised in Tables III and IV and compared with the effects of different training programmes. During the first month of training these horses were exercised daily 6 days/week and work bouts in the morning consisted of 20 minutes of exercise at trot with the rider on the flat plus 60 minutes of jumping activity over fences of 60 cm of height. In the afternoon the horses carried 90 minutes of exercise activity without rider on the flat (every second day) and over fences of 80 to 100 cm of height. During the remaining 5 months, all the horses carried 30 minutes of exercise at walk, trot and gallop, followed by 60 minutes of jumping exercises over fences between 80 and 100 cm of height. In the afternoon, they did 60 minutes of exercise without a rider on the flat (every second day) and over fences of 100 to 110 cm of height.

Most of the training schedules presented in Table III produced an hypertrophy of all fibre types, particularly in the deep region of the gluteus medius muscle. The exception was seen in the Thoroughbred racehorse in which the conventional training programme is usually associated with a reduction in size of type II fibres. Jumping training produced a significant

Table ❸ **Rate of change of the mean cross sectional areas (in percentages of relative terms) of muscle fibre types in the superficial (2-3 cm) and deep (6-7 cm) sampling depths of the M. gluteus medius of horses after different training programmes. ***

Activity	Breed	Month	Superficial region of the muscle			Deep region of the muscle		
			I	IIA	IIX***	I	IIA	IIX***
Jumpers1	Cross thoroughbred	6	↓6	↑9	↑8	↑4	↑23**	↑8
Endurance2	Arab and cross Arab	3	↑14	↑14	↑16	↑28**	↑29**	↑7
Endurance	Angloarab	3	↓13	↓7	↓13**	↑3	↓1	↑8
Carriage4	Andalusian	8	↑28**	↑14	↑12	↑35**	↑18**	↓19
Saddle6	Haflinger	6	↑33**	↑19**	↓8	↑46**	↑47**	↓9
Draugth7	Chilean cross- breed	8	↑17	↑15	↑11	↓9	↓12**	↓16**

Explanations

* The nature, frequency, intensity and duration of exercises involved in all these training programmes are explained in their respective original papers.

** The effect of training was significant with a level of significance of $P<0.05$ (at least).

1 from Islas et al (1998); 2, 3 from Rivero et al (1995); 4 from Rivero and Serrano (1999); 5 from Kissenbeck, Lindner and Rivero (unpublished data); 6 from Martí-Korff, Lindner and Rivero (unpublished data).

*** This fibre group also includes the hybrid IIAX fibres.

hypertrophy of type IIA fibres (23 %) in the deep region of the muscle. Since force generation is directly proportional to cross-sectional area of muscle fibre (López-Rivero et al 1990), this muscular adaptation is particularly important to improve the performance of show jumping horses in order to enhance muscular power in the hind quarters.

Several longitudinal training studies involving horses of various disciplines have reported significant changes after training in histochemical fibre type distribution (Table IV).

Table 4 **Rate of change of the muscle fibre type percentages (absolute values) in the superficial (2-3 cm) and deep (6-7 cm) sampling depths of the M. gluteus medius of horses after different training programmes.***

Activity	Breed	Month	Superficial region of the muscle				Deep region of the muscle			
			I	IIA	IIAX	IIX	I	IIA	IIAX	IIX
Jumpers1	Cross thoroughbred	6	↓2	↑9**	↑11**	↓1	↓2	↓6**	↑9**	↓2
Endurance2	Arab and cross Arab	3	0	↑1	↓1	↑1	↑7**	↓1	↑1	↓5
Endurance	Angloarab	3	↓4	↓2	↑14**	↓7	0	↑3	↓3	0
Carriage4	Andalusian	8	↑3	↑7	↓5	↑9	↑13**	↑1	↓8**	↓3
Saddle6	Haflinger	6	↑9**	↑3		↓12**	↑10**	↓8**		↓2
Draugth7	Chilean cross- breed	8	↑2	↑4	↓2	0	↓2	↑8**	↓5**	↓1

Explanations
* The nature, frequency, intensity and duration of exercises involved in all these training programmes are explained in their respective original papers.
** The effect of training was significant with a level of significance of $P<0.05$ (at least).
1 from Islas et al (1998); 2, 3 from Rivero et al (1995); 4 from Rivero and Serrano (1999); 5 from Kissenbeck, Lindner and Rivero (unpublished data); 6 from Martí-Korff, Lindner and Rivero (unpublished data).

The most frequently reported change is a rise in the percentage of type IIA fibres with a concomitant decrease of type IIB (termed IIX in the present report) after training. Training-induced fast-to-slow fibre transformations have also been described in horses on the basis of myofibrillar ATPase histochemistry when the duration (in total) of the training programme assayed was long enough. Most of these training programmes involved aerobic and endurance exercises, and overall the muscular adaptations found suggest a switch of muscle fibre types in the direction IIX > IIA > I. These adaptations were reversible because after detraining the muscle returned to pre-training level. The physiological meaning of these adaptations with training is a clear reduction in both the maximal velocity of shortening and tension cost of the muscle, but with a concomitant increase in fatigue resistance.

Interestingly and surprisingly a 6 month show jumping training period produced an increase in the number of hybrid fibres coexpressing MHC isoforms IIA and IIX, with a concomitant decrease of type IIA fibres (Table IV). As pure IIX fibres did not change after training, these modifications with jumping training suggest a conversion in the direction IIA > IIX. These changes were associated with significant increases of citrate synthase (CS) and 3-hydroxi-acyl-CoA-dehydrogenase (HAD) after jumping training. The enzyme CS increased by 66 % and 46 % in the superficial and deep regions of the gluteus medius muscle, respectively, whereas HAD increased by 350 % and 450 % in both regions (Islas et al 1998). These increases were directly related to a concomitant increase in mitochondrial density of muscle fibres and, therefore, to an increased oxidative capacity of skeletal muscle. The physiological meaning of the muscle fibre type adaptations with show jumping training are a clear rise in both the maximal velocity of shortening and tension cost of the muscle, together with a simultaneous increase in fatigue resistance. These muscular adaptations have a particular benefit for show jumpers, who use a considerable amount of energy in overcoming inertia, and this is a major contributor to the anaerobic nature of the sport (Clayton 1994). The effects of inertia are felt every time the horse accelerates, decelerates, or turns. Taking off and

Figure ❷ Gluteus medius muscle fibres (middle portion) from active and well-trained show jumping (A, B), endurance (C, D) and racetrack Thoroughbred (E, F) horses.

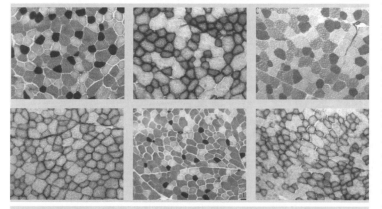

Explanations
Muscle sections were histochemically stained for demonstrated myofibrillar ATPase activity after acid preincubation at pH 4.45 (left column) and nicotinamide adenine dinucleotide tetrazolium reductase (NADH-TR) reaction (right column). Type I fibres are black in the ATPase reaction and show high oxidative capacity at the NADH-TR reaction; IIA fibres are white in the mATPase and have moderate-to-high oxidative capacity in the NADH-TR; type IIX fibres show moderate mATPase activity (grey colour) and low oxidative capacity (unstained with NADH-TR); IIAX fibres, finally, have intermediate histochemical reactions in-between pure IIA and pure IIX fibres. Jumper gluteus medius muscle biopsies are characterised by a high percentage of hybrid IIAX fibres with high oxidative capacity and moderate to high fibre size. Endurance horses have a very high percentage of type I and IIA fibres, a very high oxidative capacity and fibres with larger sizes than the other types of horses. Thoroughbred racehorses, by contrast, have numerous fast-twitch or type II fibres of a very low fibre size and moderate oxidative capacity.

landing over a jump requires intense muscular effort and is particularly expensive energetically.

Summary of show jumping training effects

Figures 2 and 3 summarise the gluteus medius muscle profile of well-trained show jumper horses in comparison with other athletic horses used for endurance rides and gallop racetrack. Jumpers have the highest relative cross-sectional area of the muscle occupied by hybrid type IIAX fibres (Fig. 3) and type II fibres of greater size than thoroughbred racehorses (Fig. 2).

Figure ③ **Figure 3: Relative cross-sectional areas (in percentages) of the gluteus medius muscle biopsies occupied by the various fibre types from three different types of athletic horses: jumpers, endurance horses and racehorses.**

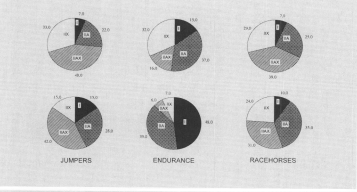

JUMPERS   ENDURANCE   RACEHORSES

Explanations

Charts in the top are from the superficial region of the gluteus medius muscle, while those in the bottom represent data of biopsies removed from the deepest sampling site. This parameter jointly takes into account fibre composition and fibre size, so it is very informative from a functional standpoint. Note the high percentage of the biopsies occupied by hybrid type IIAX fibres in both regions of the muscle in jumpers. See Figure 2's keys for further information.

From the preceeding description it can be seen that significant changes occur within skeletal muscle during training in show jumpers, and that they are mainly related to improvements in power generation (increase in type II fibre size), speed of contraction (switch of IIA to IIAX fibres) and resistance to fatigue (increase in aerobic muscle enzymes). These adaptations of equine muscle to show jumping exercise training do not follow the same general muscular changes observed with other types of long-term endurance training. It is also likely that these training effects will be more pronounced in previously untrained horses than in those re-entering a training programme, and in young horses more than in mature horses. It is not known how much training between competitions is required to maintain muscle fitness in show jumpers once optimal fitness is attained. From detraining studies made with other types of horse it would appear that all these modifications are reversible after stimulus ceases, but some of the changes can be maintained for up to several weeks.

Histopathology of muscle disorders related to show jumping activity

Numerous disorders of skeletal muscle have long been recognised as a common cause of poor performance in athletic horses (Jeffcott et al 1982). In jumpers, like in other athletic horses, most of the cases of muscle disorders suffer from a myopathy with onset occurring during or after exercise. Several factors may predispose horses to muscle strains, such as an inadequate warm-up, pre-existing lameness, exercise to the point of fatigue, and insufficient training or excessive strength training. Lumbar and gluteal muscles are frequently injured in jumpers. The pathologic conditions include local muscle strains, unspecific exertional rhabdomyolysis, polysaccharide storage myopathy, mitochondrial myopathy and malignant hyperthermia. Evaluating these skeletal muscle problems has often been limited to observing clinical signs and measuring serum enzymes. This is because a muscle biopsy has been viewed as a difficult procedure fraught with complications. In our experience, however, this technique has negligible adverse effects and can be done during and after exercise without any adverse effect on performance. Advances in skeletal muscle biopsy techniques reduce even more the risk of complications and make this procedure more acceptable to the client (Andrews et al 1993). The application of new methods of processing, staining and analysing muscle biopsies tissue samples has contributed enormously to our understanding of muscular disease processes in the horse and has also resulted in the discovery of new types of muscle disorder. In some cases, this alternative is the only way for an etiological diagnosis.

The muscle biopsy: indications and techniques

Before performing a muscle biopsy, a complete clinical examination of the patient is essential. This examination should include taking a thorough history and conducting a physical examination and locomotion examination to determine which muscle or group of muscles is involved. The most common clinical signs include atrophy and weakness, local pain to palpation, swelling, muscle tone reduced or augmented, muscle cramps, especially during or after exercise, reluctance to move, discomfort or inability to round over fences, shortened stride, and hindlimb lameness. Diseases showing some of these symptoms are considered to be myopathies, and horses with such clinical signs should be considered for muscle biopsy. Elevated serum enzyme activities (CPK AST and LDH), particularly after exercise, indicate active muscular damage. When the injury is not progressive, these values return to baseline normal values after days or weeks. Specific indications for muscle biopsy include the following: (i) to distinguish between neurogenic and myogenic causes of progressive muscle atrophy; (ii) to distinguish between acute and recurrent exertional rhabdomyolysis; (iii) to determine the extent and severity of muscle damage in cases of recurrent exertional rhabdomyolysis; (iv) to help support a diagnosis of metabolic disease in horses with suspected polysaccharide storage myopathy; and (v) to assess muscle changes in overtrained horses.

The site for biopsy is critical for successful pathologic diagnosis. The propulsive muscles of the pelvic limb (gluteus medius and semitendinosus) are commonly biopsied. If a relationship between back pain and muscle disorders is suspected, a biopsy of the longissimus dorsi muscle may be indicated. Some myopathies affect primarily postural muscles; such is the case of the equine motor neurone disease, where a biopsy of the sacrocaudalis dorsalis muscle is indicated (Valentine 1996). The site of the biopsy in the longissimus dorsi muscle is behind the saddle in the middle of the loin 5-7 cm off midline and 15-20 cm cranial to the tuber coxae. An area of the skin of approximately 2.5 cm2 is shaved, washed and cleaned. One ml of local anaesthetic (i.e. 2% mepivacaine or lidocaine) is then injected intradermally along the line of the proposed incision and into the fascia overlapping the muscle. A stab incision about 0.5 cm long is made through the skin and fascia using a small scalpel blade. A 6-mm diameter modified Bergström needle (Carl Mortensen, 4632 Bjaeverskov, Denmark) is inserted and directed vertically with a depth of 3-4 cm. The needle is pressed into the muscle belly, and several cuts are made using the inner core of the needle before it is withdrawn. After biopsying, suture is not required to close the small incision, which leaves an unnoticeable scar. Complications from this procedure are rare. The same procedure is suitable for the gluteus medius muscle. The site of biopsy is 10-15 cm along a line from the centre of the tuber coxae to the head of the tail at a depth of 6 cm. Deeper biopsies are obtained because the deeper part of this muscle is more often recruited with exercise than the superficial ones, and pathological findings associated with exertional myopathies are often found in the deepest region of the muscle.

Alternatively, an open surgical biopsy is necessary in the horse when: (i) the percutaneous needle biopsy is difficult or dangerous because the muscle is not easily accessible or vulnerable structures are on the surface; (ii) a large amount of tissue is needed and (iii) strips of muscle are required for determining in vitro muscle twitch characteristics in horses with chronic recurrent exertional rhabdomyolysis. A detailed description of this technique has been given for the horse (Andrews et al 1993). In brief, after routine surgical preparation and local anaesthesia, skin and fascia are cleft and a piece of muscle is harvested. After sampling the skin is sutured with interrupted non-absorbable material. Although the technique allows a large muscle sample to be obtained, its disadvantages include dehiscence of the suture, haematoma or seroma formation, and scar formation. This procedure is indicated for biopsying the sacrocaudalis dorsalis muscle in horses that have generalised muscle atrophy suspected to be due to equine motor neurone disease (Divers et al 1996).

Muscle biopsies can be differently processed for light microscopy, electron microscopy and biochemical studies. Most of the light microscopy analysis of muscle biopsies can be made on cryostat sections, so routine formaline fixation and processing in this way is not advised. Muscle samples for histology and histochemistry must be frozen by 30 seconds immersion in isopentane chilled to about −150 %C by liquid nitrogen. Ideally, overnight frozen samples should be shipped in dry ice or liquid nitrogen to an appropriate diagnostic laboratory for histological and histochemical evaluation. Alternatively, the patient may be referred to a clinical teaching hospital with a histopathological support laboratory for a complete neuromuscular work-up and muscle biopsy. Once at the laboratory, specimens are transferred to the cryostat, and usually sectioned at −20 %C. For routine studies in the authors' laboratories 20 successive cryostat sections are picked up on 10 coverslips and stained with a battery of histological and histochemical stains (Rivero 1999). Routine stains employed include hematoxylin and eosin (HE), periodic acid Shiff's (PAS), alpha-amylase PAS, succinic dehydrogenase (SDH), alpha-glycerophosphate dehydrogenase (GPD), myofibrillar adenosine triphosphatase (mATPase) after different preincubations and immunocytochemistry by using specific monoclonal antibodies.

Normal muscles

Transverse sections of normal equine muscle stained with HE reveal polygonal fibres tightly packed together and separated only by a thin layer or intervening endomysial connective tissue and capillaries. Muscle fibres of the same histochemical type vary little in size. The small densely staining nuclei are located at the periphery of the fibre.

Enzyme mATPase histochemistry applied to horse muscle reveals that the different fibre types are distributed according to a typical mosaic pattern as a result of the intermingling of type I, IIA and IIX fibres belonging to different motor units. The SDH reaction is used as an index of mitochondrial presence and, hence, the capacity for aerobic metabolism and, consequently, as an index of fatigability. Type I, IIA and the hybrid IIAX show moderate-to-high oxidative capacity, while pure type IIX fibres have low-oxidative capacity and, hence, they are more fatigable. The GPD reaction is used as a marker of glycolytic potential; type II fibres stain darker than type I fibres, so they have a higher glycolytic capacity. The PAS reaction is used to demonstrate glycogen content of muscle fibres; it stains II fibres more strongly than type I fibres. Finally the alpha-amylase PAS reaction is used physiologically to visualise capillaries surrounding muscle cells, and pathologically to demonstrate the presence of an alpha-amylase-resistant polysaccharide complex that is the hallmark feature found in the polysaccharide storage myopathy.

Quantitative analysis of muscle biopsies include fibre type percentages, fibre sizes, coefficients of variability of fibre sizes, atrophy and hypertrophy factors, capillary density, percentage of fibres with internal nuclei and quantitative enzyme histochemistry of oxidative capacity, glycolytic potential, speed of contraction and glycogen content (see Rivero 1999 for details).

Changes in diseased muscle may occur at different levels: (i) fibre type proportion; (ii) alterations in fibre sizes; (iii) alterations at the muscle fibre levels; and (iv) modifications at the whole muscle level.

Main events of muscle damage and muscle repair

Muscle damage in the jumpers usually occurs from excessive exertion, tearing or trauma of individual muscles, or specific diseases that produce rhabdomyolysis (Snow and Valberg 1994). Muscle tissue is regarded as having an excellent capacity to repair itself. But its ability to regenerate is related to the extent of the muscle necrosis, the preservation of the innervation and the blood supply to the area, and the degree of intactness of the architecture of the

Figure ❹ **Main cellular events during degeneration, phagocytosis and regeneration of muscle fibres.**

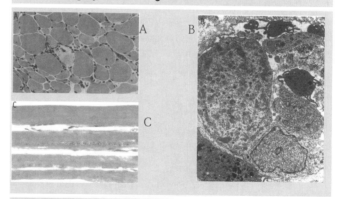

Explanation

A) This biopsy, stained with routine hematoxylin eosin (x240), shows the typical picture of a destructive myopathy. A pale necrotic fibre in the centre is surrounded by mononuclear phagocytic cells. Regenerating fibres are small with blue, basophilic cytoplasm, large vesicular nuclei and prominent nucleoli. Muscle fibres vary in size, and many are atrophic. B) Electron microscopy (x7,600). The profile of the cross-section of the original muscle fibre is outlined by the irregular basement membrane (e.g. top of picture). Densely-stained macrophages with ruffle borders are associated with cell debris (top right and bottom left). A pale regenerating myoblast (left) has bundles of myofibrils in the cytoplasm, cut in cross section and seen here as irregular dark patches in the cytoplasm. C) In this section, stained with hematoxylin and eosin, nuclear chains are seen in the centre of fibres. The upper normal fibre has peripheral nuclei, whereas the fibre below has a chain of central nuclei which are vesicular and have prominent nucleoli. A similar appearance of nuclear chains is seen in basophilic regenerating fibres.

Figure ⑤   Main cellular events during degeneration, phagocytosis and regeneration of muscle fibres.

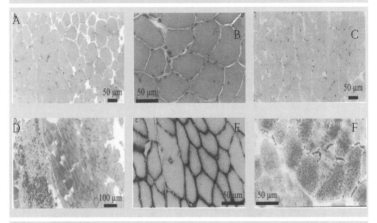

Explanation

A) local myositis; B-E) exertional rhabdomyolysis; and F) polysaccharide storage myopathy. A) Several fibres are hypercontracted, with rounded contours and very wide extracelullar spaces; muscle fibres at the left appear to be normal. B) A small basophilic cell with vesicular nucleus and prominent nucleoli is seen in the centre, together with mature fibres with central nuclei (bottom right) and middle fibrosis. C) Many fibres are seen with centrally placed nuclei, as a sign of excellent muscle repair after injury in the exertional rhabdomyolysis (hematoxylin and eosin). D) An extensive area of this biopsy, stained with hematoxylin and eosin, is occupied by a scar of connective tissue, fibroblast and macrophages, indicating a previous and very severe previous muscle injury; the rest of the biopsy has a normal appearance. E) In this mitochondrial stain (succinate dehydrogenase) there is a large IIX fibre with a target-like structure in its centre. In this case, the muscle biopsy was taken from the gluteus medius muscle with extensive denervation and reinnervation, probably as a result of severe rhabdomyolysis. F) This biopsy was stained with PAS and shows a heterogeneously distributed glycogen and numerous PAS positive inclusions that are commonly seen in the polysaccharide storage myopathy; most of these inclusions are alpha-amylase-resistant.

muscle. Complete repair of muscle fibres without any residual scarring depends on the degree of damage that occurs to the basement membrane surrounding each myofibre. Severe trauma or tearing of a muscle that results in destruction of this membrane usually results in the proliferation of connective tissue and scar formation. When exertional myopathies, by contrast, do not damage the basement membrane, complete repair of muscle tissue is possible.

After disruption or segmental necrosis of muscle fibres following exercise (Fig. 4), the damaged portion of the muscle fibre is sealed by a new sarcolemmal membrane within 10 to 20 hours.

Macrophage infiltration and phagocytosis of necrotic rests within the damaged muscle fibre can be observed within 16 hours to 4 days of injury (Fig. 4B).

Repair of the damaged segments requires activation and multiplication of satellite cells, since myonuclei are in a postmitotic stage. Satellite cells migrate along an intact basement membrane and form myoblasts which fuse together to form myotubes within 1 week following acute damage. These have a basophilic appearance in the HE stains because of their high RNA content (Fig. 4A).

As myofibrils are formed, the central nucleus of the myotube is gradually displaced, and within 1 to 2 months of the injury, it takes its customary

subsarcolemmal position. If damaged fibres lose their innervation, new neuromuscular junctions are established by sprouts from nearby axons.

Exercise-associated myopathies

Nonspecific local myositis

Local strains in the back and gluteal muscles are common injuries in jumpers because of inadequate warm-up, excessive strength training, muscle
fatigue, or insufficient suppleness exercises with training. Deep palpation
of these muscles results in pain and dorsiflexion of the spine (Snow and
Valberg 1994). They may also appear warm. In some other circumstances,
this muscular problem is secondary to an underlying disorder of the spine
or sacroiliac joint (Lindholm 1998). Clinical signs include reluctance to
move, the stride has a short anterior phase and serum activities of CPK and
AST are usually mildly elevated. Evaluation of muscle biopsies from these
horses is usually normal, although some acute inflammatory findings such
as interstitial oedema and round-shaped fibres can be observed (Fig. 5A).

Other more severe pathological changes include waxy degeneration of
muscle fibres, myonecrosis with phagocytosis and mononuclear infiltration
and low fibrosis. Diagnosis can be confirmed by thermography and/or
scintigraphy (Morris et al 1991).

Exertional rhabdomyolysis

Exertional rhabdomyolysis or "tying-up" is a quite common disease that aff-
licts all types of athletic horse, including jumpers, but appears to be more
common in mares than in stallions and geldings. In some horses, there
may be few clinical signs apart from poor performance, and the condition
may only become evident on serum or plasma biochemical tests where
elevations in muscle-derived enzymes are found. In horses performing prolonged exercise, the condition is usually acute and severe, but in jumpers
and racehorses it tends to be a recurrent, low-grade problem. In reality,
rhabdomyolysis represents a pathological description of a number of
muscle diseases that have common clinical signs (Snow and Valberg
1994).

Histopathological changes associated with acute exertional rhabdomyolysis include swelling, vacuolisation and fragmentation of muscle
fibres with loss of their striated appearance. Muscle fibres and whole fascicles may be separated due to extensive oedema. Macrophages may well
be present within 2-3 days. Regeneration may occur within one week if

the basement membrane of fibres was not intensely damaged. It includes the presence of small basophilic fibres containing large central nuclei and prominent nucleoli (Fig. 5B).

Within one month, several of these regenerating cells will be present and some may have residual, centrally located nuclei (Fig. 5C).

If trauma is severe enough to disrupt the blood and/or nerve supply to a muscle, or the architecture of the basement membrane, muscle regeneration is not possible and the muscle will be replaced with adipose and extensive scar of connective tissue (Fig. 5D)

Muscle biopsies from horses with recurrent exertional rhabdomyolysis often show evidence of recurrent waves of degeneration and regeneration. Thus, within the same sample, vacuolated, fragmented fibres, fibres with macrophage infiltration and mature fibres with centrally placed nuclei may all be observed. Affected fibres in these cases are almost exclusively type II fibres scattered throughout fascicles. In some severe chronic cases of exertional rhabdomyolysis denervation of type II fibres can occur. In the course of reinnervation, mitochondrial spatial orientation may change and target-like structures may form in the centre of some of these fibres (Fig. 5E).

Modest to high increases in muscle glycogen staining may be evident in horses with recurrent exertional rhabdomyolysis. The recurrence of rhabdomyolysis in these cases suggests an underlying defect in muscle function. Recent evidence suggests that the defect in these horses is inherited and involves abnormal regulation of muscle contraction and intracellular calcium regulation. Myogenic atrophy with massive loss of muscle fibres is usually a sequeala to severe rhabdomyolysis. In these cases a high percentage of hybrid type IIC fibres, i.e. fibres coexpressing type I and IIA myosin heavy chains, is frequently observed, in connection with evident loss of muscle mass.

Polysaccharide storage myopathy

An additional pathological feature of muscle biopsies from certain breeds of horses with clinical signs of recurrent exertional rhabdomyolysis (Quarter horse, Warmblood, draught horses, Andalusian and Arab) is the presence of PAS positive crystalline inclusions in fast twitch fibres together with a very high intracellular and heterogeneously distributed content of glycogen (Fig. 5F). The PAS positive inclusion bodies are resistant to alpha-amylase digestion (Valberg et al 1997). Other additional histopathological findings usually observed in this disease, together with its differential diagnosis with non-specific recurrent exertional rhabdomyolysis are considered in another article of the current book (López and Glitz 2000).

Neurogenic myopathies

Spinal and gluteal muscles of show jumpers may show profound and rapid atrophy due to several neuropathies. Muscle atrophy is frequently not confined to the muscles of the spine, but may also involve other skeletal muscles. Epaxial atrophy is, however, often most readily noted due to the prominence of the spinous apophysis processes of vertebrae. Most commonly, neurogenic atrophy occurs with equine motor neurone disease (Divers et al 1996), but unilateral atrophy of back or proximal limb muscles can also result from peripheral neuropathies.

Figure 6 Myopthic changes seen in the gluteus medius muscle from a 7 year-old pony diagnostised with equine motor neuron disease.

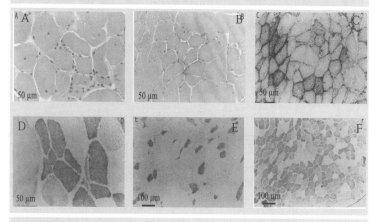

Explanations

Figure 6. A) Several fibres are necrotic and hypercellular due to invasion by phagocytes whereas other cells have a round shape and centrally placed nuclei; there is prominent fibrosis (hematoxylin and eosin). B) Centrofascicular atrophied and compensatory hypertrophy of surrounding fibres; the consequence is a very high increased variability in fibre size (hematoxylin and eosin). C) Decreased oxidative capacity of muscle fibres is a typical picture of denervated muscle; in addition many moth-eaten fibres are observed (NADH-TR). D) Angular atrophied fibres with concave sides and triangular section (immunohistochemistry with anti-MHC IIA monoclonal antibody). E) Predominance of type II fibres is also to be expected in denervated muscles (immunohistochemistry with anti-MCH I monoclonal antibody). F) Predominance of fibres expressing IIA MHC isoform (immunohistochemical reaction).

Neurogenic atrophy is characterised by angular atrophied muscle fibres of both types I and II (Fig. 6).

An angulated fibre is small in diameter and has concave sides. Fibres such as these may occur singly or in groups in certain stages of denervation atrophy. A variable number of motor units will contain atrophied fibres whereas other motor units may contain fibres undergoing compensatory hypertrophy (Fig. 6B). As a consequence, the coefficients of variability of fibre sizes are significantly increased over 25 % in neurogenic myopathies. The checkerboard pattern of fibre types is altered when denervated muscle is reinnervated. Following the denervation of muscle, sprouts of adjacent intact motor axons reinnervate the muscle fibres. During this process, the random distribution of fibre types is so altered that an increased number of fibres of the same histochemical type appear immediately adjacent to each other. Such a histochemical change is termed "fibre type grou-

ping" and provides an unequivocal means of early recognition of neurogenic muscle disorders. When the bi-directional dialogue between muscle
fibres and motor neurons is deficient, such as in the equine motor neuron
disease, muscle becomes less oxidative (Fig. 6C), more glycolytic and with
a very high percentage of fast twitch fibres (Fig. 6C, E, F). Target fibres are
also often found in neurogenic processes, as well as "moth-eaten fibres" a
term applied to myofibres that show multiple patches of decreased oxidative enzyme activity (Fig. 6C). Eventually, chronic neurogenic processes
may result in end stage changes of fatty infiltration and fibrosis (Fig. 6A).

Mixed neuropathy/myopathy is also found in athletic horses. Muscle
biopsies with this problem are characterised by angular atrophied muscle
fibres, selective hypertrophy of type I fibres, moth-eaten fibres and degeneration with phagocytosis.

The work of a national show jumper equipe veterinarian

In this article I describe my work as a team veterinarian of the german show jumping team. As an actual example I will take the year 2000. It is the year of the World Cup Final in Las Vegas and the Olympic Games in Sydney in September 2000.

In Germany there are team veterinarians since the beginning of the sixties. First there was just one veterinarian for all disciplines. With the high number of international competitions today, each discipline has its own veterinarian. I am working as a team veterinarian since the first World equestrian Games 1990 in Stockholm.

In Germany the DOKR (German olympic committee for riding) is responsible for the nomination of the show-jumping - team for any CSIO or major championship as the European Championship, the World Championship or the Olympic Games. The nomination is done by the show-jumping committee. Members are officials of the federation, the chef d´ equipe, the trainer, representants of the riders, jumping judges and the team veterinarian. My role can be defined by the following statements:

- I have a contract with the DOKR. I am adviser for the DOKR. It is my job to work out every information necessary to achieve a complete picture about each horse that may be nominated.
- I am only responsible to the DOKR, not to riders, horse owners or sponsors.
- I am responsible for the horses competitive fitness, and have to give advise in case of health problems concerning treatment matters carefully considering FEI rules on medication control.

Every year I start my work around march. On a meeting with the national team trainer we work out the list of horses and riders that may be interesting for the yearly championship. Hereby we consider the results obtained by horses and riders in the former year and latest competitions. Because of the large number of international riders in Germany this list contains often more than ten horses.

Then I start to get in contact with the riders. We discuss their competition plan for the year. I try to get into contact with the home veterinarians. They know the horses best. I need every information that is necessary for my work as the team veterinarian. After several years of interaction this is nowadays done in a friendly attitude, and is completely confidential. The home-veterinarians know that I am not taking away their clients.

From the moment the riders and their horses are on the list I try to stay in close contact with them. A lot of telephone calls are done after each weekend. The results are discussed. How did the horses do and feel ? Did any problems occur with them. Orthopedic problems are of major interest. The yearly World Cup Final (former VOLVO World Cup Final) is always a good chance to watch new or young horses. During a week of competition with them you get a lot of information as a team veterinarian.

On the way of nomination to the championship we have two trials:
- German Championship (16th to 18th of June 2000)
- CHIO Aachen (11th to16th of July 2000)

After the German Championship the list of candidates is reduced to the ones with the best auspices. I examine all horses very closely to get their health status. The evaluation includes a thorough clinical examination, lameness exam, blood hematology and biochemical screening. Quite often I have an-in depth discussion concerning training management, warm-up, and feeding.

After the CHIO Bad Aachen the definitive nomination will be carried out. At this point the team veterinarian needs to have every little detail concerning health status, fitness, training or injuries. He will be always asked if there is any problem or not. After the nomination I prepare and coordinate the journey to the city where the championship will take place. This requires involvement of the transport enterprises, health papers to suffice international hygiene regulations, and equipment.

In my opinion, the team veterinarian does not need to be the best specialist in equine medicine, but he/she needs to be well trained in this matter. The team-vet has to be also an adviser, organizer, driver, groom and psychologist. She/he needs to win over the confidence of all persons involved with the selected horses. We have a system in which chef d´ equipe, trainer and team veterinarians form a team. This system has been very succesful in the past, and I hope that it will continue to be an asset for success.

How can the rider help show jumpers to have better performances?

1 Summary

The purpose of this paper is to review current knowledge concerning the effect of the rider on jumping performance in horses. Although some important research has been conducted on equine jumping biomechanics over the past two decades, there is still much to learn about the role of the rider in controlling the horse's motion. There are many determining factors involved in the assessment of rider effects. These factors need to be highlighted in order to ensure appropriate evaluation and improve jumping performance in horses and riders. This paper examines previous research in jumping horse mechanics, and provides a theoretical framework to aid future analyses on the effects of the rider on performance in jumping horses.

2 Introduction

Showjumping is a competitive international event, and is one of the world's most popular equestrian sports. Despite this, it is a relative newcomer to equestrian competition. Jumping events were not recorded as an official event until 1865, when the Royal Dublin Society's annual show held a jumping competition for high and wide fences. This was followed in 1866 by a competition at the Paris Show, where riders jumped over a cross-country course, rather than fences in an arena. By the turn of the century show jumping was growing in popularity on a world-wide basis, and three competitions for individual riders were held at the Paris Olympic Games in 1900 (Hartley Edwards 1994).

Little research into equine locomotion mechanics was done before the mid-1980s. A review of literature on equine locomotion research at that time revealed that the knowledge of locomotion was far from complete, especially concerning the mechanics involved in jumping horses (Leach and Dagg 1983). Even less scientific research has been conducted into the effects of the rider on jumping performance in horses. On the other hand, countless coaching articles and books have been written on jumping horses and what the rider can do to improve jumping performance and ability in horses (for example: Serio 1992; Hadley 1987).

Additionally, many riders and coaches of show jumping horses have gained knowledge through years of experience and word of mouth, and not through scientific evaluation. This is where science meets the artisan, and it is up to the scientists to answer the very real questions that are found in practical situations.

This review aims to evaluate the effects and influences of the rider on jumping ability in horses. Several aspects will be examined:
- The role of the rider
- Phases of the jump sequence
- Theoretical models for jumping horses and rider effects
- Experimental data on the effects of the rider
- Avenues of future research in equine biomechanics

2.1 The Rider

It is well known that riders of different calibre exist, and the better riders typically produce a better performance from their mounts. Experienced riders of sport horses have a tremendous ability to control the movement and locomotion of their horses. There is also a matching process involved in that some horses perform to a higher standard with a particular rider. In coaching literature, it is generally acknowledged that the rider has much influence over the horse's jumping ability and technique (Klimke 1989). The exact nature of this has not been scientifically investigated.

Show jumping rarely relies on the physical strength of the rider. Even small light rider can achieve as successful a performance as a bigger, stronger rider can. In many cases the response of the horse is not controlled by the size of the rider. In fact equine competitions are probably one of the only sports where men and women compete on an equal basis. The way the rider sits on the horse, for example leaning forward or sitting out of the saddle, has an important role in controlling the movement of the horse. By altering his/her body position, the center of gravity (CG) position of the whole horse-rider system can in turn be altered. There is however, an optimum range of positions for the rider on the horse's back, and for the rider's hands on the horse's neck. Perpetually incorrect posture and position of the rider can cause acute disease and permanent injury in horses (Meyer 1996).

There are many factors involved during jumping. To thoroughly assess the rider's influence it is necessary to understand some of the important factors that determine rider effects and how these factors interact with each other. In order to do this a theoretical understanding of all the determining factors is required. In the absence of an established theoretical model for equine jumping, it is appropriate to draw upon existing knowledge in human biomechanics. The deterministic models of Hay (1985) were adapted and used as a basis for examining equine jumping. The deterministic model process involves two steps:
1. Divide the activity into discrete elements or phases (e.g. Approach, Take off, etc).

2. Identify those factors that interact to produce the required outcome
    during each phase.
It is recommended that the factors included should be mechanical quanti-
ties and should be linked in a hierarchical structure by:
*   Mathematical relationships, which use simple addition and subtrac-
    tion, for example the height achieved by a high jumper is the sum of
    the take off height, flight height and clearance height.
*   Mechanical relationships which, examine factors such as the time
    taken to cover a certain distance or an optimum angle of take off.
There are many similarities between the techniques used by equine
jumpers and their human counterparts, principally long jumpers and high
jumpers. Similar characteristics are found during the approach and take off
strides for both humans and horses. To contrast with human high and long
jumpers, however, the equine jumper does not have a straight, measured
run up to just a single jump, but has to jump a series of fences of different
types, heights and widths all of which will have different approach angles
and lengths. The stride length must therefore be regulated (usually by the
rider) to allow the horse to take off from a suitable position. Likewise after
landing, the human athlete is finished until their next turn, whereas the
equine jumper has to adjust itself as the following route is also variable in
length and direction. There may even be another fence within another stride of two, in which case a successful landing and recovery is vital. It is felt
for these reasons that the equine jumper must be somewhat more flexible
and adaptable than his human counterpart when it comes to jumping competitions (Clayton and Barlow 1989).

An examination of the literature and knowledge in equine jumping
helped in the development of a series of models for use in analyses involving equine jumping (Powers and Harrison 1999). For the purposes of this
paper, these models have been adapted to highlight the important areas of
rider effect.

2.2 Phases of the jump

A showjumping competition can be classified as a continuous skill, with
many fences of different sizes and configurations that have to be negotia-
ted in order to complete the course. When examining/evaluating the horse's jump, five discrete parts are evident. These are: Approach, Take off,
Suspension (i.e. flight), Landing and Departure and are illustrated in
Figures 1a and 1b.

The rider's influence during the various phases of the jump may vary
considerably. Previous research has examined characteristics of the
approach (Leach et al 1984; Clayton and Barlow 1989; Clayton and Barlow

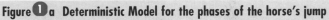

Figure **1**a Deterministic Model for the phases of the horse's jump

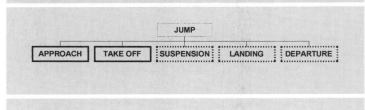

Figure **1**b Stick figure illustration of a horse and rider showing the jump phases

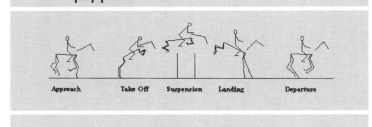

1991; Deuel and Park 1991); take off (Clayton et al 1995; Colborne et al 1995; Clayton et al 1996; Powers et al 1999); suspension (Galloux and Barrey 1997); landing (Clayton and Barlow 1989; Clayton 1997), and departure phase (Clayton and Barlow 1991; Deuel and Park 1991). Review of all this literature shows that the rider effects are most important during the approach and take off, since the factors involved in these phases will primarily determine the jump outcome.

2.3 Models for the kinematic evaluation of jumping horses

The following models examine the factors involved during the approach and the take off. For each of the models shown, the determining factors are highlighted to indicate their importance or otherwise of the rider. The ranges of effects, based on literature are:
- Factors within rider control with scientific evidence
- Factors outside of rider control
- Factors with unknown level of rider control – no scientific evidence

2.3.1 Approach

The model for the approach phase is shown in Figure 2. In a showjumping competition, the approach is typically conducted at a canter. The purpose of the approach is to generate optimal conditions for take off, such as, appropriate body position, velocity and control of angular momentum. The fence dimension and the distance between the fences are not within the control of the rider, however they determine how high and far the horse and rider system have to jump.

From coaching literature it is generally recommended that the approach to a fence should be "controlled and balanced", and that the rider's position and weight distribution will have an effect on the horse's movement and performance during jumping (Blignault 1997). However, little empirical data is available on these factors.

A rider can regulate the horse's lead and stride pattern through instruction and adjustments in his/her body position. By altering the stride length and velocity, the rider can extend or collect the horse's stride and these alterations in stride characteristics can assist the horse in attaining the most appropriate distance from the fence at take off.

Important elements of the approach are the velocity and accuracy of the approach. The velocity is determined by stride length and stride frequency. The maximum stride frequency is governed mainly by physiological factors such as muscle forces (strength), phasic muscle activity patterns, and the elasticity of the muscle and tendon unit (Alexander and Bennett-Clarke 1977). Therefore, the rider does not directly affect the maximum stride frequency, however it can be improved through appropriate training.

It is important that the velocity of the approach is optimised. Every horse will have a functional limitation in its muscle force generation capacity, i.e. strength. If the horizontal velocity is large, the ground contact time at take off will be reduced. The product of force and time applied, with body mass held constant governs the velocity at take off. Therefore, maximum jumping capacity is fully determined by the impulse at take off, which in turn is an optimisation between approach speed (which reduces the time for force production) and muscle strength (which limits the magnitude of force generated). The rider can largely control the approach speed. Through training, the horse can be taught to lengthen and/or shorten its stride as demanded, thus optimising the horizontal velocity (speed), stride pattern and accuracy.

2.3.2 Touchdown phase

Much of what occurs at take off, depends on the ability of the rider to control the horse at the touchdown phase of the final approach stride. It is at this point that the linear velocities and angular momentum required to optimally clear the fence are generated. In order to activate the stretch shortening cycle (Komi and Bosco 1978) an optimum downward force is required at touchdown to generate the optimal upward impulse to clear the

Figure ❷   **Deterministic Model for the Approach**

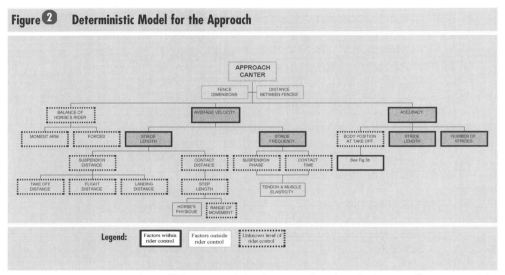

fence. If the approach has been too fast, then the horse will use most of the touchdown phase as a breaking mechanism, thus inhibiting the generation of upward impulse. If the approach has been too slow, then this downward force at touchdown will be insufficient to activate the stretch shortening cycle and the horse is unlikely to generate its maximum muscular tension. Clearly, there are optimum touchdown forces, which must be achieved, but no research to date has fully evaluated the size of these forces or impulses, or the factors which interact to determine them in show jumping horses. For example, muscle tendon elasticity and stiffness, body mass, and time of force development.

Generally a more experienced equine jumper can cope with a faster approach, due to having greater muscle strength and increased control of the motor skills (Clayton 1990). If the horse approaches the fence too fast, there may not be enough time to generate sufficient velocity to clear the fence successfully. As a result the horse may either hit the fence or use compensatory movements to clear it such as rolling a shoulder or the hind limbs, or twisting in the air (Clayton 1990). Clayton and Barlow (1991) found that the horizontal velocity of the approach to a fence 1.55 m in height is less than 50% of the horse's estimated maximum velocity at the gallop. When jumping a water jump, although the approach speed is a good deal faster than the approach to a higher fence (Deuel and Park 1991), show jumpers do not approach a water jump at very high speeds. This contrasts with human long jumpers who accelerate to speeds greater that 90% of the maximal possible for the athlete (Hay 1986). However, if the horse's long jumping ability were being tested as in human athletes, perhaps greater approach velocities would be required.

The balance of the horse and rider is an important element for many phases of the jump. Balance is a term that is frequently used by horse trainers, but in biomechanical terms it has a precise meaning. It is not clear whether the trainer's definition of balance is the same as the biomechanist's. Mechanically, balance is defined as the ability to control equilibrium. When a body is motionless, it is in static equilibrium. However, a body in motion is in dynamic equilibrium when inertial factors are considered (Hall 1995). The mechanical behaviour of a body subject to force(s) is influenced by the position of its CG. The mechanical stability of a body is its resistance to both linear force and torque. If the CG of the horse and rider are out of alignment, for example during the approach or at the point of take off, unfavourable forces will be generated, which are likely to destabilise the equilibrium of the horse and rider system. Although the rider may weigh less than 10% of the mass of the horse, any deviation in the vertical alignment of the rider's CG from the horse's CG will affect the state of equilibrium. The larger the deviation, the greater the effect on the horse's ability to move naturally. Even a light rider sitting in an inappropriate position may, in practise, effect the horse's balance and movement quite significantly. There is, however, little if any quantitative research on this area, which may have important implications for horse trainers and riding coaches.

2.3.3 Take off

The model for the take off is presented in Figures 3a and 3b. The take off encompasses the stance phase of the two pelvic limbs (Clayton 1989). The purpose of the take off is to obtain optimum vertical velocity and rotation, while retaining a suitable amount of horizontal velocity. This is the most important phase because it is at this phase that the trajectory of the horse's flight is determined. Much research has rightly focused on the take off parameters in their research (Clayton et al 1995; Colborne et al 1995; Clayton et al 1996; Powers et al 1999). This research has shown that many of the take off factors are subject to the influence of a rider.

Figure 3a Deterministic Model for the Take Off

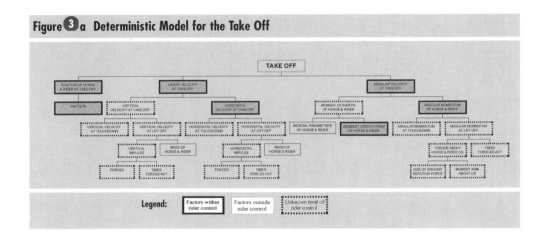

Figure 3b Deterministic Model for body position at take off

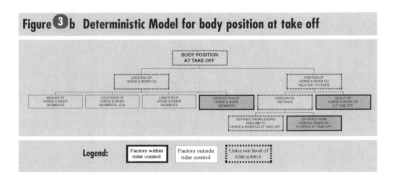

2.3.3.1 Linear considerations

An experienced rider can position a horse at a specific distance from the fence by adjustment of the stride length and frequency during the approach strides. The CG height the horse achieves at take off can be influenced by the rider's own position at this point. The velocity of the approach will influence the same take off velocities, and therefore the angle of take off.

At take off the horse and rider system becomes a projectile. Two important components involved in projectile motion are translation of the whole body CG and rotation of the horse and rider system about the CG. During the suspension phase of a jump, the translational component is curvilinear, i.e. parabolic. The flight trajectory is determined at the moment of take off by the horizontal and vertical velocity components at take off (Hay

1985). Figure 3c shows the main linear factors involving the horse's centre of gravity at take-off.

2.3.3.2 Angular considerations

Equally important to the jump outcome are the angular motion factors. The importance of angular momentum in the jumping horse has been briefly discussed (Clayton 1990; Clayton and Barlow 1991). Angular motion during the suspension phase is generated by eccentric force at take off (i.e. force not acting through the centre of mass of the horse and rider system). The position of the body segments of the horse and rider system will effect the moment of inertia, i.e. the resistance to rotate, and the level of angular momentum generated. It is angular momentum that causes the jumping

Figure 3 c Diagram illustrating some of the main factors involved during the take off

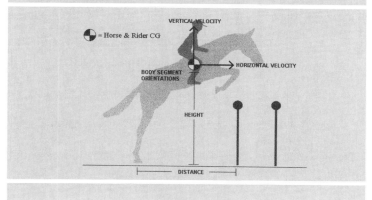

horse to rotate during flight over a fence and land on it forelimbs. The amount of angular momentum, during the suspension phase tends to remain constant, although there may be some minor effects caused by variations in air resistance, and forces due to the horse hitting the fence. The rate of rotation, i.e. angular velocity, can be altered if the moment of inertia of the horse rider system is changed during flight. This can be achieved by the horse and rider redistributing body mass, by movements of the body segments during flight.

During the jump the CG of the horse and rider system needs sufficient velocity at take off to clear the fence, i.e. appropriate trajectory of the CG; and sufficient control of rotational motion to land successfully, i.e. the body rotation around the CG.

The models presented here show the chains of dependency of observable factors on performance. The importance of each factor will vary from being relatively trivial to being of major importance. The importance of the rider's influence on the factors in the model will also vary, and further scientific research is required to establish the true nature of the rider's effect on jumping horses. The models attempt to identify the important elements of jumping, but should be subjected to continued academic scrutiny and review. Once the models have been tested, and refined if necessary, they can be used to provide direction and assistance in training and research.

2.4 Experimental studies into the effects of the rider

2.4.1 Linear motion

Although some research has been conducted on the kinematics of the CG of ridden jumping horses (Clayton et al 1995; Clayton et al 1996), in these studies the rider was not digitized. The rider effect was accounted for only by raising the height of the CG in the trunk of the horse by 10% (Clayton et al 1995) and the cranial/caudal positioning of the CG was left unaltered. In most kinematic analyses, however, the horse and rider are in motion, with constantly changing body segment orientations that may alter the positioning of the CG.

Powers (2000) examined the effects of the rider on the linear kinematics of the horse during the take off, suspension and landing. In order to fully evaluate the effects of the rider, three jumping conditions were examined. These were: Loose (i.e. no rider or tack); Ridden (rider included); Riderless (rider data removed). The three different effects were estimated as follows:

Total effect = Ridden horse data minus Loose horse data

Mechanical effect = Riderless horse data minus Loose horse data

Behavioural effect = Ridden horse data minus Riderless horse data

The results revealed that the rider's effect on the CG positioning was considerable less than was calculated by raising the CG of the trunk by 10% The ridden horses were positioned closer to the fence, had higher CG positions at take off and over the fence, and hit the fence on fewer occasions.

2.4.2 Angular motion

Studies in angular momentum in the jumping horse are very rare. Clayton (1990) briefly considered the importance of angular momentum in the jumping horse, however little has been discussed since. One exception (Galloux and Barrey 1997) examined the contribution of each segment of

Figure ❹ Stimuli affecting the horse during jumping

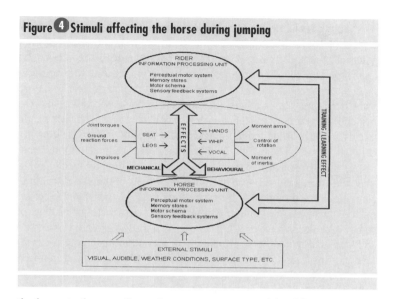

the horse to the overall angular momentum around the CG. Inertial para-meters for this study were derived from the geometric modelling approach. All the horses were ridden, and the riders were included in the analysis. Although the experiment evaluated various components of overall angular momentum, the nature of the rider's effect on control on the rotation was not fully investigated. A later study on the effects of the rider on angular momentum was conducted and revealed substantial differences between loose and ridden horses, i.e. the total effect of the rider was examined. The ridden horses had an increased angular momentum and angular velocity during the suspension phase of the jump (Powers 2000).

Examining both linear and angular effects, it is interesting to note that the main effect of the rider was found to be behavioural rather than mechanical (Powers 2000). This implied that the rider effect was due to the way the horses were ridden and the instructions given, rather than the weight or body position of the rider. This is an important concept, and is one that has not been previously examined in the scientific domain.

2.5 Future work

A theoretical basis is an important fundamental step in any scientific evaluation. Future evaluations of rider effect and control on show jumping should work from proposed theoretical models, which have been subject to academic scrutiny. Figure 4 provides an initial attempt to develop a theo-retical framework for rider control during jumping. The framework considers the horse and rider system during competition. The horse in particular is subject to a wide range of stimuli, not just from the rider, but from external stimuli. Both the horse and rider have to process the information and respond optimally to produce a satisfactory result. All the factors in Figure 4 may affect the horse's performance to some degree, obviously some factors more than others. An experienced horse will be less likely to respond to external stimuli, however highly likely to respond to the commands and instructions from the rider. The opposite will probably be the case for the novice horse who will find the external stimuli far more interesting than responding to his rider. This indicates the presence of a training and learning effect on moderating the effects of the various stimuli. How the horse responds to the rider's instruction is critical to the performance outcome. The horse processes signals via a number of lines of communication as indicated in Figure 4. How these signals are processed and amplified by the horse are important areas that may require experimental investigation. The flow chart in Figure 4 is typical of the approach used in motor control theory and information processing in human research. In order to evaluate and understand the effects of these stimuli, it may be necessary to develop instrumented devices to measure the flow of information across the lines of communication, e.g. forces generated by the rider through the reins, legs and seat, etc.

3 Conclusions and recommendations

Presently equine jumping mechanics is in its infancy compared with research in human sporting activities. However, this means that there are many relevant avenues of research available to researchers in this field. We can draw upon the knowledge of human biomechanics and motor control to form the basis of testable theoretical frameworks. Advances in technology have provided equine researchers with many useful experimental techniques and methods, for example motion analysis, force plates and force transducers; all of which can assist the equine researcher in answering some of the many questions that exist in equestrianism. This is an exciting time for jumping horse research, and with the help of trainers and riders alike, we can more fully understand, and hopefully improve performance in jumping horses.

Acknowledgements

The authors wish to thank Teagasc and the Walsh Fellowship for funding research projects into equine jumping biomechanics at the University of Limerick; and Dr. Hilary Clayton of Michigan State University for her advice and support throughout this research.

1.2 Articles

Plasma parathyroid hormone concentration in horses after long term exercise

Take home message

Endurance exercise causes both hypocalcemia and an increase in parathyroid (PTH) hormone secretion. However, decreased plasma PTH levels have been detected in some horses after racing for 80 km.

Introduction

A decrease in blood ionized calcium (Ca^{2+}) and an increase in plasma PTH have been previously described in horses performing short-term exercise (show jumping). Exercise-associated hypocalcemia has also been reported after endurance raids. Moreover, it has been speculated that the decrease in Ca^{2+} could be related to abnormalities which are commonly found after long term exercise (e.g. exertional rhabdomyolysis, synchronous diafragmatic flutter and fatigue).

Objective

The aim of the study reported here was to determine the effect of endurance exercise on plasma Ca^{2+} and PTH concentrations in horses.

Material and methods

Samples were obtained during two endurance raids. Twenty-eight Arabian or mixed-Arabian horses were studied (16 horses in raid 1 and 12 horses in raid 2). Two venous blood samples were obtained from each horse: one the day before the ride (during the pre-ride veterinary examination) and the other after the horse completed 80 kilometers (just after getting out of the "vet gate"). All horses passed successfully the veterinary control after racing for 80 km. Plasma Ca^{2+} was measured using a selective electrode and plasma PTH concentration was quantified with an immunoradiometric assay previously validated for use in horses.

Results

A significant decrease in plasma Ca^{2+} (from 1.6 ± 0.02 to 1.41 ± 0.02 mmol/l) and a significant increase in plasma PTH (from 49.9 ± 5.7 to 148.1 ± 34.6 pg/ml) concentrations were found after exercise. While all horses showed hypocalcemia after exercise, the PTH response to exercise was not homogeneous, allowing differentiation of two groups of horses. Group I horses (n=20) showed an increase in plasma PTH concentration after exercise (from 46.5 ± 7.1 to 196.5 ± 44.1 pg/ml) associated with the decrease in plasma Ca2+ (from 1.61 ± 0.02 to 1.39 ± 0.02). A decrease in plasma PTH concentration (from 58.2 ± 9.4 to 27.4 ± 8.0 pg/ml) was detected in Group II horses (n=8), even though plasma Ca^{2+} decreased (from 1.61 ± 0.04 to 1.46 ± 0.03 mmol/l).

Discussion

Previous reports of hypocalcemia after long-term exercise are confirmed by this study. Concerning PTH secretion, most horses (Group I, n=20) showed a logical PTH response to hypocalcemia (i.e. an increase in PTH concentration which is commensurate with the decrease in Ca^{2+}). The increase in plasma PTH concentration found after endurance exercise is similar to what has been previously reported after show jumping competitions. However, the decrease in plasma PTH concentration detected in the other 8 horses (Group II) is contradictory and difficult to explain. Plasma ionized calcium and PTH are known to have a reciprocal and inversal relationship which is described by a sigmoidal curve – the PTH-calcium curve. A decrease in extracellular Ca^{2+} results in an increase in plasma PTH concentration up to a maximum (maximal PTH) and vice versa, although a minimal non suppresible PTH concentration is still present at high calcium levels. It is tempting to speculate that in Group II horses there was an inadequate PTH response to hypocalcemia and that the lack of PTH secretion would impair their capacity to regulate blood Ca^{2+} levels. However, it is also interesting to note that despite having lower PTH values hypocalcemia was not more pronounced in Group II horses. Apart from their different PTH response after exercise, no other differences were evident between Group I and Group II horses. Group II horses were uniformly distributed in the two rides studied and their athletic performance was apparently similar to Group I horses – all Group II horses finished the rides and no differences in body condition after the race or in finishing position could be found between groups. In conclusion, further work needs to be done to clarify the significance of the low PTH concentrations found in the plasma of some horses after performing endurance exercise.

Three dimensional kinematic analysis of jumping horses: A preliminary study

Take home message

Kinematic variables could be used to study jumping ability of horses. The results have to be confirmed with more horses of different jumping ability and on higher jumps.

Introduction

Previous studies of jumping horses have already described the temporal and linear stride characteristics of horses clearing different kinds of fence during show jumping (Leach et al 1984; Leach and Ormod 1984; Clayton et al 1991; Deuel et al 1991) or under experimental conditions (Clayton et al 1989). Other studies have examined the hind limbs push off (van den Bogert et al 1994) and the relation between variables of the total body centre of gravity (speed, height, distance of the impact) and the horses´ performance (Clayton et al 1995; Colborne et al 1995; Clayton et al 1996). All these studies have been carried out with two-dimensional (2-D) kinematic analysis and with riding horses. Only one 2-D study have used free jumping horses (Dufosset et al 1984).

The kinematic analysis provides quantitative and objective information on sport motions. Its use in the study of show jumpers is interesting for the horse professional set, in assessment of the horses ability, as for the veterinary set, and in the investigation of performance disorders.

The purpose of this investigation is to describe the movement of the horse jumping and to assess interest in the 3-D kinematic analysis for the evaluation of a show jumper skill. In this preliminary study, we apply ourselves to:
- adjust a method for the 3-D reconstruction of the horse jumping motion,
- determine kinematic variables to study,
- illustrate these variables with experienced horses.

Material and Methods

Subjects – Five French Warmblood horses of a riding school were used in this study. These horses had different levels between bad and medium. They were graded according to their competition level. The three best horses (Horses 3, 4, 5) were competing at low levels while the two others (Horses 1 and 2) were of limited skill and were only used as teaching horses.

The mean age (± S.D.) was 11 (± 2) years and the mean height at the withers (± S.D.) was 166 (± 4) cm.

Recording area: A 30-m long and 4-m wide track was laid out in an indoor arena. Four video cameras and projectors were placed on 1.5-m high platforms surrounding the track. They were focused in order to image a 10-m long field of view. Two dark vertical fences were placed on the track. The first fence was 60 cm high and placed at the beginning of the field of view. The second fence was placed a stride after the first one, and its height was 1 m.

Recording procedure: Thirty-one reflective markers were stuck to the skin of the horses on specific anatomical landmarks demarcating the different bone segments (4 on the head, 5 on each forelimb, 6 on each hind limb, and 5 on the back). The horses were led by a handler to the entrance of the track and let free on the fences. Each horse performed several jumps until all of them realised 5 successful jumps.

Film analysis: The video recordings of the trials were digitalised. The positions of the markers were determined by the EKAS system (Pourcelot et al, 1997). The jumps were 3-D reconstructed using the direct linear transformation method (Abdel-Aziz and Karara, 1971).

Variables considered: The following variables were studied
*   withers trajectory,
*   back and neck angle with respect to the horizontal,
*   shortening of the limbs.

Results

Withers' trajectory: A typical trajectory of the withers is presented in Figure 1. The minima of the trajectory occurred at the overlap phases of the forelimbs inducing the withers to be lowered preceding the jump.

The raising of the withers at takeoff was performed in two phases. The first phase started when the trailing forelimb lifted off. The pushoff of the leading forelimb and the bringback of the hindlimbs under the body led to the back elevation. This first phase of the withers' rise finished with the impact of the hindlimbs at takeoff. The second phase was produced by the extension of all the articulations during the hindlimb push off. After the liftoff, only a residual elevation of the withers occurred for the 1-m high jump.

The impact of the forelimbs on landing occurred during the downward slope of the withers. This slope finished by a minimum associated to the overlap phase of the forelimbs.

Examples of withers trajectories of five successive jumps are represented for 2 horses of different skill in Figures 2 and 3. The repeatability obser-

Figure ①   Withers' trajectory for a 1m high fence

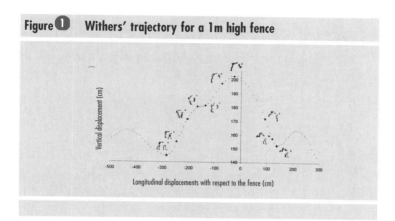

Figure ②   Withers' trajectories of Horse 3 for five 1m high jumps

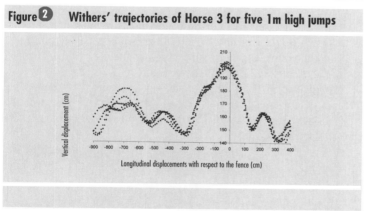

Figure ③   Withers' trajectories of Horse 2 for five jumps at 1m high

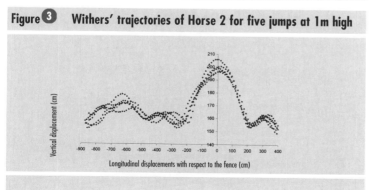

ved on the curve of a good horse (Horse 3) was higher than the repeatability observed for the worst one (Horse 2).

Figure ❹ **Back (withers-tuber sacrale line) and neck (withers-temple line) angle (withers-temple line) angle with respect to the horizontal**

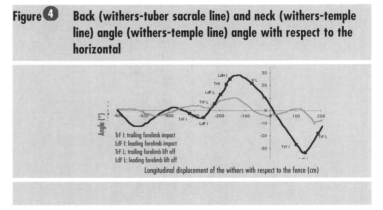

Trunk and neck movement: These movements were illustrated by the angle between the back line (withers-tuber sacrale) and the horizontal (α_{B-H}) for the trunk, and by the angle between the neck (withers-temple) and the horizontal (α_{N-H}) for the neck (Figure 4).

The righting of the trunk started with the impact of the leading forelimb. The back swing was initiated by the stance phase of the forelimbs allowing the bringback of the hind limbs under the body and a constant increase of α_{B-H}.

At hind limb impact, the increase of α_{B-H} slowed down rapidly. The maximum of the angle opening occurred when the flexion of the hind limbs was maximal during the pushoff.

Figure ❺ **Angle of back and neck with respect to the horizontal of a good horse (five 1m high jumps)**

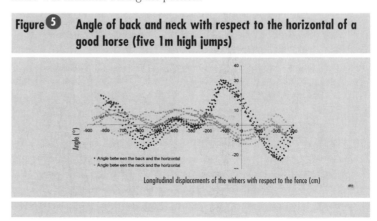

The extension of the hind limbs induced the inversion of the trunk rotation. After the hind limb liftoff, α_{B-H} regularly decreased until the forelimbs' overlap phase at landing, which induced an inversion of the trunk rotation.

The α_{B-H} curve's layout had a similar pattern for all the horses. The maximum at takeoff and the minimum at landing of α_{B-H} differed in particular between horses. As opposed to the trunk movement, the neck movement had no clear pattern (Figure 5).

Shortening of the forelimbs: The distance between the withers and the forelimb fetlocks (D_{W-f}) was used for the study of this variable (Figure 6). The D_{W-f} was maximal at impact. It decreased rapidly during the first part of the stance phase due to the extension of the fetlock and the flexion of the elbow and shoulder. In the second part of the stance phase, the forelimb pushoff induced a less important shortening.

After the liftoff, the D_{W-f} was rapidly shortened during takeoff. It was minimal before the withers got over the fence. This minimum occurred at the hind limb impact. A difference of shortening could be observed between the two forelimbs; this agreed with a dissymmetry of the horse during its jump.

Shortening of the hind limbs: This variable was illustrated by the distance variation between the tuber sacrale and the hind limb fetlock (D_{ts-f}) (Figure 6). During the first half of the stance phase at takeoff, the hind limb flexion induced a decrease of D_{ts-f}. It increased again during the extension of the hind limbs.

During the airborne phase, the D_{ts-f} was minimal as the trailing forelimb lift off at landing.

Figure ❻ Shortening of forelimb and hind limb on a 1m high jump

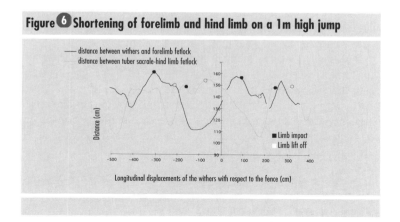

Longitudinal displacements of the withers with respect to the fence (cm)

Discussion

The three good horses achieved their five successful jumps successively whereas the two other horses had either done refusals or knocked down the rail during their trials before succeeding with five jumps.

The choice of the studied variables relied on main criteria usually used by professionals to assess jumping horses. The choice of the fence height was made so that all horses were able to jump it easily. The small elevation of the withers during the airborne phase suggested that a 1 m high jump did not require any great vertical propelling

The withers' trajectory was a bell-shaped curve. The two phases of the withers' rise were separated by an intermediate phase in which an inflexion point of the curve was included. This transition part occurred during the hind limb flexion at takeoff. For the 1m high jumps, the intermediate phase observed for the three good horses was well marked, looking like a plateau. For the two other horses, this intermediate phase was not very marked or even absent. This reduction of the intermediate part could also be observed in the 3 good horses for higher jumps. It could be supposed that a marked intermediate phase on the withers' trajectory when jumping low fences, associated with a good repeatability, characterised horses of easier skill at jumping.

The α_{B-H} curves had a typical shape for all the horses. Only the angles' range and their distance with respect to the fence varied between the horses. On the other hand, the α_{N-H} curves were more random. Any pattern of the neck movement was clearly noticeable between the horses and even between the jumps of one and the same horse (only one horse showed a clear pattern of its neck movements). Hypothesis could then be expressed on the importance of the neck movements during the jump. Either the neck was not very involved in jumping over the low fence, leading to a higher liberty for the horse in its neck movements, or the horse fitted its neck movement to adapt the trunk rotation.

D_{W-f} and D_{ts-f} were extremely synthetic variables and were more difficult to explain because they involved many joints. For example, the shortening of the D_{ts-f} at take off was produced by the flexion of the hock and stifle and the extension of the fetlock but was limited by the hip joint's opening, allowing trunk rotation at takeoff. This result had already been observed in the study of van den Bogert et al (1994) who had shown that the final pushoff of the hind limbs at take-off was the most important part of the jump.

These first results are indicative of what is actually undertaken in this study. It is useful to illustrate some kinematic variables that can be used for the study of jumpers. Although horses had slight level differences, some differences in their kinematics could already be observed as they were tested on low fences. However, these first observations have been obtained on a small sample of horses clearing low fences and do not afford any definitive conclusion. Nevertheless, it seems attractive to confirm these results with a larger sample and to study the modifications of these variables on higher jumps.

Acknowledgements

The authors wish to acknowledge their gratitude to Jean-Paul Valette, Céline Robert and Fabrice Audigié for their important contributions for the data collection and analysis.

Effects of different types of exercise and training on plasma catecholamines in young horses

Take home message

Training seems to induce a higher noradrenaline response during prolonged low-speed exercise as well as a reduced adrenaline reaction during high-speed exercise with a concomitant decrease in lactate in young horses.

Introduction

It has been demonstrated that catecholamines play an important role in (Snow et al 1992, Kurosawa et al 1998). Furthermore the catecholamines are useful indicators for estimating exercise stress and physical fitness. The purpose of this study was to investigate plasma catecholamine reactions during different types of exercise and training in young horses.

Material and methods

Seven Standardbred horses, age 2 years, were used in this investigation. All exercise took place on a highspeed treadmill without incline. Standardized exercise test (SET) consisted of six steps of five minutes' duration each. The velocity in the first step was 5 m/s, each consecutive step was increased by 1 m/s, and between two consecutive steps there was a resting period of 60 s for blood sampling. SET was followed by a lactate-guided training where horses had to perform two different types of exercise: 1) High-speed exercise: start by $v_{4.0}$, the running velocity was increased continuously by 0.3 m/s every 60 s, total running time: 15 minutes. 2) Prolonged low-speed exercise: constant velocity by $v_{2.5}$, total running duration was calculated based on the equal energy requirement during the high-speed exercise to achieve equal energy demand for both types of exercise (~60-90 min). The type of exercise changed every second day. The training program consisted in total of 8 workouts of prolonged low-speed exercises and 8 workouts of high-speed exercises. A second SET (same conditions like first SET) was done after finishing the whole training program. Blood samples (V. jugularis externa, indwelling catheter) for catecholamines and lactate were collected before, during and after SET, at the beginning and at the end of the training period (before and after prolonged low-speed and high-speed exercise, respectively). Heart rate (Polar Sport®) was monitored continuously during all types of exercise. Catecholamines in plasma were analysed by HPLC (Fa. Biometra), and whole blood lactate analysis was done enzymatically with Accusport® (Boehringer

Table ❶   **Changes in adrenaline, noradrenaline in plasma (ng/ml) and lactate (mmol/l) in whole blood during SET**

	before training program		after training program	
	Start	End	Start	End
adrenaline (ng/ml)	0.11 ± 0.06a	3.29 ± 1.89b	0.08 ± 0.03a	1.91 ± 0.90b
noradrenaline (ng/ml)	0.09 ± 0.06a	1.88 ± 1.53b	0.14 ± 0.06a	0.14 ± 0.61b
lactate (mmol/l)	1.7 ± 0.2a	12.7 ± 0.9b	1.5 ± 0.1a	9.3 ± 1.8c

Explanation
means with the same letter are significantly different at p<0.05

Table ❷   **Changes in adrenalin, noradrenaline in plasma (ng/ml) and lactate (mmol/l) in whole blood during high-speed and prolonged low-speed exercise**

	first training bout		first training bout	
	Start	End	Start	End
high-speed exercise				
adrenaline (ng/ml)	0.10±0.05a	2.99±1.22b	0.08±0.04a	2.35±1.05b
noradrenaline (ng/ml)	0.10±0.03a	1.40±0.47b	0.10±0.03a	1.83±0.83b
lactate (mmol/l)	1.7±0.4a	12.3±1.5	1.6±0.2a	10.3±1.7c
prolonged low-speed exercise				
adrenaline (ng/ml)	0.10±0.05a	0.24±0.10b	0.09±0.04a	0.22±0.07b
noradrenaline (ng/ml)	0.11±0.02a	0.25±0.05b	0.12±0.04a	0.37±0.12c
lactate (mmol/l)	1.8±0.3a	2.2±0.2b	1.6±0.3	2.3±0.4b

Explanation
means with the same letter are significantly different at p<0.05

Mannheim GmbH, Art. Nr. 1463667).

Results were analysed by an analysis of variance for repeated measures according to the program of Statistica® to evaluate the effect of exercise and training. Post hoc analyses were made by Scheffé test. Differences were considered to be significant when p<0.05. All results are presented as mean±s.d.

Results

Mean plasma catecholamine and whole blood lactate concentrations are presented in Table 1 and 2. Under resting conditions adrenaline and noradrenaline concentrations varied about 0.1 and 0.2 ng/ml. SET resulted in a significant rise in adrenaline and noradrenaline concentration (moderate up to 7 m/sec and exponential increase between 8 and 10 m/sec).

During high-speed exercise there was a similar increase in catecholamine concentration compared to SET in spite of a higher treadmill speed. Prolonged low-speed exercise resulted only in a moderate rise, but in contrast to SET and high-speed exercise, the increase in noradrenaline concentration exceeded adrenaline levels in the last training bout. Significant lower lactate concentrations were observed after training during SET and high-speed exercise. In contrast higher noradrenaline concentrations were analysed after the training period (overall 16 training units), and during the last prolonged low-speed exercise (first training bout: 0.25±0.05, and last training bout: 0.37±0.12 ng/ml, p<0.05).

Discussion

The present study is the first one to describe the influence of training and different types of exercise on plasma catecholamine concentration under standardized conditions in young horses. In accordance with previous findings the increase in catecholamine levels is more pronounced during high-speed exercise compared to low-speed exercise or endurance riding (Snow and Rose 1981, Snow et al 1992, Gonzalez et al 1998 and Kurosawa et al 1998). The increase in catecholamines plays a major role in mediating the cardiovascular and metabolic responses to exercise that are responsible for increasing the supply of oxygen and fuel to the working muscle. Reactions in adrenaline tended to be lower after training during SET and high-speed exercise, but failed to get significant ($p < 0.12$). In contrast to these results, whole blood lactate decreased significantly after training.

During SET and high-speed exercise there was always a higher release of adrenaline relative to noradrenaline, but after training noradrenaline levels exceeded adrenaline concentrations during prolonged low-speed exercise. In humans it is well documented that the adrenaline response to all types of exercise is smaller compared to the increase of noradrenaline (Lehmann et al 1984, Mazzeo and Marshall 1989), and it is reported that training results in a blunted noradrenaline response to exercise. It is speculated that the greater noradrenaline response is mediated by the recruitment of a larger muscle mass, resulting in stimulation of more afferent nerves (Greiwe et al 1999). Although the origin of circulating noradrenaline in the horse has not been clarified yet, plasma noradrenaline levels may result from active sympathetic fibers as well as from the adrenal medulla (Snow et al 1992). The moderate increases in catecholamines during prolonged low-speed exercise emphasise the importance of other factors in mediating energy metabolism. Cortisol is known to increase during exercise (Dybdal et al 1980, Desmecht et al 1996), but glucagon might be another important factor for mobilizing energy fuels during prolonged exercise.

In conclusion, the current findings indicate a training related effect by a higher noradrenaline response during prolonged low-speed exercise as well as a reduced adrenaline reaction after training during high-speed exercise with a concomitant decrease in lactate in young horses.

Takeoff mechanics of olympic show jumping horses over a fan jump

Take home message

Horses jump over fan jumps differently depending on chosen takeoff position. Despite the apparent preference to jump this obstacle at the fan end, the takeoff mechanics involved seem to involve significantly more effort.

Introduction

A fan jump presents the show jumper with several alternatives. At one end, the rails are vertically placed on a single standard, while at the other end, they are fanned horizontally on several standards, giving the appearance of a ramped spread jump. The rider has to choose between jumping the fence as a vertical, an oxer, or in the middle. In theory, jumping the fence at the spread end should present the rails less abruptly; however, the horse might have to jump a greater horizontal distance and this might require a different approach and takeoff mechanics. The purpose of this study was to investigate takeoff variables related to the chosen approach.

Material and methods

At the 1996 Summer Olympics in Atlanta, 53 of 82 contestants in the Team competition jumped Fence 9 at its fanned end, while 15 jumped in the middle. The remaining 14 jumped midway between the middle and fanned end. Horses were videotaped sagittally at 60 Hz as they attempted to jump Fence 9. The video data were digitised and analysed with the PEAK5 kinematic system. Twenty points on the camera-side of the horse were used to define body segments and the position of each horse's centre of mass was calculated from the centres of mass of these segments in each frame of the video. Data were compared between two groups: the 15 horses that jumped the middle position (MID), and 15 randomly chosen horses that jumped the spread end (FAN).

Results

All horses in both groups approached the fence on a wide, sweeping right turn from Fence 8 and were all on the right lead. None of the horses had a fault at the fence. One-tailed t-tests revealed significant differences between groups for horizontal distance jumped (MID: 5.57 ± 0.52m, FAN: 6.07 ± 0.39m; $p<0.01$), horizontal distance of the hind hooves from the base of the fence at takeoff (MID: 2.35 ± 0.29m, FAN: 2.64 ± 0.31m; $p<0.01$), maximum height jumped (MID: 2.19 ± 0.07m, FAN: 2.30 ±

0.07m; p<.001), resultant velocity of the horse's centre of mass at takeoff (MID: 6.29 ± 0.46m/s, FAN: 6.75 ± 0.51m/s; p<.01), horizontal velocity of the horse's centre of mass at takeoff (MID: 5.70 ± 0.40m/s, FAN: 6.19 ± 0.56m/s; p<.01), and horizontal distance of the hind hooves from the horse's centre of mass at takeoff (MID: 1.00 ± 0.06m, FAN: 1.06 ± 0.09m; p<0.05). There were no significant differences between groups for vertical velocity at takeoff (MID: 2.63 ± 0.37m/s, FAN: 2.68 ± 0.28m/s), nor angle of projection of the horse's centre of mass at takeoff (MID: 24.7 ± 2.6 deg, FAN: 23.6 ± 3.0 deg).

Discussion

On the basis of these results, there appear to be differences in the way horses jump this type of fence that depend on the chosen takeoff position. It is likely that more effort was required to jump the fan end, as indicated by the greater horizontal and vertical distances jumped, and by the greater horizontal and resultant velocities. Therefore, despite the apparent preference for the fan end, the takeoff mechanics involved seem to involve significantly more effort.

Fibre type composition of the gluteus medius compared with the semitendinosus muscle of Dutch warmblood foals and the effect of exercise

Take home message

The type of exercise applied did not affect fibre type composition of semitendinosus and gluteus medius muscle. The gluteus medius muscle appeared to become more slow and fatigue resistant in the course of aging. The muscle fibre composition of the semitendinosus muscle was stabile, except for the decrease in type IId fibre type percentages from 22 to 48 weeks of age.

Introduction

The aim of our study was to describe and compare the expression of myosin heavy chain (MHC) isoforms in the gluteus medius and semitendinosus muscle of Dutch warmblood horses during the first year of life and the effect of exercise on this expression. The Dutch warmblood horse is a rather new race that was defined in 1958. This race is a mixture of many different breeds and has therefore a broad genetical background. The Dutch warmblood horse is used for riding, jumping or as a draught horse. The gluteus medius is a muscle of exceptional size and power. It is primarily an extensor of the hip, so its main function is propulsion. Secondly, it has a major function as stabiliser of the hip joint during weight bearing. The semitendinosus muscle is included in the hamstring group. The actions and uses of the hamstring muscles are complicated. When the hindlimb bears weight they extend the hip and knee joint, moving the horse forward. When the hoof is raised from the ground, they flex the knee joint.

To generate power, a muscle has to contract. The main determinant of contraction speed is myosin heavy chain (MHC), which exists in different isoforms. With the help of monoclonal antibodies raised against MHC, equine muscle fibres were shown to express three isoforms of MHC: I, II a and II d , well known from other mammals. MHC II b was absent. Expression of one MHC isoform per fibre is the rule, but multiple expression of MHC in single fibres occurs, particularly during growth and after a change in training regime. For this reason, fibre typing on basis of monoclonal antibodies is superior to the classic methods, e.g. ATP-ase techniques, which are less able to distinguish the fibres with multiple expression. The isoforms differ in their ATP-ase reaction speed and consequently engender differences in contraction speed. Contraction speed increases in the order I, II a, II d. Type I and II a fibres are the most slow contracting fibres, but they can contract for a long time (fatigue resistant). The fibre with the most opposite characteristics, type II d, is the fastest contracting and the most fatiguable fibre type. In the first months after birth, mammalian muscle fibres undergo changes in innervation and MHC expression. External factors like the amount of exercise in this period may have an effect on the muscle fibre composition and hence on the capacity for later athletic performance. Therefore, exercise in early life may create better possibilities for further adaptation during the conventional training period later in life. How muscles adapt to exercise depends on their function. Since the gluteus medius and the semitendinosus muscle act in moving the horse forward, an exercise effect can be expected in both muscles.

Material and methods

Thirty-eight foals were exercised according to the following protocol: 0-22 weeks: one third were given boxrest, one third did a daily increasing number of gallop sprints, and one third were kept in the pasture. 22-48 weeks: half the foals were euthanised at 22 weeks and the other half were kept in a paddock. Biopsies were taken at birth, at the age of 22 weeks and at the age of 48 weeks. Monoclonal antibodies were used to determine the muscle fibre composition. The four predominantly detected fibre types ($>$ 96.5 %) were fibres expressing type I, type II a and type II d MHC and fibres co-expressing type II a and II d MHC (= fibre type II ad).

Results

Gluteus medius muscle (fig.1): Statistical analysis (General Linear Model – repeated measures : multivariate tests) showed that the three groups (boxrest-, boxtraining- and pasture group) differed in their fibre type composition (group effect). This difference already existed at birth and did not change in time. Therefore, the group effect can not be explained by exercise. Since there was no exercise effect, the three training groups could be considered as one single group. The MHC expression of the gluteus medius muscle changed in time (age effect). From 0 to 48 weeks there was an overall increase in type I and II a fibres and a decrease in type II d and II ad fibres.

Semitendinosus muscle (fig.1): The MHC expression of the semitendinosus muscle did not change in time from 0 to 22 weeks of age. From 22 to 48 weeks there was a small age effect, due to a statistically significant decrease of the percentage type II d fibre in this period. From 0 to 22 weeks, the three groups differed in their fibre type composition. Again, this difference already existed at birth and did not change in time. This means that also in the semitendinosus muscle a clear exercise effect could not be demonstrated.

When we compared the muscle fibre type composition of the semitendinosus with the gluteus medius muscle, the mean percentages of fibre type I and II d differed. In the gluteus medius muscle the percentages of fibre type I were higher and of fibre type II d were lower compared with the semitendinosus. This difference could first be detected at the age of 22 weeks and increased up to the age of 48 weeks

Figure ❶ **Mean percentages of the four main fibre types (±SD) at the age of 0, 22 and 48 weeks of age in the semitendinosus and the gluteus medius muscle (n=38).**

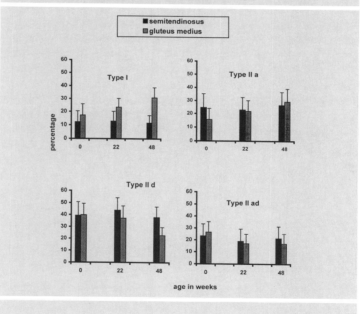

Discussion

It can be concluded that the gluteus medius muscle becomes more slow and fatigue resistant in the course of aging. Because of its function as stabiliser of the hip joint this is most likely caused by the adaptation to weight bearing. The muscle fibre composition of the semitendinosus muscle is rather stabile, except for the decrease in type IId fibre type percentages from 22 to 48 weeks. The exercise performed can best be described as an anaerobic sprint training. This kind of exercise first affects the muscle fibre areas and the oxidative capacity of the existing fibres before a change in MHC expression occurs. We observed no exercise effect with respect to the fibre type composition of both muscles. The difference between the three training groups in the muscle fibre composition of both muscles must be caused by other factors like the genetical background.

Effect of performance success on blood ß-endorphin, ACTH and cortisol levels in Show Jumping horses

Take home message

Competitive factors and jumping ability influence serum cortisol concentration changes after show jumping. This does not hold for serum ACTH and ß-endorphin concentrations because of a very large inter- and intra-individual variability.

Introduction

Cortisol levels of sport horses are affected by emotional stress prior to show jumping (Ferlazzo et al 1993) and post-exercise increases are usually detected (Lekeux et al 1991; Linden et al 1991), depending on intensity of exercise and individual fitness (Linden et al 1991; Foreman and Ferlazzo 1996), and on competition experience of horses (Clayton 1989). Earlier serum cortisol concentration increases after show jumping have been documented in horses performing clear rounds compared to horses with penalties (Ferlazzo et al 1998).

Blood ß-endorphin and ACTH may be markers of horse fitness, and higher values post-exercise have been described (McCarthy et al 1991). Ferlazzo et al (1998) found a tendency for higher values of these hormones with increasing fence height.

This study was done to collect further information on the effect of jumping performance during competition and training on the hypophyseal-adrenocortical response of horses.

Materials and methods

A total of 36 horses were examined during show-jumping competitions, and 6 were studied performing the same jumping circuit on three consecutive days once every day. According to their jumping performance, horses of both groups were divided into two groups: a) horses clearing the jumping circuit without penalties (clear round); b) horses with at least one fault during a circuit (penalty round).

Blood samples were collected from jugular vein prior to exercise (07.00 – 09.00 a.m.) and 5 and 30 minutes post-exercise. Serum cortisol concentrations were analysed by immuno-enzymatic assay (Boehringer Mannheim Immunodiagnostic, Art. No. 1288946). Serum ACTH concentrations were analysed by RIA (ELSA-ACTH, CIS Diagnostics). Plasma ß-endorphin concentrations were analysed by RIA (Peninsula Lab, Inc Cod 03086160), as reported (Ferlazzo et al 1998).

Statistics: Data are presented as mean standard deviation (SD). To determine the effect of exercise an analysis of variance for repeated measures was applied. To compare post-exercise with basal values the paired t-test was applied, and the comparison between groups was done with the t-test for unpaired samples. The level of significance was set at <0.05.

Results

Exercise increased serum cortisol concentration in all horses 5 minutes after exercise regardless of whether they performed a clear or a penalized show-jumping circuit during competition (table 1). In the horses submitted to a show-jumping circuit for three consecutive days during training an increase of cortisol levels was observed only in horses performing clear rounds. Cortisol concentration continued to increase 30 minutes post-exercise in the horses which were penalized during competition. In the clear round horse groups mean cortisol concentration 30 minutes after exercise was lower than 5 minutes post-exercise (table 1).

Table ❶   Blood concentrations (mean ± SD) of cortisol, ACTH and ß-endorphin in horses before and after show jumping

Variables	n	Success in round	Basal	5 min	30 min	ANOVA F	p
During competion							
Cortisol (µg/dl)	14	clear	3.88±1.45	5.92±2.13^c	5.76±1.72^c	11.83	<0.01
	22	penalized	3.73±0.91	5.27±1.38^d	5.46±1.44^d	13.37	<0.01
ACTH (pg/ml)	8	clear	11.14±6.95	24.14±8.76^c	15.25±3.76	8.60	<0.05
	15	penalized	10.84±6.06	24.43±18.20^b	14.41±11.89	6.45	< <0.05
ß-endorphine (pg/tube)	8	clear	3.35±1.28	7.21±6.43	4.14±1.19	2.66	n.s
	15	penalized	4.27±1.41	5.04±4.35	6.11±3.61^b	1.56	n.s
During training							
Cortisol (µg/dl)	14	clear	3.78±1.33	5.51±0.84^d	4.57±0.84^a	14.05	<0.01
	4	penalized	4.36±2.54	5.15±1.44^d	4.42±0.68	0.60	n.s.
ACTH (pg/ml)	14	clear	11.82±3.22	17.99±14.19	12.76±5.75	3.22	n.s
	4	penalized	11.27±4.00	13.22±3.49	8.80±2.99	6.62	< n.s.
ß-endorphine (pg/tube)	14	clear	4.49±0.71	4.81±1.23	4.16±0.82	2.84	n.s
	4	penalized	4.32±0.53	4.42±0.62	3.92±0.51	0.73	n.s

Explanation
vs basal: ^{a}p=0.05; ^{b}p<0.05; ^{c}p<0.01; ^{d}p<0.001; n=number of horses

The serum ACTH concentration increased 5 minutes post-exercise and fell back towards basal values 30 minutes post-exercise in all competing horses regardless of their success (table 1). There were no differences between groups. The ACTH concentration in the horses performing the show-jumping circuits during training did not change after exercise.

The serum ß-endorphin concentration in horses tendentially increased 5 minutes after exercise, but due to high individual variability it did not reach the significancy level (table 1). Thirty minutes after exercise its concentration was significantly above basal values in those horses which completed the show-jumping circuit with faults.

The ß-endorphin concentration did not change in horses performing show-jumping circuits during training.

Discussion

The distinct behaviour of serum cortisol concentration after show-jumping competition and after show-jumping in training with or without penalties seems to indicate an additional stress effect due to competition and jumping success. This assumption is supported by a report of Clayton (1989) describing smaller increases of plasma cortisol in experienced jumping horses than in unexperienced horses during competition.

Competition stress may also influence serum ACTH concentration, but performance success does not seem to play an important role. The reaction of plasma ß-Endorphin concentration to exercise and performance success had a very high individual variability, not allowing for clear conclusions regarding the conditions of this study to be drawn.

Neuronal coordination
during jumping in the horse

Take home message

A central pattern generator for jumping sequence, integrated with input and output reflexes, is proposed. This implies an involvement of innate mechanisms in this motor act control that can be only partially modified by teaching and training.

Introduction

It is largely demonstrated by photographs, videotapes and drawings that jump phases are very similar in horses. A confirmation of this common observation was also obtained by our electromyography-video-synchronised technique (video-EMG) analysis on a total of 160 jumps (performed by 30 different horses). It was amazing to again observe that horses show the same general trend in their EMG patterns and thus their general co-ordination, substantially invariable among all of them. In spite of this striking invariability and the evidence of a common muscular recruitment sequence of jumping, there are as yet no scientific papers explaining the reason of this locomotor expression. The aim of this paper is to build a theory that could explain the basis of a neuronal control, common to all horses, during jump phases.

Physiological basis of neck and vestibular reflexes

In physiology books it is common to find the historical research work of Charles Sherrington on symmetric tonic neck reflexes, usually described in decerebrated cat models. Neck dorsal flexion develops foreleg extension and hindleg flexion (Fig. 1/A).

Neck ventral flexion develops foreleg flexion and hindleg extension

Figure ❶ Symmetric tonic neck reflexes in a decerebrated cat model

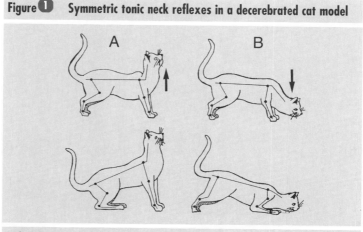

Explanation
A) with neck dorsal progressive flexion
B) with neck ventral progressive fexion

(Fig. 1/B). However, there are other fundamental reflexes that are integrated with symmetric tonic neck reflexes as well as vestibular, visuospatial, and other ones. To simplify, we will only take the vestibular reflex into consideration, leaving the other ones out. Because horses normally approach the obstacle upright and perpendicularly, the vestibular reflexes achieved by asymmetric horizontal movements will be disregarded. After these considerable simplifications, it appears that the macular symmetric reflexes can induce opposite leg actions to those previously exposed about symmetric tonic neck reflexes. Head dorsal flexion develops foreleg flexion and hindleg extensions; while head ventral flexion develops foreleg extension and hindleg flexion.

The most interesting considerations are drawn from the interaction between these two reflexes. In the central column of Fig. 2 (B, E and H) symmetric tonic neck reflexes are reported; the common reference is the maintaining of the head's horizontal position. In other words, the ventral angle between neck and head is unvaried (macular inputs remain constant). These three pictures differ only for the neck position with respect to the trunk position, and therefore leg muscle tonus follows the symmetric tonic neck reflexes (Fig. 1).

The horizontal stripe in the middle (Fig. 2/D, E and F) shows vestibular symmetric reflexes.

The common reference is the preservation of the neck's natural position (neck inputs remain unvaried). D, E and F pictures differ only for the ventral angle between neck and head, while the angle between neck and trunk remains unvaried; therefore leg muscle tonus only follows vestibular symmetric reflexes. In the remaining drawings it is possible to recognise the reciprocal opposition of the two reflexes

Figure ❷ **Synthetic scheme of symmetric tonic neck reflexes, symmetric macular reflexes and their possible interactions. Detailed explanation in the text.**

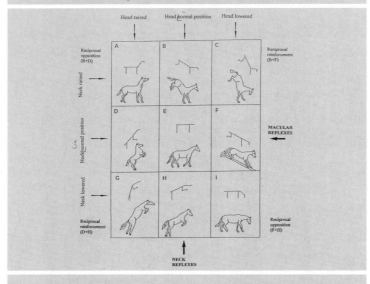

when there is neck and head dorsal flexion (Fig. 2/A) or neck and head ventral flexion (Fig. 2/I). Because there is a reciprocal opposition of the two reflexes in these two situations, muscle tonus is equally distributed on the four legs. The reciprocal reinforcement of the two reflexes is achieved when there is neck dorsal flexion with head ventral position (Fig. 2/C) and when there is neck ventral flexion with head dorsal position (Fig. 2/G).

Central pattern generators

The reflexes previously mentioned can be integrated with the outputs of a central pattern generator, similar to those proposed by Grillner and Wallén (1985) for interlimb co-ordination. This new central pattern generator simplifies the neuronal co-ordination scheme that the horse develops during jumping. The proposed pattern here (Fig. 3) allows to confirm the experimental results (Giovagnoli et. al, 1998) and agrees with the various theories proposed in literature on postural and locomotor mechanisms (e.g. Robert, 1967; Grillner, 1985). Moreover, by using this presumed pattern,

Figure ❸ **Presumed mechanisms of interlimb and neck co-ordination in the jump (modified from S. Grillner, 1985). The original pattern proposed by Grillner consisted only of interlimb co-ordination. Here the interaction between limbs and neck are proposed as well.**

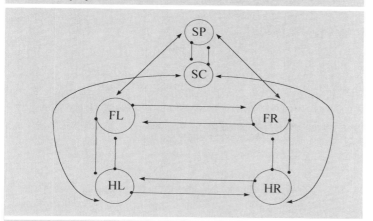

Explanations
FL= left foreleg; FR= right foreleg; HL= left hindleg; HR= right hindleg; SP= Splenius muscles and, as extension, all dorsal flexor muscles; SC= sternocephalicus muscles and, as an extension, all ventral flexor muscles. Inhibitory connections between centres are represented by lines with filled circles and excitatory connections by arrows.

the transition from jump to gaits such as trot (Fig. 4) and vice-versa, can be achieved in a very simple way: by switching from one set of command neurons co-ordinating legs to the other, where one set utilises reciprocal inhibition (Fig. 4) and the other set mutualexcitation(Fig. 3).

Figure 4 **Presumed mechanisms of interlimb and neck co-ordination in the trot (based on S. Grillner, 1985). The original pattern proposed by Grillner only consisted of interlimb co-ordination. Here are as well proposed the interaction between limbs and neck.**

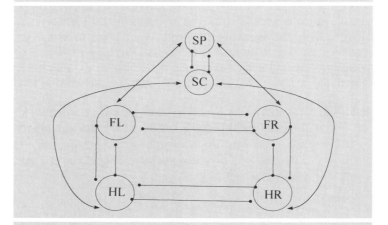

Explanations
FL= left foreleg; FR= right foreleg; HL= left hindleg; HR= right hindleg; SP= Splenius muscles and, as an extension, all dorsal flexor muscles; SC= sternocephalicus muscles and, as an extension, all ventral flexor muscles. Inhibitory connections between centres are represented by lines with filled circles and excitatory connections by arrows. In the "trot pattern", reciprocal inhibition between fore- and the hindlimbs, respectively, assures that each diagonal pair will alternate. Correspondingly, the reciprocal connections between fore and hindlimbs at the same side will make these limbs alternate. By changing just one set of connections between the two forelimbs and two hindlimbs from inhibitory to excitatory (Fig.3) each pair of limbs will instead become active in synchrony.

Presumed neuronal co-ordination arrangement during jumping sequence

During the end of the approach to the obstacle, the take-off phase begins. With the last canter step splenius muscles begin their activity, to lighten the weight on the forelegs. Only one leg is touching the ground, which is what happens in a canter step (Fig. 5.1). Then the typical take-off phase follows in which splenius muscles are recruited: head, neck and forelegs rise. Meanwhile both hindlegs touch the ground simultaneously (Fig. 5.2).

The horse has switched from canter to a jump central pattern (Fig. 3). The head, neck and forelegs complete rising, and splenius muscles start to end their activity. The hindleg movements (from drawing 2 to 3) occur without active recruitment of the middle gluteus (EMG silent, personal observations), probably caused by a "passive contraction" due to elastic muscle and tendon properties. Longissimus thoracis and middle gluteus muscles are next to be recruited (Fig. 5.3) (personal observations). Splenius muscle activities end completely; longissimus thoracis and middle gluteus activities start (personal observations) by suggested neck reflex participation (Fig. 2/H and 5.4). Middle gluteus activity is ending, hindlegs are in a complete extension and about to leave the ground (Fig. 5.5).

The middle of the parabola has been reached. Because all legs are without ground contact, the myostatic reflexes are eluded; furthermore neck and vestibular reflexes are reciprocally eluded as well (Fig. 2/I). Thus, while head and neck are in a lower position, the legs can be flexed. Longissimus thoracis muscles then prolongue their activity, probably to support hindquarters (Fig. 5.6) (personal observations).

The landing phase is starting. Longissimus thoracis muscles progressively reduce their activity until the end of their contraction. The forelegs are still flexed, but are about to show a progressive extension. Synchronuously the neck takes on a higher position than the body's, which goes down because it is heavier than the neck; in this way the neck elevation is obtained without active muscle recruitment (splenius EMG activity is still silent) (Giovagnoli et al., 1998). At this point neck reflex routes begin to be used (Fig. 2/B). Jump central pattern works with an excitatory connection

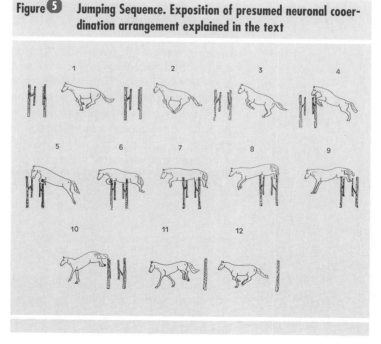

Figure 5 **Jumping Sequence. Exposition of presumed neuronal cooerdination arrangement explained in the text**

between both forelegs (Fig 5.7 and 5.8), and splenius active contractions start (Fig. 3) (Giovagnoli et al., 1998), strengthening neck reflexes; thus extreme leg extension is observed (Fig. 2/B). Foreleg extension is equal both for the left and right side as the central pattern generator commands (Fig. 5.9). A typical landing phase is then performed. The horse switches from jump to canter central pattern so that only one foreleg touches the ground. In Fig. 5.10 the right foreleg is shown touching ground first. The hind legs will be next to touch the ground. And finally the left foreleg will be the last one to touch the ground (Fig. 5.11 and 5.12). Subsequently the left foreleg will leave the ground as a canter step on the left hand.

Discussion

The capacity to initiate and generate the complex repertoires of movements is a peculiarity of the central nervous system (i.e. brainstem control). Subsequently the control process is developed and supported by central pattern generators, afferent sensorial inputs (vestibular, ocular, proprioceptive, etc.) and cerebellum co-ordination. Without this complex integration and considering only the reflexes and central pattern generators, exposed here, the sequences of the jump would appear stereotyped. The sensory information is probably an integrated part of the control system and is of crucial importance during critical situations such as rapid changes of speed or during turning, not only through the spinal cord reflex, but especially through cerebellum refinement. After this processing, the cerebellum influences the motoneurons by indirect and direct projections via vestibulo-, rubro- and reticulo-spinal pathways. Therefore these signals contribute to perfecting the movements and maintaining the equilibrium.

The factors considered until now have permitted to draw a complex picture of the neuronal co-ordination of jumping in the horse. In fact, we could synthesise the jumping action as a sequence of complex voluntary movements, also composed by the involvement of the central pattern generator integrated with a sort of arrangement of chain reflexes (Fig. 5). This mechanism, constantly controlled through sensory inputs, allows to develop all jump phases in a fluent and harmonious sequence and would represent a very simple and efficient strategy of control from the point of view of higher nervous co-ordination centers, requiring only little extra information.

Acknowledgements

We are happy to thank Micromed s.r.l. who kindly supplied the necessary technical instruments and equipment that were essential for our researches. We would also like to thank Dr. Arno Lindner, Dr. Sonia Boyazoglu and Mrs. Federica Alba for their precious help.

Enzyme patterns in muscles and half life periods of intravenous injected, homologous muscular enzymes in horses

Take home message

Evaluation of time course of CK, AST and ALD activities in plasma and calculating their quotients are useful for determination of the extent of muscular damage, and to differentiate the fibre types that are mainly concerned.

Introduction

Myopathies in horses occur regularly, and in many cases the clinician is at first restrained to the clinical examination and taking blood samples. The clinical symptoms are typical in some cases (stiffness, painful and swollen muscles, sweating, etc.), and there is often an elevation of the activity of muscular enzymes due to the muscular damage.

The purpose of this study was to get further information from bloodchemistry by determination of muscle enzyme patterns and elimination of intravenous injected, homologous muscular enzymes in horses.

Material and methods

In the first part of the study tissue samples were taken of different muscles (diaphragm, M. masseter, M. glutaeus medius superficial and deep part, M. semitendinosus) and of the liver and the heart of 17 warm-blooded and small horses. Homogenates were made out of these samples, and the activities of CK, ASAT, ALD, LDH and HBDH were determined. Besides the concentrations of hemoglobin and myoglobin were measured together.

In the second part of the study the kinetic behaviour of the cellular enzymes CK, ASAT, ALD, LDH und HBDH were examined. The determination of the enzymes' elimination rates was performed on six horses (four adult and two young animals) after intravenous injection of a homologous extract from skeletal muscle and repeated blood sample collections.

Results

Table 1 shows the enzyme activities in the tissue homogenates of the horses. In homogenates of muscle tissue with a higher percentage of type II B fibres (M. semitendinosus, M. glutaeus medius superficial part) significantly higher contents of glycolytic enzymes ALD and LDH were found.

Table ❶   Enzyme activities (U/g), myoglobin- and hemoglobin values (nmol/g) in different homogenates (x ± s; n = 10)

tissue	CK	ASAT	ALD	LDH	HBDH	Myo+Hb
heart	1496 ± 318	101.6±15.3	17.62±4.94	192.8±44.3	127.1±25.9	0.54±0.12
	a	a	a	a	a	a
M. mass.	3178±520	96.0±21.6	19.53±6.10	186.9±37.1	112.8±26.9	0.60±0.17
	b	a	a	a	a	a
dia-phragm	2584±520	116.1±35.2	49.4±13.4	237.9±58.5	87.8±13.3	0.53±0.16
	c	a	b	a	b	a
M. glut. deep	3279±630	128.5±33.7	73.5±24.7	414±119	102.2±23.6	0.54±0.19
	b	b	c	b	b	a
M. glut. superf.	3379±590	99.0±43.0	112.9±45.7	640±224	133.5±37.0	0.39±0.24
	b	a	d	c	a	b
M. semi-tend.	3185±530	78.7±39.0	118.6±31.1	637±137	117.4±29.8	0.19±0.14
	b	a	d	d	a	c
liver [1]	6.94±1.44	58.91±0.98	2.21±0.59	66.1±15.6	27.7±12.5	–
	d	a	e	d	c	

Explanation
different letters within a column show a significant difference (multiple t-Test. $p < 0.05$).
[1] n = 2. - = not determined

Table ❷   Quotients of enzyme activities (U/g) in different tissue homogenates (x ± s; n = 10)

tissue	CK/ASAT	CK/ALD	ALD/ASAT	LDH/ASAT 1)	HBDH/LDH
heart	15.21±4.77	93.4±39.1	0.177±0.058	1.97±0.71	0.665±0.063
M. masseter	33.77±6.76	171.8±51.5	0.224±0.131	2.06±0.68	0.598±0.123
dia-phragm	23.88±7.40	57.9±17.9	0.458±0.211	2.29±1.07	0.388±0.102
M. glut. deep	26.36±4.32	47.7±11.3	0.612±0.261	3.62±1.98	0.263±0.084
M.glut. superf.	38.08±11.78	38.5±26.6	1.388±0.725	8.05±4.07	0.240±0.125
M.semi-tend.	47.61±15.83	28.2±5.9	1.785±0.734	9.99±4.03	0.183±0.024
liver [1]	0.12±0.02	3.1±1.1	0.040±0.010	1.12±0.25	0.404±0.097

Explanation
[1] n = 2

Those with a higher content of type I fibres had significantly higher values of myoglobin and hemoglobin.

Table 2 gives the results of the quotients of enzyme activities in homogenates. Muscles with a higher percentage of type I fibres (heart, diaphragm, M. masseter, M. glutaeus medius deep part) show significant differences to muscles with predominant percentages of type II B fibres. There was a significant difference between the quotients of enzyme activities in the liver and all other tissues.

After intravenous injection of a muscle extract the elimination of the enzymes CK, ASAT, ALD, LDH and HBDH showed a two compartment kinetic. The half-life periods of the enzymes were CK 9.07 ± 3.30 h, ASAT 58.28 ± 17.10 h, ALD 17.40 ± 2.67 h, LDH 7.65 ± 2.98 and HBDH 12.76 ± 8.23 h. There were no significant differences between adult and young horses.

Conclusions

The determined half life of CK in this study is slower than those calculated in other studies (~2 h). Half-life periods of ASAT, ALD, LDH and HBDH were measured for the first time in the present study.

In a model the time course of enzyme activities and the

quotients of enzyme activities (figure 1) in blood plasma after a damage of 20 gramm muscle over a time period of 48 hours was calculated. For this the M. masseter was taken as a muscle with a predomination of type I fibres and the M. semitendinosus as a muscle with more type II B fibres. Figure 1 shows that enzyme quotients of ALD/ASAT > 0.2 show a predominant participation of type II B fibres while a quotient of ≤ 0.2 indicates damage of type I fibres. In this way exertional myopathies can be distinguished from nutritional and poisonous myopathies. Out of the model calculations it can be concluded that CK is useful for determination of the extent of muscular damage, while measurement of ASAT and ALD enables the clinician to differentiate the fibre types that are mainly concerned.

Figure ❶ **Modell calculation of the course of the quotients of enzyme activities over a time period of 48 hours with a damage of 20 grams of muscular tissue (left: M. masseter, right: M. semitendinosus)**

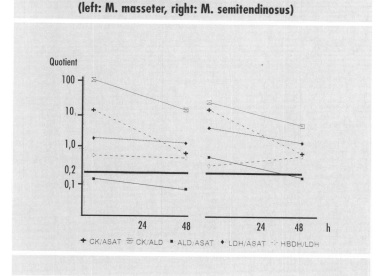

Effect of photobiological oxidation of blood on plasma lactate levels, arterial partial pressure of oxygen, and running time of Thoroughbred horses

Take home message

HOT/UV therapy was applied to horses 10 times within five weeks. Plasma lactate concentration after exercise was lower in treated horses, and their maximal speed over a distance of 300 m during a period of six weeks remained more constant than in horses of the control group.

Introduction

Due to the interest in improving running efficiency of Thoroughbred horses, it was decided to examine the effect of photobiological oxidation therapy with ultraviolet light (HOT/UV). The hypothesis of Standtländer (1980) is that tissues with poor irrigation and therefore lacking or reduced oxygen supply would benefit of an extra oxygen supply. Thus we hypothesized that an extra amount of oxygen available to Thoroughbred horses during racing could improve their performance. The therapy is a combination of blood oxidation (HOT), and blood ultraviolet light irradiation (UV). We used animal´s own blood, treated it and returned it to the same horse. The effect of this therapy is supposed to be cumulative (Stadtlaender, 1980; Holesch 1993).

To test our hypothesis, lactate concentration in blood plasma and P_aO_2 in blood, and running speed in horses treated was compared with untreated horses.

Material and methods

Fourteen unconditioned Thoroughbred horses between 3 and 5 years old were used. They were walked and trotted daily for 6 weeks before starting trial. Thereafter horses were galloped daily over 1,200 metres. The first 900 metres were at canter speed, and the last 300 meters at maximal speed. HOT/UV treatment started with gallop training. Blood samples for measuring lactate (jugular vein) and P_aO_2 concentration (facial artery) were taken one minute after finishing the workout at maximal speed. Time for covering the 300 m distance was clocked with a hand chronometer. Blood samples for plasma lactate analysis were collected in vacutainer tubes containing acetate lithium iodine. Plasma was separated immediate-

Table ❶ Plasma lactate concentration of HOT/UV treated and untreated horses after exercise (mean ± standard deviation SD; mmol/ l)

First Determination	T	12.7 ± 3.9
After 4th treatment	C	15.4 ± 4.5
Second Determination	T	11.6 ± 5.9
After 6th treatment	C	13.4 ± 6.5
Third Determination	T	14.4 ± 2.9
After 8th treatment	C	15.8 ± 2.7
Fourth determination	T	16.1 ± 3.1*
After 10th treatment	C	20.5 ± 3.5

Explanations
T = with HOT/UV treated group
C = not treated control group
* = $p < 0.10$ between groups; Kruskal Wallis Test

Table ❷ Partial oxygen pressure in arterial blood of HOT/UV treated and untreated horses after exercise (mean ± standard deviation SD; mmHg).

First Determination	T	133 ± 40
After 4th treatment	C	124 ± 32
Second Determination	T	116 ± 19
After 6th treatment	C	112 ± 25
Third Determination	T	105 ± 19
After 8th treatment	C	101 ± 10
Fourth determination	T	116 ± 37
After 10th treatment	C	99 ± 6

Explanations
T = with HOT/UV treated group
C = not treated control group

ly by centrifugation and kept refrigerated until analysis. Samples for P_aO_2 were collected by taping the facial artery. The heparinised 3 ml syringes were refrigerated and processed within one hour after sampling.

The treated group consisted of eight animals and the control group of six animals. HOT/UV was applied ten times to horses of the treatment group, on a rate of two treatments per week for five weeks. Blood samples of each horse were taken four times beginning after the fourth HOT/UV treatment, and consecutively always after two further treatments.

For treatment 240 ml of blood were drawn from the jugular vein. Then the blood was mixed with 48 ml of sodium citrate (24.7 g/l) as an anticoagulant. This mixture was subjected to the HOT/UV process using type C ultraviolet waves during 45 minutes in a HOT/UV machine. The re-injection of the treated blood was through the jugular vein and took approximately 2 minutes each time.

Plasma lactate concentration was measured using an analyzer (model ACA #4 Dupont, USA). P_aO_2 was measured with a gas analyzer model 1306 (Instrumental Laboratory, IL, USA).

Data of plasma lactate concentration and P_aO_2 were not normally distributed. Therefore comparison between groups was done with the Kruskal-Wallis test, within groups with the Wilcoxon test (Steel and Torrie,

1992). P < 0.10 was accepted to denote significant differences. Galloping time over 300 m at maximal speed was not examined statistically.

Results and discussion

The average values of plasma lactate and P_aO_2 in the horses are shown in the tables 1 and 2. Tendentially the plasma lactate concentration was always lower in horses of the treated group compared to horses of the control group. After the 10th treatment the difference was significant. P_aO_2 behaved in the opposite way but never reached significancy.

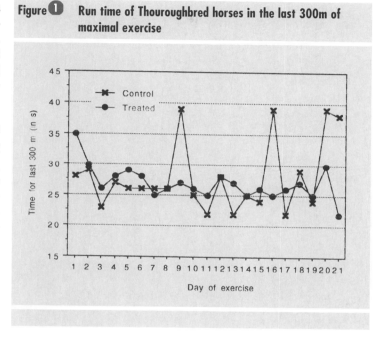

Figure ❶ Run time of Thouroughbred horses in the last 300m of maximal exercise

Running time of the final 300 meters of the track seemed more stable in the treated group than in the control group (figure 1).

There is no information available of other investigations on this subject. The results of this study do not indicate large effects, if any, of the HOT/UV therapy. Stadtlaender (1980) and Holesch (1993) believe that through HOT/UV therapy, there is an increase in the availability of oxygen which produces beneficial effects in the tissues of patients. Of course this hypothesis was formulated for patients with a disease compromising blood perfussion to tissues only (Turowski et al 1991). We believed it to be an interesting hypothesis also for the maximally exercising horse. Maybe more than ten applications have to be given or larger blood volumes need to be treated before effects are measurable.

Oxidative stress and antioxidant systems in horses

Take home message

The level of oxidative stress imposed on horses during an endurance race can be estimated by measuring the concentration of thiobarbituric acid reactive substances (TBArS) and carbonylated proteins in bloodplasma as well as the activities of glutathione reductase and catalase in haemolysate. All these may provide a useful indicator "stress threshold" for adjusting intensity levels during training to prevent tissue damage due to overtraining, or to follow recovery after competition to avoid premature return to intensive training.

Introduction

The disruption of intracellular homeostasis in response to physical exercise leads to metabolic and physiologic conditioning. Indeed, this seems to be the main stimulus responsible for a series of events finishing with a new cellular homeostasis (1). Under this new condition, many enzymes show activity levels higher than those previous to exercise in a compensatory way (2). Intense exercise without the corresponding rest period can lead to an overtraining condition. This will later result in poor performance, and a variety of tissue damage is likely to occur, causing a decrease in the level of or even the complete interruption of the physical activity (2). The success of adaptation is related to the ability of the muscle fibres to tolerate the applied stimulus.

There is a strong correlation between physical exercise and the production of reactive oxygen species (ROS) (3). The main targets of these –species are: the cellular membranes, which undergo lipid peroxidation, the proteins exposed to proteolytic attack after carbonylation or oxidation; and both nuclear and mitochondrial DNA that suffer disruption or cross linking (4).

Although all aerobic cells generate ROS and consequently free radicals, the natural antioxidant defenses usually prevent the cellular damage caused by these highly reactive species. When the generation of these species is increased, and/or the activity of the antioxidant systems is decreased, an oxidative stress is established, resulting in cellular damage or even cellular death.

Since 1982, when Davies et al (3) showed that intramuscular oxidative damage is a consequence of ROS generation, several papers began to describe a cause-effect relationship between oxidative stress and fatigue and/or muscle damage (5).

In this paper we followed the oxidative stress level of 9 horses during a 210 km endurance competition lasting three days. The chosen parameters were two biomarkers of oxidative attack and two of the antioxidant defence systems.

Materials and methods

Nine horses were followed during an endurance competition developed in three stages of 70 km each (table 1).

Blood samples (4 ml) were collected just before the start of the competition and at the end of each daily stage and immediately placed in ice. The samples were centrifuged for plasma isolation and the pellet was resuspended and submitted to hemolysis. All samples were then kept frozen at -700 C before the analysis.

The level of thiobarbituric acid reactive substances (TBARS) (6) and carbonylated proteins (7) were determined in the plasma fraction. The activities of the enzymes glutathione reductase (8) and catalase (9) were measured in the hemolysate.

Statistical analysis was made by ANOVA (one-way) and Tukey HSD tests.

Table ❶ Horse characterization

Horse	Breed	Age (years)	Sex (*)	Overall distances raced km	Winning history	Competitive lifetime (months)	Rest before ride (days)	Rider weight (kg.)
Horse 1	A. Arab	11	G	250	1x1th, 1x3th	48	10	75
Horse 2	A. Arab	15	M	380	2 x 3th	95	15	75
Horse 3	Arab	6	S	245	1 x 3th	23	30	80
Horse 4	Arab	6	G	130	-	12	7	80
Horse 5	Arab	6	S	190	1 x 3th	24	7	95
Horse 6	A. Arab	8	G	0	-	7	3	75
Horse 7	Arab	10	G	60	-	8	5	85
Horse 8	A. Arab	9	G	90	-	12	5	75
Horse 9	Arab	5	G	60	-	6	7	75

Explanations
* (S) Stallion; (G)Gelding; (M) Mare

Results and discussion

Table 2 summarizes the results of the endurance race, showing that the animals that obtained the better places were those with previous good performance and a longer period of training.

Table ❷ Results of multi-day race. The speeds shown are the average speeds in km/h, and the horses marked as out had been eliminated on the previous day.

Horses	Day 1 65 km Speed	Classif.	Day 2 65 km Speed	Classif.	Day 3 80 km Speed	Final results Speed	Classification	Best condition
Horse 1	13.3	1th	12.5	4th	13.7	13.2	1th	–
Horse 2	13.1	2th	12.2	5th	13.4	13.0	2th	–
Horse 3	12.7	6th	11.6	7th	13.8	12.9	6th	2th
Horse 4	11.9	12th	12.5	3th	13.7	12.9	7th	1th
Horse 5	9.6	22th	9.6	15th	12.2	10.8	14th	–
Horse 6	11.8	10th	12.2	9th	out	–	–	–
Horse 7	11.4	16th	11.9	6th	out	–	–	–
Horse 8	12.9	8th	10.5	13th	out	–	–	–
Horse 9	8.7	23th	out	–	–	–	–	–

Table ❸ Concentration of oxidative biomarkers in plasma of horses at different days of a multi-day race

Horses	TBARS (nmol/mL) * Before	Day 1	Day 2	Day 3	Carbonylated proteins (μmol/mL) Before	Day 1	Day 2	Day 3
Horse 1	0	8.2	8.2	8.9	97	104	107	85
Horse 2	0.49	8.2	10.0	10.4	76	109	112	49
Horse 3	0	11.1	11.1	11.1	68	83	68	62
Horse 4	0.49	16.1	13.3	16.6	103	77	137	86
Horse 5	0.42	8.9	8.9	7.8	64	80	76	72
Horse 6	0	10.4	15.5	out	89	82	47	out
Horse 7	0	7.8	9.4	out	65	97	50	out
Horse 8	0	10.4	10.4	out	69	100	80	out
Horse 9	0	7.8	out	-	68	107	out	-
	*	* +	* +	* +				

Explanations
(*) Analysis of Variance, p<0,05. (+) p<0.05 relative before group

The oxidative stress level induced by the competition was measured through the analysis of the biomarkers shown in Table 3 and the activities of the enzymes shown in Table 4.

The plasma levels of TBARS showed an initial increase followed by stabilization (p<0,05), which was better observed in the successful horses (1, 2, 3 and 4). The same pattern was observed for carbonylated protein levels, with a slight decrease on the last day.

The results shown in Table 4, support the hypothesis that the antioxidant capacity is the limitation for the response to stress, as those animals that finished the competition (horses 1, 2, 3, 4 and 5) showed a compensatory adaptation (3), probably induced by the aerobic exercise stimulus on the antioxidant enzymes, mainly glutathione reductase (p<0.05). The rest period between stages lasted approximately 15 hours. There is a tendency towards a decrease in the enzymatic activities for horses 7, 8 and 9 and an absence of response for horses 1, 5 and 6 after the first day of competition. However, an increase in the activity of these enzymes can be observed from the second day on.

Horses 1 and 2, respectively first and second classified on this race, presented a decreased in the antioxidant activities in the last day, either in comparison to their own levels on the second day or compared to the results of the other horses that finished the competition. These results could point to a higher stress imposed on these two horses to win the endurance race. This hypothesis is supported by the results shown by horses 3 and 4, which placed 6 th and 7 th respectively, but won first and second places for best condition.

Table ❹: Enzymatic activities in haemolysate of horses at different days of a multi-day race

Horses	Catalase (k/gHb)				Glutathione reductase (UI/gHb) *			
	Before	Day 1	Day 2	Day 3	Before	Day 1	Day 2	Day 3
Horse 1	0.55	0.44	0.71	0.74	30.7	30.8	293.5	161.2
Horse 2	0.27	0.67	0.79	0.69	48.4	11.8	148.1	120.3
Horse 3	0.36	0.41	0.65	0.93	96.9	27.0	113.8	458.5
Horse 4	0.26	0.55	0.84	0.45	22.5	85.4	178.8	187.1
Horse 5	0.38	1.40	0.62	0.77	24.0	20.2	129.8	363.0
Horse 6	0.45	0.45	0.22	out	62.6	26.1	119.9	out
Horse 7	0.68	0.56	0.40	out	51.0	28.4	173.2	out
Horse 8	0.43	0.27	0.51	out	159.1	91.0	71.1	Out
Horse 9	0.68	0.51	out	–	90.6	19.8	out	–
					*	*++	*	*+

Explanations

(*) Analysis of Variance, p<0.05. (+) p<0.05 relative before group. (++) p<0.05 relative Day 2 and Day 3 groups.

Conclusions

The level of oxidative stress imposed on horses during an endurance race can be estimated by these four chosen biomarkers.

The comparison between the activity of the antioxidant system at rest and during or after the competition can be used to estimate the ability to overcome the competition stress.

All these parameters when analyzed together can provide a useful indicator - stress threshold - which permits adjustments of intensity levels during training. This is extremely important to prevent tissue damage due to overtraining (2). This method can also be useful during the post-competition rest period, to follow the recovery and to avoid a premature return to heavy training.

Financial Support

Fapesp (97/03889-4) and CNP_q

Effects of exercise on plasma haptoglobin composition in control and splenectomized Thoroughbred horses

Take home message

Hp composition: Hb free Hp and Hb binding Hp in plasma is a clinical indicator of red cell membrane fragility and haemolysis in blood vessels.

Introduction

Haptoglobin (Hp) is an acute phase protein which is synthesized in the liver , and its synthesis is induced by haemoglobin (Hb) concentration in plasma (Putnum 1975). Hp has a specific binding activity to Hb, and supports an efficient treatment for collection of free Hb to the liver and prevents external leak of iron (Putnum 1975).

Plasma Hp proved to be a useful indicator of infection/inflammation and haemolytic disease in the horse (Kent & Goodall 1991, Mills et al. 1998). Increase of osmotic fragility of red cells and plasma Hb concentration after exercise in Thoroughbred horses suggests the release of Hb from red cells into plasma by haemolysis based on acceleration of red cell membrane permeability (Hanzawa et al. 1992). Splenectomy significantly decreased osmotic fragility of equine erythrocytes (Hanzawa et al. 1998). These results suggest that splenectomy decreases the plasma Hp level and haemolysis in blood vessels during exercise. Therefore, in this experiment, changes of plasma Hp composition with exercise were compared between control and splenectomized horses.

Material and methods

Six Thoroughbreds, five 2-year-olds and one 5-year-old (3 males, 1 gelding and 2 females) weighing a mean $\pm$ s.e.m 462 ± 14 kg were used. These animals were divided into two groups of three each: control (Group C) vs. splenectomized horses (Group S) (Hanzawa et al. 1995). The spleen of Group S horses was surgically removed after removal of the 18th rib on the left side. In Group C horses only the 18th rib was removed, and the wound was immediately sutured. These procedures were conducted 6 months before the exercise test.

The treadmill (Mustang-2200, Kagra, Switzerland) exercise test was defined as 1.5 min at 80% of peak speed (determined during the preliminary test) and 1 min at both 90 and 100% of peak speed, and the treadmill speed was increased by 5% of peak speed every min until the point of fatigue. Each horse performed two exercise tests within a 3-week period.

Heart rate (HR) was recorded throughout the study using a commercial heart rate computer (PE-3000, Polar, Finland). Blood samples were collected by jugular venipuncture from each horse into heparinized test tubes: 30 min before the start of the treadmill program and immediately (within 30 s) following exercise test. Blood lactate [La-] was measured with an automated lactate analyzer (YSI-1500 Sport, Yellow Springs, USA). Packed cell volume (PCV) was measured using a microhaematocrit centrifuge. Osmotic fragility of the erythrocytes after washing with ice-cold Dulbecco's phosphate buffered saline was determined by the haemolysis rate (HL) in a hypotonic salt solution (0.56%) with the equipment described earlier (Hanzawa et al. 1995).

Electrophoretic analysis of haptoglobin (Hp) was done with 10 % polyacrylamide gel in tris glycine buffer solution (pH 8.8) on a slab electrophoretic system (PAGE). Hp: Hb free, 1/2Hb binding Hp and Hb binding Hp, were detected through immunoblotting with rabbit anti horse Hp serum produced in the authors' laboratory. Plasma Hp concentration (total Hp level) was measured by single radial immunodiffusion technique (SRID) using the anti horse Hp serum. Hb binding Hp (including 1/2Hb binding Hp) level in plasma was calculated by the calibration curve between Hb binding Hp concentration and density of Hb binding Hp band which was detected by orthodianisidine staining of peroxidase activity from Hb on PAGE.

Results

Table 1 shows exercise induced changes of some physiological parameters in Groups C and S. The peak speed and PCV in Group C was significantly higher than in Group S, but HR in Group C was significantly lower than in Group S. Insignificant

Table ❶ Exercise induced changes (mean ± s.e.m) in heart rate (HR), blood lactate concentration [La-], packed cell volume (PCV) and haemolysis rate (HL) of circulating red cells washed in PBS in control (Group C) and splenectomized (Group S) horses

Group	Before	After
Maximum velocity (m/s)		
C	-	$9.8 \pm 0.48b$
S	-	$8.1 \pm 0.42a$
HR (bpm)		
C	$30.4 \pm 2.2a$	$199.0 \pm 1.8b$
S	$27.3 \pm 2.9a$	$216.3 \pm 3.5c$
[La-] (mM)		
C	$0.49 \pm 0.05a$	$10.8 \pm 1.8b$
S	$0.43 \pm 0.06a$	$11.7 \pm 1.4b$
PCV (%)		
C	$37.4 \pm 1.2a$	$57.2 \pm 0.64b$
S	$40.4 \pm 0.49a$	$41.4 \pm 0.56a$
HL (%)		
C	$52.7 \pm 3.0c$	$68.4 \pm 11.5d$
S	$12.0 \pm 2.0a$	$22.7 \pm 6.3b$

Explanations
Differences from each other: $a<b<c<d$, $p<0,05$ (LSD)

difference was observed in [La-] between Groups C and S. Exercise significantly increased HL in both groups. HL in Group C was significantly higher than in Group S, regardless of exercise.

From the cathode side of transferrin in polyacrylamide gel three bands of Hp were isolated: Hb free Hp, 1/2Hb binding Hp and Hb binding Hp. The regression line and correlation coefficient between the square of diameter of precipitate ring (x, mm2) on the SRID and Hp concentration (y, g/l) was significant and positive: $y=-0.1537+0.0143x$ and $r=1.00$ (P<0.001), respectively. The regression line and correlation coefficient between density of Hb binding Hp band detected by ortho-dianisidine staining on PAGE (x, %) and Hb binding Hp concentration (y, g/l) was also significant and positive: $y=0.00267+0.01189x$ and $r=1.00$ (P<0.001), respectively.

Table 2 shows effects of sham and splenectomized operation on plasma Hp concentration (total Hp levels) of horses. In the first week after the operation, total Hp levels were significantly increased in both Groups C and S. Total Hp level in Group C decreased and thereafter returned to the level before operation during the second month, while, in Group S, total Hp level at the end of the second month decreased. No significant differences were ob-served in the total Hp level before, and in the first week after operation between Groups C and S, but in

Table ❷ Changes (mean ± s.e.m.) in haptoglobin concentrationof plasma (total Hp level) in control (Group C) and splenectomized (Group S) horses before and after splenectomy

Time(months)	Group C	Group S
-1	0.88± 0.094b	1.19 ± 0.11b
0 (Surgery)	0.94 ± 0.086b	1.03 ± 0.10b
0.25	2.53 ±• 0.18c	2.82 ± 0.26c
2	0.80 ± 0.093b	0.18 ± 0.091a

Explanations
Differences from each other: a<b<c<d, p<0,05 (LSD)

Table ❸ Exercise induced changes (mean ± s.e.m) in haptoglobin concentration of plasma (total Hp level) and haemoglobin binding haptoglobin concentration (Hb binding Hp level: including 1/2Hb binding Hp) of plasma in control (Group C) and splenectomized (Group S) horses.

Group	Before exercise	After exercise
Total Hp (g/l)		
C	0.98±0.092b	1.24±0.12b
S	0.20±0.091a	0.18±0.093a
Hb binding Hp (g/l)		
C	0.090±0.081a	0.51±0.10b
S	0.10± 0.082a	0.13± 0.091a

Explanations
Differences from each other: a<b<c<d, p<0,05 (LSD)

Group C the total Hp level two months after operation was higher than in Group S.

Table 3 shows the effects of exercise on total and Hb binding Hp levels of Groups C and S horses. In Groups C and S, exercise did not change total Hp levels. There was no difference in Hb binding Hp levels before exercise between Groups C and S. Thereafter, in Group C, exercise significantly increased Hb binding Hp level, while, in Group S, exercise had no effect. After exercise, Hb binding Hp level in Group C was significantly higher than in Group S.

Discussion

In both groups, total Hp level increased just after the operation. A synthesis of Hp in the liver will be accelerated by the increase of plasma Hb level due to haemolysis induced by the operation (Kent & Goodall 1991, Putnum 1975). Total Hp level in Group C thereafter returned to the level before operation, while, in Group S, it decreased. Splenectomy in Group S horses significantly decreased HL (Hanzawa et al. 1998). In Group S, the increase of osmotic resistance of red cells inhibited haemolysis in blood vessels during exercise, and controlled synthesis of Hp in liver.

HL and Hb binding Hp level after exercise in Group C were significantly higher than in Group S. A functioning spleen increases fragility of red cell membrane and induces larger haemolysis during exercise (Hanzawa et al. 1998). Haemolysis during exercise increases Hb binding Hp level in plasma (Hanzawa et al. 1992, which suggests that osmotic sensitive red cells are more prone to haemolyse than osmotic resistant red cells.

Conclusions

These experimental results suggest that: 1) spleen accelerates the fragility of red cell membrane; 2) osmotic sensitive red cells are prone to haemolysis during exercise; 3) haemolysis during exercise increases Hb binding Hp level in plasma; and 4) haemolysis accelerates synthesis of Hp in the liver. Therefore, Hp composition: Hb free Hp and Hb binding Hp in plasma is a clinical indicator of red cell membrane fragility and haemolysis in blood vessels.

Exercise capacity and post-exercise blood lactate disappearance

Take home message

Horses in good condition do not have faster post-exercise blood lactate disappearance during walking recovery than horses in poor. Fast blood lactate disappearance may indicate inefficient movements and therefore increased use of lactate as energy.

Introduction

During high-intensity exercise, oxidative metabolism is pushed to the limit, and additional energy must be derived from anaerobic glycolysis producing large amounts of lactate in muscle. Facilitated diffusion by the monocarboxylate transporter exports the major part of the lactate out of the muscle, which in turn increases blood levels (Poole et al 1993).

The ability to rapidly remove metabolites during exercise from both muscle and blood could be considered a distinct physiological advantage to an athlete. Post-exercise lactate disappearance is increased with walking compared to standing and with slow trotting compared to walking (Marlin et al 1987). Therefore, post exercise activity has to be standardised, and a walking recovery was used in this study. Also, lactate concentration at the end of the exercise needs to be considered when lactate disappearance is evaluated (Marlin et al 1991).

The aim of this study was to investigate the effect of performance capacity on post-exercise blood lactate disappearance.

Material and methods

147 trained Standardbred trotters, 34 stallions, 44 geldings and 69 mares, with an age range of 3-9 years, were used. 131 horses had raced. Horses performed a standardised exercise test (SET) on a high speed treadmill (Haico treadmill, Loimaa, Finland) with a 3o incline. The SET consisted of a 15 minute warm-up period at 1.7 m/s (walk), followed by 3-5 exercise intervals, 2 minutes each, at speeds of 6, 7, 8, 9, 10 m/s (trot), and ended with a 20 minutes recovery period at 1.7 m/s (walk). Heart rate was monitored continuously with a pulse meter (Polar, Kempele, Finland).

Blood samples were collected during the last 15 s of each exercise speed and at 5, 10 and 15 minutes of the walking recovery period through a catheter placed in the jugular vein. Blood samples were analysed for blood lactate and total circulating haemoglobin (Hb).

Post-exercise blood lactate disappearance was calculated as decrease in blood lactate concentration during the first 10 minutes of post-trot walking (ΔLaD).

Heart rate per minute at treadmill speed 8 m/s ($P_{8m/s}$), blood lactate at treadmill speed 8 m/s ($La_{8m/s}$), best race time and race time in the last race before the SET were used as indicators of exercise capacity and condition.

Statistical analysis: All results are expressed as means $\pm$ s.e. Significance of differences was tested with least square analysis of variance. Correlation between variables were tested using linear regression analysis.

Results

At the end of the fastest trot heart rate per minute was 198 ± 1 and blood lactate concentration (La_{max}) was 5.2 ± 0.2 mmol/l. After 10 minutes of post-trot walking lactate concentration was 2.4 ± 0.1 mmol/l. ΔLaD was lower in stallions than in mares and geldings (2.4 ± 0.2; 2.8 ± 0.1; 3.1 ± 0.2; $p<0.05$). La_{max} had a very significant effect on ΔLaD ($p<0.001$) (Table 1).

Horses with La_{max} 4 mmol/l or higher were divided in two groups: higher and lower than average ΔLaD. There was a significant difference between the groups in best race time (high ΔLaD $1.20,4 \pm 0,5$ and low ΔLaD $1.18,5 \pm 0,6$) and time in the last race (high ΔLaD $1.23,3 \pm 0,4$ and low ΔLaD $1.21,5 \pm 0,5$) ($p<0.05$; $p<0.01$). In these horses the regression coefficient between ΔLaD and heart rate at 10 minutes of post-trot walk was 1.9 ± 0.9 ($p<0.05$). When the 3, 4 and 5 year olds were compared, age had a significant effect on $La_{8m/s}$ ($p<0.05$), $P_{8m/s}$ ($p<0.001$), Hb ($p<0.001$) and

Table 1 **Blood lactate concentration at the end of exercise (La_{max}) and blood lactate disappearance during first 10 minutes of walking (1.7 m/s, 3o incline) recovery (ΔLaD) in 147 trained Standardbred trotters, mean $\pm$ s.e.**

n	La_{max} (mmol/l)	ΔLaD(mmol/l)
6	< 2.0	1.0 ± 0.2
25	2.0 – 2.9	1.5 ± 0.1
20	3.0 - 3.9	2.2 ± 0.1
27	4.0 – 4.9	2.7 ± 0.1
23	5.0 – 5.9	3.2 ± 0.1
20	6.0 – 6.9	3.7 ± 0.1
8	7.0 – 7.9	4.4 ± 0.2
11	8.0 – 8.9	3.6 ± 0.2
5	9.0 – 9.9	4.2 ± 0.3
2	10.0 – 10.9	3.6 ± 0.4

Explanations
La_{max} had a significant effect on ΔLaD ($p<0.001$).

best race time (p<0.05), but age had no effect on ΔLaD (Table 2).

Discussion

Although blood lactate disappearance was significantly affected by Lamax, it seems to occur at a fairly linear rate when maximal blood lactate concentration is between 4 and 10 mmol/l as described by Marlin et al (1991). However, even when Lamax was taken into account, horses had considerable individual differences in post-exercise blood lactate disappearance. The hypothesis was that horses in good condition have faster blood lactate disappearance than horses in poor condition.

Table 2 **Blood lactate concentration at 8m/s ($La_{8m/s}$), heart rate at 8m/s ($P_{8m/s}$), haemoglobin (Hb), best race time and blood lactate disappearance during first 10 minutes of walking recovery (ΔLaD) in 84 trained Standardbred trotters aged 3 to 5 years, mean ± s.e.**

Age	n	$La_{8m/s}$ (mmol/l)	$P_{8m/s}$	Hb (g/l)	Best race time (time/kilometre)	ΔLaD (mmol/l)
3	23	4.5 ± 0.4*	196 ± 3 ***	192 ± 2***	1.22,9 ± 1.1*	3.1 ± 0.2
4	33	3.8 ± 0.3	185 ± 2	206 ± 2	1.20,0 ± 0.5	3.2 ± 0.2
5	28	3.0 ± 0.3	183 ± 2	206 ± 2	1.19,1 ± 0.6	2.7 ± 0.2

Explanations
* Significantely (p<0.05) different to 5 year olds
*** Significantely (p<0.001) different to 5 year olds

The main finding of this study was that the condition of the horse does not affect post-exercise blood lactate disappearance. Improvement of La8m/s, P8m/s, Hb and best race time with age in the young trotters are attributed to training effects (Persson 1983). Lack of significant improvement in ΔLaD indicate that blood lactate disappearance during walking recovery was not improved by training. In fact horses with fast racing times tended to have slower than average blood lactate disappearance. One explanation could be that although training improves maximal aerobic capacity and probably increases the exercise speed during which lactate can still be used as energy substrate, during walking recovery horses would not benefit from the improved maximal capacity to use lactate because their need for energy is limited.

The finding that horses with fast racing times tended to have slow blood lactate disappearance could be explained by the efficiency of movements and the need for lactate as an energy substrate. There was a significant positive relationship between ΔLaD and recovery heart rate after 10 min of walking. Heart rate is highly correlated with work effort (Fregin and Thomas 1983). When walking at the same speed horses with efficient walking movements would have a lower heart rate and less need for energy and lactate as a substrate during the recovery compared to horses with less efficient movements. Assuming that horses with an efficient walk also have an efficient trot, they would be expected to have good racing results.

The differences in efficiency of movements accounted only partially for the individual differences in blood lactate disappearance. Another explanation could be differences in lactate transport through membranes. It has been shown that individual horses have different amounts or activities of lactate transporters on red blood cell membranes (Väihkönen et al 1999). This may also be true for muscle membranes. Maybe future studies of lactate transporters will also explain the finding that ΔLaD was lower in stallions than in mares and geldings.

Although post-exercise blood lactate disappearance can not be used as an indicator of fitness, it has practical value when training sessions are designed. The intensity of interval training is affected by the speed and duration of the exercise bouts and the time between the bouts (Hyyppä and Pösö 1996). Therefore the individual post-exercise blood lactate disappearance should be considered, particularly because recovery heart rate can be misleading, when the times between the exercise bouts of the interval training session are planned.

In conclusion the hypothesis that during walking recovery horses in good condition have faster post-exercise blood lactate disappearance than horses in poor condition was not true because lactate disappearance was not improved by training. In fact fast blood lactate disappearance may indicate inefficient movements and therefore increased use of lactate as energy.

Post-partum bone and collagen markers in Arabian mares and foals

Take home message

Assessment of bone turnover indicators Osteocalcin (OC), carboxy-terminal telopeptide region of type I collagen (ICTP), and pyridinoline (PYD) and deoxypyridinoline (DPD) cross-links may be helpful for monitoring post-partum skeletal adaptation in mares and foals.

Introduction

Mature horses undergo bone turnover to maintain a structurally superior skeleton. During lactation, the demand for calcium is great and mares may resorb calcium from bone to meet this increased demand. Additionally, foals experience modeling, or growth of total bone, coupled with remodeling, or turnover, to develop strong bones that will adequately prepare them for their active lives. In equine research, there is a need to assess bone metabolism by a non-invasive, non-terminal method. Biochemical markers can be analyzed in the laboratory by utilizing commercially available assays. For example, biochemical indicators of bone turnover have been increasingly used in the area of equine exercise physiology to determine the extent of formation and resorption occurring. The objective of this study was to assess bone and collagen metabolism in post-partum mares and newborn foals using serum indicators of bone and collagen metabolism.

Material and methods

Three commercially available tests were utilized to determine serum concentrations of osteocalcin (OC), carboxy-terminal telopeptide region of type I collagen (ICTP), and pyridinoline (PYD) and deoxypyridinoline (DPD) cross-links to evaluate bone and collagen metabolism in the mares and foals. Osteocalcin is a non-collagenous protein formed by osteoblasts, or bone building cells. Therefore, measurements of serum osteocalcin can be taken to indicate bone formation. Bone is 90% type I collagen, and as bone is degraded ICTP is released into circulation. Serum ICTP levels can be determined as a marker of bone resorption, or breakdown. An evaluator of collagen turnover is the concentration of serum PYD/DPD cross-links. These cross-links occur in collagen to provide the helical molecule with strength. When collagen (type I or II) is degraded, these cross-linking structures are released into blood. Deoxypyridinoline tends to be more bone type I specific.

Twelve aged Arabian mares were fed individually to maintain body condition score and meet NRC requirements (1989). The mares and foals were maintained on paddocks for 8 h during the day and in stalls at night for 16 h. Serum samples were collected at 16:00 from the mare and foal on d 0, d 15, d 30, and d 45 post-partum. Day 0 was defined as the day of foaling (if foaled prior to 15:30) or the following day if foaled after 1600. Twenty ml of blood were collected from both the mares and foals using two 20 ml vacuum tubes with no additive (Becton Dickinson, Franklin Lakes, NJ). The blood was allowed to clot at room temperature, centrifuged and then serum was collected and stored at $-20°C$.

Serum was analyzed for OC and PYD/DPD using a competitive enzyme immunoassay (ELISA) (Novocalcin, Serum PYD, respectively, provided by Metra Biosystems, Mountain View, CA). Serum was also analyzed for ICTP using a radioimmunoassay (RIA) (Diasorin, Inc., Stillwater, MN). Data was analyzed for repeated measures using the Proc Mixed procedure of SAS (6.12).

Results

A significant decrease in ICTP values was observed in the mares from d 0 (16.01 $\pm$ 1.21 mg/ml) to d 30 (10.89 $\pm$ 1.21 mg/ml) (P = 0.0001) and to d 45 (9.08 $\pm$ 1.19 mg/ml) (P = 0.0001). Additionally, d 30 and d 45 were lower than d 15 values (16.59 $\pm$ 1.20 mg/ml) (P = 0.0001 for both) and there was an overall time difference (P = 0.0001). Pyridinoline: deoxypyridinoline ratios in the mare on d 15 (1.87 $\pm$ 0.14 ng/ml) were higher than d 0 (1.06 $\pm$ 0.14 ng/ml) (P = 0.0001). Also, d 30 (1.04 $\pm$ 0.15 ng/ml) and d 45 (0.92 $\pm$ 0.16 ng/ml) were lower in PYD:DPD values than d 15 (P = 0.0001 for each). Post-partum OC values in mares were not significantly different over time.

Foal OC had an overall increase over time (P = 0.003). Values from d 0 (58.56 $\pm$ 12.1 ng/ml) increased at d 15 (113.16 $\pm$ 9.05 ng/ml) (P = 0.0004), d 30 (117.63 $\pm$ 9.70 ng/ml) (P = 0.0007), and d 45 (106.99 $\pm$ 9.45 ng/ml) (P = 0.004). Foal ICTP values decreased from d 15 (37.94 $\pm$ 1.34 mg/ml) to d 30 (33.82 $\pm$ 1.30 mg/ml) (P = 0.0005) and then increased from d 30 to d 45 (37.08 $\pm$ 1.50 mg/ml) (P = 0.01). Additionally, there was a trend to decrease from d 0 (36.25 $\pm$ 1.40 mg/ml) to d 30 (P = 0.09). Pyridinoline: deoxypyridinoline ratios in the foals decreased from d 0 (18.75 $\pm$ 1.28 ng/ml) to d 15 (6.16 $\pm$ 1.36 ng/ml) (P = 0.0001) and remained at this low level through d 30 (6.10 $\pm$ 1.21 ng/ml) and d 45 (6.71 $\pm$ 1.21 ng/ml) when compared to d 0.

Discussion

This data suggests that bone formation in the mare is unaffected but bone resorption is occurring. This resorption is likely due to the increased Ca demand during lactation, and bone is breaking down to release Ca into circulation to be utilized for milk production. Also, the significant PYD:DPD increase at d 15 may be due to uterine involution, which yields a higher PYD release into circulation.

Foal OC dramatically increased over the first 15 d to adapt to the demands placed on the growing bone. The reason behind the decrease in ICTP at d 30 and then an increase again to d 45 remains unclear. The decrease in PYD:DPD is likely due to a decreased resorption rate to allow net bone gain.

Understanding the skeletal developmental patterns of young foals may help the industry better manage and reduce the incidence of bone growth-related diseases. Additionally, these patterns may help researchers understand the growth curve for young foals. Because of the high rate of modeling and remodeling in foals, it is difficult to determine if the animal is "normal" compared to growth of others. It is also inappropriate to assume that the fluctuations in the bone markers are indicative of abnormalities or excess formation or resorption.

The indicators of bone health in mares may be useful in also developing a curve for skeletal adaptation to foaling. Sometimes, high quality mares are used in competition before and soon after parturition, and an expedient return to optimal skeletal health often is desirable. If the mare and foal must be confined to the stall after foaling, bone metabolism may be altered. Therefore, assessment of these bone turnover indicators may be useful in monitoring post-partum skeletal adaptation.

The left ventricular mass measurement through guided M-mode echocardiography in the horse

Take home message

Echocardiography is a non-invasive, simple and reliable technique to determine the left ventricular mass in horses.

Introduction

The selection of the outstanding horse for a particular form of sport prior to beginning training is a dream of those connected with the horse industry. Athletic performance requires a complex interaction of metabolic and physiological mechanisms of the musculoskeletal, respiratory, nervous and cardiovascular systems.[7] The structure and function of the equine cardiovascular system is fundamental to the superior athletic performance of the horse. Indeed, heart size is a major determinant of maximal cardiac output and maximal aerobic capacity.[4] It is known that the heart mass and the heart mass to body weight ratio are a function of breed (racing horses: 0.86; drafts horses: 0.62).[3,11] Therefore techniques to assist in determination of heart size could be important to evaluate the performance potential. In the horse, the initial technique to measure the heart size was based on measurements derived from electrocardiographic recordings.[9]

The mean QRS duration (in msec) in the three bipolar limb leads of the ECG, the value known as "Heart Score", has been found in one study to be highly correlated with postmortem heart weight.[10] Actually the use of the "Heart Score" in evaluation of performance potential is controversial. However, it is apparent that for many athletic horses, those with the largest hearts are often the better performers, whereas those with small heart sizes perform poorly.[2]

Echocardiography has become an invaluable diagnostic tool to represent the equine heart since the first description of its use in horses. Echocardiography has been employed to assess the size of the cardiac chambers and the thickness of ventricular walls and interventricular septum, both in normal and diseased horses. O'Callagham [5] found a positive correlation between body mass and left ventricular size determined through M-mode echocardiography and corroborated it with necropsy measurements.

Our current research has two parts. In the first part we attempt to verify whether the left ventricle mass values obtained through guided M-mode echocardiography have a good correlation with body weight or body surface. In the second part we will investigate whether horses with higher left ventricular mass are also superior performers. In this article we present the results of the first part of our research.

Material and methods

A total of 27 Thoroughbred horses 13-18 months old of several farms in Argentina were studied. The group consisted of 15 females and 12 stallions. Their body weight was between 300 and 510 kg. None of the animals had clinical, electrocardiographic or echocardiographic evidence of cardiovascular disease. None of the horses had undergone training.

Equipment – A Kontron 1C Sigma Cardio ultrasound machine with a 3.5 MHz. mechanical sector scanner was used. The frame rate was 18 frames/s at a depth of display of 23 cm, working at sector angles of 80° and 120°. The setting of parameters was the following: TGC maximal at all levels; General gain for B-mode: 50% and for M-mode: 60%; Reject: 50%; Enhance: 0; Image focus: far field; focus depth: level five.

Measurements – All measurements were made to the nearest 1 mm according to the "leading-edge to leading-edge method", as recommended by the American Society of Echocardiography.[8] In order to reduce variability between investigators, all measurements were made by the same operator. Recording of images was made from the right side of the chest. The following measurements were made: interventricular septal thickness in diastole (IVSd) and in systole (IVSs), left ventricular internal diameter in diastole (LVIDd) and in systole (LVIDs), left ventricular wall thickness in diastole (LVWd) and in systole (LVWs).

All measurements were made in short axis views in M-mode guided with the M-mode cursor positioned between the chordae tendinae. The measurement of left ventricular diastolic diameter was made at the level of the q wave of the electrocardiogram and the left ventricular systolic diameter in the point of maximal distal excursion of the interventricular septum. The thickness of the left ventricular wall and the interventricular septum were measured at the same level that ventricular diameters had been.

We employed the following formula: $IVSd + LVIDd + LVWd)^3 - (LVIDd)^3$ to the left ventricular mass measure[6] and the Teichholz corrected cube formula to measure the left ventricle internal dimension $(7(LVIDd)^3 / 2.4 + LVIDd)$.

Statistical Analysis – We proposed a non-linear model $Y = aX^b$, supposing an allometric relationship between the left ventricular mass and body weight or body surface. We adjusted the linear regression model $logY = log$

(a) + b log(X). The 95% confidence limits to regression line was obtained in each of the adjusted functions.

Results

1- Left ventricular mass value (n = 27)

Mean:	2349 g
Standard deviation:	484 g
Coefficient of variation:	20.6 %
Minimum value:	1518 g
Maximum value:	3398 g

2- Relationship between left ventricular mass and body weight

Proposed model = Left Ventricular Mass = a x Weight^b

Adjusted linear model: log(Mass) = log(a) + B log(Weight)

Estimated line regression obtained: log(Mass) = 0.39 + 1.24 x log(Weight), being the regression significant (b ≠ 0; p<0.001) and the relation between the variables non-linear (b ≠ 1; p<0.005). The coefficient of determination indicated that 90 % of the total variation was explained by the regression (R^2 = 0.90; Residual standard error = 0.065 with 25 degrees of freedom). The coefficient of correlation demonstrated a significant positive correlation between log(Left Ventricular Mass) and log (Weight) (r = 0.95; p<0.0001). Transformed variables had a normal distribution which was not the case for the raw data.

The allometric relationship obtained was: Left Ventricular Mass = 1.48 x Weight $^{1.24}$

The 95% confidence limits of the regression line for log(Left ventricular mass)-Body weight: are:

Inferior limit = 0.39 + 1.24 x log(Weight) - 2.06 x
√ (1.58 x 10-4 + 6.53 x 10-3(log(Weight) - 5.93)^2

Inferior limit = 0.39 + 1.24 x log(Weight) - 2.06 x
√(1.58 x 10-4 + 6.53 x 10-3(log(Weight) - 5.93)^2

Superior limit = 0.39 + 1.24x log(Weight) + 2.06 x
√(1.58 x 10-4 + 6.53 x 10-3 (log(Weight) - 5.93)^2

The confidence limits of the regression line for Left ventricular mass (derived from previous formula) are:

Inferior limit = Exp.(0.39+1.24xlog(Weight)-2.06
√(1.58 x 10-4 + 6.53 x 10-3 (log(Weight) - 5.93)^2))

Superior limit $= $ Exp.$(0.39+1.24$x$\log$(Weight)$+2.06$x
$\sqrt{(1.58 \times 10\text{-}4 + 6.53 \times 10\text{-}3 \, (\log(\text{Weight}) - 5.93)^2)}$

Figure ❶ Function of Left ventricular mass $= 97.20$ x Body Surface$^{1.86}$ and confidence limits to regression line.

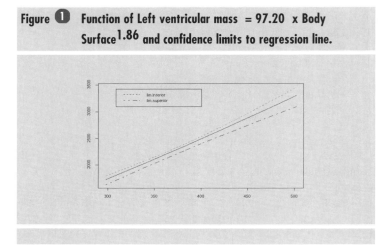

3- Relationship between Left ventricular masses and Body surface
Proposed model $=$ Left Ventricular Mass $=$ a x B. surface^b
Adjusted linear model: $\log$(Mass) $= \log$(a) $+$ B $\log$(B. Surface)
Estimated line regression obtained: $\log$(Mass) $= 4.58 + 1.86$ x $\log$(B. surface), being the regression significant (b $\neq$ 0; p$<$0,001), and the relationship between the variables non-linear (b $\neq$ 1; p$<$0,001). The coefficient of determination indicated that the regression explained 90 % of the total variation ($R^2 = 0.90$; Residual standard error $= 0.065$ with 25 degrees of freedom). The coefficient of correlation showed that relation between $\log$(Left Ventricular Mass) and $\log$(B. Surface) was positive and significant ($r = 0.95$; p$<$0.0001). Again only transformed data sufficed the requirement of normal distribution.

The allometric relationship obtained was: Left Ventricular Mass $= 97.2$ x Body Surface $^{1.86}$

The confidence limits to regression line for the relationship Left Ventricular Mass: The 95% confidence limits of the regression line for $\log$(Left ventricular mass-Body Surface) is given for the expression:

Inferior limit $= 4.58 + 1.86$x$\log$(B.Surface)-2.06x
$\sqrt{1.58 \times 10\text{-}4 + 1.51 \times 10\text{-}2 \, (\log(\text{B. Surface}) - 1.70)^2}$

Superior limit $= 4.58 + 1.86$x$\log$(B. Surface)$+2.06$
$\sqrt{1.58 \times 10\text{-}4 + 1.51 \times 10\text{-}2 \, (\log(\text{B. Surface}) - 1.70)^2}$

The confidence limits to regression line for Left ventricular mass (derived from previous formula) are:

Inferior limit $= Exp.(4.58 + 1.86 \times log(B.Surface) - 2.06 \times \sqrt{(1.58 \times 10^{-4} + 1.51 \times 10^{-2}(log(B.Surface) - 1.70)^2))}$

Superior limit $= Exp.(4.58 + 1.86 \times log(B.Surface) + 2.06 \sqrt{(1.58 \times 10^{-4} + 1.51 \times 10^{-2}(log(B.Surface) - 1.70)^2))}$

Figure ❷   Figure 2-function of Left ventricular mass = 97.20 x Body Surface$^{1.86}$ and confidence limits to regression line.

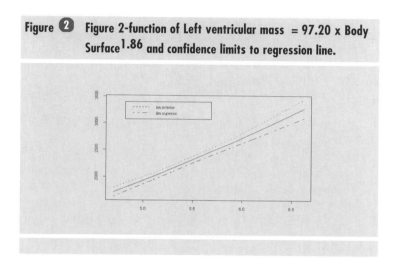

Conclusions

1   There were highly significant allometric relationships between left ventricular mass and body weight as well as between left ventricular mass and body surface.
2   Applying the obtained formula, any one of the relationships can be used because   quality of correlation was similar.
3   The echocardiography is a non-invasive, simple and reliable technique to determine the left ventricular mass in horses.

Acknowledgements

This paper is part of Research TV-021 approved and supported by SCyT, University of Buenos Aires.

The effect of velocity on temporal variables of the equine walk

Take home message

Stride duration and stance time of both the hind and forelimbs decreased with increased velocity. The faster the horses traveled the less time the horses spent in a tripedal support phase with a compensatory increase in the amount of time in both a diagonal and lateral support phases. Understanding these gait variations due to velocity will assist in the evaluation of performance particularly in the breeds noted for walking rapidly while maintaining a regular rhythm.

Introduction

The walk is a regular, four-beat stepping gait. The footfall pattern is right hind limb, right forelimb, left hind limb, and left forelimb. Typically, the walk stride alternates between phases of bipedal and tripedal support. For a regular walking rhythm, the bipedal support is equally distributed between periods of diagonal support and periods of lateral support.

Material and methods

To determine the relationship of velocity and gait variables, the temporal characteristics of a range of walking speeds were measured. The velocities ranged from 0.97 m/s to 2.89 m/s. Data were obtained from videotapes analyzed on a frame-by-frame basis using an Ariel Performance Analysis System. The frames of ground contact and lift off were determined. Stride duration was measured as the time between successive impacts of the right hind limb. The following stride variables were calculated as a percentage of stride duration: diagonal and lateral step durations, hind and forelimb stance time, and the durations of the different types of support phases (bipedal diagonal, bipedal lateral, tripedal with two hind limbs and one forelimb, and tripedal with one hind limb and two forelimbs). Data were collected for 12 strides for each of the nine horses (height range: 142.4-159.2 cm, weight range: 392 kg-510 kg). Strides demonstrating an inequality between diagonal and lateral step durations of greater than 10% of the stride duration were determined to represent a loss of the regular walking rhythm and were excluded from the study. Correlations between velocity and stride duration, hind limb stance time, forelimb stance time, and percentage of tripedal support were evaluated in a simple regression test.

Results

The stride duration decreased from 1483 ms to 629 ms from the slowest to fastest walk. Stride frequency increased with velocity from 0.71 strides/sec to 1.6 strides/sec. Hind and forelimb stance times were similar to each other and ranged from 950 ms to 367 ms as the velocity increased. The time spent in a tripedal support decreased from 788 ms to 173 ms as velocity increased. Total percentage of tripedal support decreased from 83% at the slowest velocity to 47% at the fastest. Tripedal support with two hind limbs and one forelimb decreased from 40% to 26% as velocity increased, and tripedal support with one hind limb and two forelimbs decreased from 43% to 21%. The bipedal diagonal and bipedal lateral support times increased from 9% to 28% and 8% to 26%, respectively, as the velocity increased. Correlations were determined between velocity and stride duration ($r = -0.996$, $p = 0.002$), hind limb stance time ($r = -0.954$, $p = 0.023$), forelimb stance time ($r = -0.977$, $p = 0.011$), and total percentage of tripedal support ($r = -0.992$, $p = 0.004$).

Discussion

The results show that as velocity increased the horses decreased the stride duration and the stance time of both the hind and forelimbs. The faster the horses traveled the less time the horses spent in a tripedal support phase with a compensatory increase in the amount of time in both a diagonal and lateral support phases. Understanding these gait variations due to velocity will assist in the evaluation of performance particularly in the breeds noted for walking rapidly while maintaining a regular rhythm. Theses breeds include the Peruvian Paso, the Paso Fino, the Racking horse, the Icelandic horse, the American Saddlebred, and the North American Single-Footing horse. Measurement of temporal variables at a range of velocities for the fore mentioned breeds might indicate pathological gait if deviations from the described gait variable measurements are detected. An increase in tripedal support or an inequality between diagonal and lateral support as velocity increases may indicate lameness. A greater percentage of stance time on either the hind or forelimbs as velocity increases may also indicate a lame limb. Further research in temporal variables of equine gaits should include the measurement of other four-beat stepping gaits including those demonstrating either diagonal or lateral couplets.

Long-term pasture housing promotes bone mineral deposition in the third metacarpus of previously stalled weanlings

Take home message

Short-term stall housing can have a negative effect on the mineral content of the third metacarpus of weanling horses. This can be mitigated by access to free exercise at pasture for 12 hours per day, and reversed upon return to pasture at an early age.

Introduction

Wolff's Law states that the structure of a bone will change to accommodate stresses as its function is altered (Norwood 1978). These changes arise via the processes of modeling and remodeling. In the juvenile skeleton modeling is the primary method of increasing bone strength by adding mass and improving geometric properties (Kimmel 1993). In the adult skeleton, remodeling is the replacement of immature or damaged bone by healthy mature bone, a process that continues throughout life (Jee 1988). Only through modeling can net deposition of bone occur and, since modeling only occurs during growth, it is critical that bone mass be deposited in the skeletal system of the young horse during early growth.

Unfortunately, common management of horses may predispose them to poor skeletal development and injuries. Horses maintained in stalls are often prevented from taking any fast strides, thus initiating demineralization and retardation bone development. Hoekstra et al (1999) found that yearling and 2-year-old horses housed on pasture had greater bone mineral content in the third metacarpus than horses housed in stalls. An initial decrease in serum osteocalcin, a marker of bone formation, and an increase in urinary deoxypyridinoline, a marker of bone resorption, was shown when these young horses were confined to stalls. Likewise, Bell et al (1999) concluded that confining weanlings to stalls caused a reduction in third metacarpal bone mass in comparison to pastured weanlings. This decrease in bone mineral content may predispose the young horse to skeletal injury once training begins. However, it is not known if horses initially confined to stalls then later moved to pasture will be able to gain bone mineral content to equal that of horses raised on pasture.

In foals and weanlings, the rate of bone formation greatly exceeds that of resorption (Maenpaa et al 1988). Any alteration to this growing process may have a large impact on bone strength later in life (Nunamaker et al 1990). Immature bone is more responsive to stress than mature bone so exercise at an early age is advantageous to young skeletal development (Raub et al 1989). Consequently, the hypothesis of this study was that weanlings housed in stalls and subsequently returned to long-term pasture housing would not restore bone density to equal that of weanlings housed on pasture continuously.

Material and Methods

To test the hypothesis, radiographs were acquired of the left forelimb third metacarpus of 18 yearling Arabian horses to determine radiographic bone aluminum equivalence (RBAE) (Meakim et al 1981). As weanlings, all horses were part of a study described by Bell et al (1999) to determine the effect of housing on bone mineral content. As weanlings, these horses were pair-matched by age and randomly assigned to one of 3 treatment groups: Pastured (P, n=6, 4 colts, 2 fillies, mean age = 136 d), Stalled (S, n=5, 3 colts, 3 fillies, mean age = 134 d), and Partial Pastured (PP, n=4 colts, 2 fillies, mean age = 135 d). One S filly died in an accident, resulting in 17 horses completing the project. Pasture and S horses remained in their assigned housing scenario for 56 d. Partial Pastured horses were housed in stalls for 12 h and pasture for 12 h daily.

Dorsal-palmar radiographs of the left third metacarpus were taken on d 0, 28 and 56. At the conclusion of the 56 d Bell et al study (1999), all horses were returned to pasture for 284 d. On d 340 of the study, all horses were once again radiographed. All radiographs were taken at 70 kV, 17 mA, .08 sec at 70 cm focal film distance using mobile x-ray equipment and medical x-ray film. The radiographic cassette was positioned against the palmar surface of the leg allowing the beam to be parallel to the ground and centered at the mid-point of the metacarpus. An aluminum stepwedge penetrometer was exposed with each radiograph as a reference standard. Radiographs were scanned at the nutrient foramen using the Bio-Rad GS-700 Imaging Densitometer (Bio-Rad Laboratories, Hercules, CA).

Logarithmic regression was used to determine the lateral and medial RBAE using the thickness of the stepwedge and the maximal optical density readings of the cortices (Meakim et al 1981). Total RBAE was determined using the total area of the bone divided by the total area of the aluminum stepwedge (Nielsen and Potter 1997). Differences between treatments, day of study and day*treatment interactions were determined using a two-factor ANOVA (PROC MIXED) appropriate for repeated measures in SAS 6.12 (1997). LSMEANS was included in the analysis to obtain treatment means, differences between means and standard errors. A P-value $< .05$ was considered significant while a trend was investigated at a P-value < 0.1.

Results

Pastured horses had greater lateral RBAE than did stalled horses (P=.02). This difference was primarily due to group P having a greater lateral RBAE than S on d 28 (P=.01) and on d 56 (P<.01). Additionally, on d 56, P was greater than PP (P=.04). Group P showed a trend to increase to d 28 from d 0 (P=.08) and a definite increase by d 56 (P<.01). By d 340, all treatment groups had increased in lateral RBAE (P<.01) but did not differ from each other. Medial RBAE showed a trend to be greater in PP horses than in S horses (P=.06). Partial pastured horse increased from d 0 to d 56 (P=.03) while P horses tended to increase from d 0 to d 28 (P=.09). Pastured horses had greater medial RBAE (P<.01) and PP horses tended to have a greater medial RBAE (P=.08) than S horses on d 28. All treatment groups had increased in medial RBAE by d 340 (P<.01) but did not differ from each other. The total RBAE of P horses increased from d 0 to d 56 (P=.05) and tended to be greater than S horses on d 28 (P=.08). The PP horses increased from d 0 to d 56 (P=.08) and was greater than the stalled weanlings on d 28 (P=.05). The total RBAE of S horses increased from d 0 to d 56 (P=.04). As with the lateral and medial RBAEs, the total RBAEs of all treatment groups had increased by d 340 of the study (P<.01) and did not differ from each other.

Discussion

This study emphasizes the negative effect short-term stall housing can have on the mineral content of the third metacarpus of weanling horses. Fortunately, this can be mitigated by access to free exercise at pasture for 12 hour per day. This study also demonstrates that the negative effects of housing weanlings in stalls can be reversed upon return to pasture. The lack of differences between the three treatment groups at d 340 demonstrates the dynamic ability of the third metacarpus to adapt to strain in the young growing horse. How long it takes for these adaptations to occur is yet unanswered. However, this study has provided evidence that the undesirable loss of bone mass due to decreased loading in the juvenile skeleton may be reversed and it does not appear to limit the horse's skeletal development.

Cardiac parameters of the evaluation of performance in the athlete horse

Take home message

Heart score, resting heart rate and P wave duration are influenced by the type of activity, by sex and age of horses.

Introduction

In the field of equine sports medicine, the cardiological functional evaluation of the athletic horse has an increasingly important role. This is facilitated by contemporaneous progress in clinical-physiological techniques and by the knowledge relating to the adaptations of the cardiovascular system to training. A significant effort is required of the cardiovascular system during physical exercise; this effort is expressed in a series of transitory functional mechanisms - adjustments - which vary in relation to the type and intensity of the exercise. From a qualitative point of view, the adjust-

Table ❶   **Mean value (±SD) of the heart score (msec), heart rate (beat/min) and of the P wave duration (sec), together with the fiducial limits at 95% (F.L.) and the significance of the statistic comparison, in horses with varying activity, sex and age.**

	Heart Score (msec)	F.L. (95%)	H.R. (beat/min)	F.L. (95%)	P wave duration (sec)	F.L. (95%)
Sprinters (26)	120.0±14.5a,b,c	95.9-144.3	36.5±5.5 b*, c	29.2-44.0	0.13±0.02	0.12-0.14
Jumpers (18)	104.0±15.0d	78.8-130.0	36.3±5.9 d	27.4-45.2	0.12±0.02 x	0.11-0.13
Stayers (16)	112.0±6.4e	83.3-141.3	32.6±5.4 e	24.1-41.1	0.14±0.009 e	0.13-0.14
Sedentaries (40)	82.6±6.0	69.4-96.0	47.3±4.4	39.8-102.5	0.12±0.02	0.12-0.13
Males (38)	102.0±22.4	84.9-119.3	42.4±8.1g	35.3-49.5	0.12±0.02 f	0.11-0.13
Females (43)	97.7±17.6	82.4-113.0	40.2±7.8h	33.8-46.5	0.14±0.02	0.13-0.14
Geldings (19)	105.4±13.4	80.4-130.4	36.0±6.1	27.4-44.6	0.13±0.02	0.12-0.14
1st Group (2-5 years)	111.5±19.1i,l	91.8-131.1	38.6±7.7	31.8-45.5	0.13±0.02	0.12-0.14
2nd Group (6-8 years)	95.7±16.7	81.2-110.2	40.4±7.7	34.3-46.5	0.13±0.02	0.12-0.13
3rd Group (9-15 years)	94.7±16.3	72.6-116.7	42.5±8.4	32.5-52.4	0.13±0.02	0.12-0.14

ments do not vary greatly between a sedentary subject and an athlete. However, the latter's cardiovascular performance is much better: when training is done systematically the athlete's organism - and in particular the cardiovascular system - is induced to "adapt itself" to the new "overworking" conditions. This adaptation develops through a series of durable morphological and functional modifications called "training-related cardiovascular adaptation". The aim of our investigation was to study the influence of some qualitative (activity and sex) and quantitative (age) variables on heart score, heart rate and P wave duration to provide further knowledge for the utilisation of cardiovascular parameters in the performance evaluation of the athletic horse.

Material and methods

The study was carried out on 100 horses: 26 "sprinters" (10 females, 14 males and 2 geldings; Thoroughbreds; average age 4 ± 1 years, trained to sustain races of 1000-2400 meters), 18 "jumpers" (7 females and 11 geldings; Sella Italiano breed; average age 9 ± 3 years), 16 "stayers" (6 females, 4 males and 6 geldings; Arab breed; average age 6 ± 1 years), and 40 "sedentaries" (20 females and 20 males; various breeds – Sella Italiano, Thoroughbred, Arab and Sanfratellano –; average age 7 ± 1 years). At the time of the study all the animals were clinically healthy. All subjects were divided according to activity (sprinters, jumpers, stayers and sedentary), sex (female, male and geldings) and age group (1st group: 2–5 years; 2nd group: 6–8 years; 3rd group: 9–15 years). Some ECG recordings were carried out on each subject at rest by means of a monopen electrocardiograph with microprocessor (Personal C1 Esaote Biomedica) with a deflection of 10 mm/mV and paper speed of 25 mm/sec. The leads were: I, II, III, aVR, aVF, aVL. The heart score, the heart rate and the P wave duration were calculated. The heart score was calculated on the individual tracings by measuring – in the three bipolar derivations – the average duration of the QRS complex, expressed in milliseconds: to this end we recorded 25 QRS complexes without registration errors.

Table ❷   Significance of results in table 1

activity	sex	age group
Sprinters vs Jumpers a=P<0.001	Males vs Females f=P<0.002	1st group vs 2nd Group: i=P<0.0001
Sprinters vs Stayers b=P<0.04 b*=P<0.02	Males vs Geldings g=P<0.003	1st group vs 3rd Group: l=P<0.001
Sprinters vs Sedentaries c=P<0.001	Females vs Geldings h=P<0.04	
Jumpers vs Stayers x=P<0.001		
Jumpers vs Sendentaries d=P<0.001		
Stayers vs Sendentaries e=P<0.001		

Results

Table 1 reports the mean value (SD) of the heart score (msec), of the heart rate (beat/min) and of the P wave duration (sec), and table 2 the statistic comparison, in horses of varying activity, sex and age groups.

Discussion and conclusions

Our results show that cardiac performance is greatly influenced by physical activity. There are, in fact, significant differences between athletes and sedentaries in all the cardiac parameters tested. Specifically, the heart score was highest in sprinters (120 ± 15 msec) and decreased progressively from stayers (112 ± 6), to jumpers (104 ± 15) to sedentaries (83 ± 6). This is in line with what other authors have observed - i.e. that horses with more intensive physical effort have a higher heart score. An increase in heart weight, which has been reported to be more marked in sprinters, is believed to be responsible for longer activation times and hence for an increase in QRS complex duration (Physick-Sheard and Hendron 1982; Steel et al 1976; Rose 1997).

Resting mean heart rate was significantly lower in horses with athletic activities than in sedentary ones (47 ± 4). It rose from 33 ± 5 beat/min in stayers, to 36 ± 6 in jumpers, to 37 ± 6 in sprinters. These results seem to confirm that physical exercise reduces resting heart rate. Of course there may be also breed effects. In literature there are several reports documenting lowered resting heart rates in horses undergoing long periods of hard training (Rose 1997).

Our results for P wave duration showed significantly higher levels for stayers than for jumpers and sedentaries. This differs from other authors' findings. Beckner and Winsor (1954), McKrichnie et al (1967), and Nakamoto (1969) did not observe variations in atriogram duration, morphology and voltage related to physical exercise respectively.

Sex-related differences in cardiac parameters were significant for heart rate and P wave duration. We observed that the former was lower in geldings than in males and females, while the latter was higher in females than in geldings and males.

Moreover, higher mean heart scores were noted in geldings (105 ± 13 msec) and males (102 ± 22) than in females (98 ± 18), although the differences were not statistically significant. Other authors found that heart score in males is about 5 msec higher than in females and that the best performance is seen in males (Steel and Stewart 1978; Nielsen and Vibe-Petersen 1980; Physick-Sheard and Hendron 1982).

Age significantly influenced heart score only. Its levels decreased progressively with ageing. We observed the highest levels (112 ± 19) in animals under 5 years, as have other authors (Steel and Stewart 1978), and the lowest in animals over 10 years (95 ± 16).

In conclusion it seems obvious that the cardiac parameters we studied, which may be useful for evaluation of performance potential in the athletic horse, are influenced by the type of activity, by sex and age.

Plasma cortisol progressive response during standardised exercise test on treadmill

Take home message

Plasma cortisol changes during and after exercise cannot be predicted. Thus repetitive blood sampling is necessary if this variable is used as an index to estimate exercise-induced stress, to adjust training programmes, and for performance diagnosis.

Introduction

Adrenocortical involvement in physical exertion has been studied both in human and equine subjects for the evaluation of physiological responses to exercise stress. The most important glucocorticoid in the horse is cortisol, whose plasma levels show diurnal variations, the highest levels being measured in the morning between 6:00 and 9:00 am, and the lowest between 6:00 and 9:00 pm (Irvine and Alexander 1994). Cortisol plasma levels are affected by physical effort, but there are conflicting data about the characteristics of these modifications. In a review Thornton (1985) reports that short exercise periods and low workloads are associated with constant or decreasing plasma cortisol concentrations, whilst exercise of increasing duration and workload will increase the levels. In humans, the critical workload intensity necessary to induce a response by adrenal cortex has been identified in 60% of VO_2max maintained for 1 hour (Davies and Few 1973).

Recently, post-exertion plasma cortisol levels have been proposed as a reliable index to estimate exercise-induced stress, particularly cortisol values measured 2 min after exercise (Linden 1991); moreover, simultaneous measurements of post-exertion plasma cortisol and lactate levels have been suggested to discriminate between different types of exercise and to be useful to adjust training programmes (Desmecht 1996). But, there are many reports describing the behaviour of cortisol levels after exercise, and interpretation of data is very difficult. An extensive review was published by Ferlazzo and Fazio (1997). For a correct utilization of this variable it is necessary to exactly know its changes during and after physical effort. Thus, it is necessary to standardize the sampling procedure, because a difference in timing will affect the result. The aim of this work was to demonstrate this measuring of plasma cortisol levels within short periods of time during and after standardized exercise on a treadmill.

Materials and methods

The study was done with four untrained two-year old Haflinger mares. They were adapted to treadmill exercise for 5 days before the test. The test was performed in the morning (9:00-10:00 am), after overnight fasting, as an incremental submaximal exercise with 5 steps: 1st) 4 min 30 sec treadmill speed 1.8 m/sec, 2nd) 2 min speed 3.5 m/sec, 3rd) 2 min speed 5.5 m/sec, 4th) 2 min at the necessary speed to maintain a constant heart rate 200 b/min, 5th) 4 min 30 sec at 1.8 m/sec; steps 1-4 at slope 3.5%. Blood was drawn every 60 seconds using an HEBC (haematic extrabody circuit) method (Berthoud 1986; Martin 1993; Tedeschi 1998) into heparine sodium tubes for cortisol assay and in EDTA-F for plasma lactate assay. Cortisol was measured by RIA (CORT-CT2, CIS®, previously validated for equine) while plasma lactate was measured using an enzymatic method (n.735-10, SIGMA). Each sample was double assayed. Heart rate was monitored each 30 sec during the test with a Polar Sport Tester((Polar Electro Oy, Finland).

Results

Plasma cortisol responses induced by incremental exercise are reported in the graph (Fig. 1). The study of data points by regression, Pearson's correlation coefficient and ANOVA of the regression has permitted us to characterize the curve. We observed different phases of cortisol response during and after exercise. Between the 1st and the 12th min (1.5 min after the end of the exercise, $r=0.47$, $p>0.05$) plasma cortisol concentration did not change. Between the 13th and 19h min (2.5 to 8.5 min after the end of exercise, $r=0.82$, $p<0.05$) there was a linear increase of the cortisol concentration. At the 13th min lactate reached its peak value (20.5 min after the end of the exercise). Between the 21st and 41st min after exercise the mean plasma cortisol concentration remained at the same level ($r=0.19$, $p>0.05$), and it only decreased after the

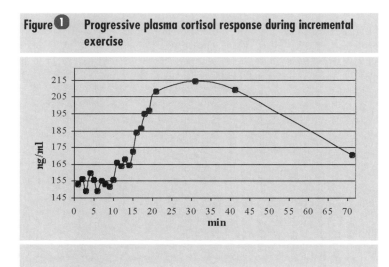

Figure ❶   Progressive plasma cortisol response during incremental exercise

41st min (r=0.99, p<0.05). One hour after exercise, cortisol plasma levels were still 11% above the basal value.

Discussion

These data on the progressive changes of cortisol concentration in plasma during and after standardized exercise show the importance of repetitive blood sampling, whether it is wanted to use cortisol measurements as an index to estimate exercise-induced stress (Linden 1991), to adjust training programmes (Desmecht 1996), or for performance diagnosis (Ferlazzo and Fazio 1997).

Changes in plasma PTH and calcium during different types of exercise and training in young horses

Take home message

Intensive exercise was associated with a marked rise in plasma PTH concentration and a decrease in ionized calcium in blood in young horses. Lower intensity and training did not influence plasma PTH and ionized calcium levels in whole blood. The increase in PTH and the decrease in ionized calcium during exercise may increase risk of skeletal injury in young racehorses.

Introduction

In humans it is well established that physical exercise can influence plasma concentrations of intact PTH and other parameters related to calcium metabolism. In horses there is still little information on the hormonal regulation of calcium metabolism during exercise. Aguilera-Tejero et al (1998) reported about an increase in plasma PTH by a concomitant decrease in whole blood ionized calcium after a show jumping competition in horses. The purpose of this study was to investigate the effects of different types of exercise and training on changes in plasma PTH and calcium in young horses.

Material and methods

Seven Standardbred horses, age 2 years, were used in this study. The horses were fed hay and a commercial concentrate providing an average daily intake of 90 MJ of digestible energy and 500 g digestible protein. Standardized exercise tests (SET) and training were done on a highspeed treadmill without incline. SET consisted of six steps of five minutes' duration each. The velocity in the first step was 5 m/s, each consecutive step was increased by 1 m/s, and between two consecutive steps there was a resting period of 60 s for blood sampling. SET was followed by a lactate-guided training where horses had to perform two different types of exercise:

1. High-speed exercise: start by $v_{4.0}$, the running velocity was increased continuously by 0.3 m/s every 60 s, total running time: 15 minutes.
2. Prolonged low-speed exercise: constant velocity by $v_{2.5}$, total running duration was calculated based on the equal energy requirement during the high-speed exercise to achieve equal energy demand for both types of exercise. The kind of exercise changed every second day, and in between there was a rest. In total, the training program consisted of 8 workouts of prolonged low-speed exercises and 8 wor-

kouts of high-speed exercises. A second SET (same conditions like first SET) was done after finishing the whole training program. Blood samples for intact PTH and total calcium in plasma and ionized calcium and lactate in whole blood were collected before and after SET, at the beginning and at the end of the training period (before and after prolonged low-speed or high-speed exercise, respectively). Intact PTH in plasma was determined with a radioimmunoassay (intact PTH, Nichols Institute Diagnostics, Estepa et al 1998), ionized calcium (corrected to pH of 7.4) was measured in whole blood using ion-sensitive electrodes (AVL 988-4, Bad Homburg), total calcium in plasma was determined by AAS (Unicam Solar 969), and whole blood lactate was done enzymatically by Accusport® (Boehringer Mannheim GmbH, Art. Nr. 1463667). All results are presented as mean±s.d. Results were analysed by an analysis of variance for repeated measures according to the program of Statistica® to evaluate the effect of exercise and training. Post hoc analysis were made by Scheffé test. Differences were considered to be significant when $p < 0.05$.

Results

During SET and high-speed exercise there was a significant increase in plasma PTH by a concomitant decrease in ionized calcium in whole blood. However total calcium in plasma was not affected by exercise (Table 1 and 2).

No exercise related changes in PTH, ionized calcium and total calcium were observed during prolonged low-speed exercise. Training seemed to have no influence on PTH, ionized calcium and total calcium during rest and exercise. There was a close relationship between PTH in plasma and ionized calcium in whole blood which is best described by the linear equation $y = 1.72 - 0.0078x$ ($r = -0.77$; $p < 0.05$)

Table ❶   Changes in PTH in plasma (pg/ml), ionized calcium in whole blood (mmol/l) and plasma total calcium (mmol/l) during SET

	before training program		after training program	
	Start	End	Start	End
PTH (pg/ml)	9.0 ± 2.6a	32.2 ± 9.4b	9.2 ± 4.7a	29.3 ± 10.1b
Ca++ (mmol/l)	1.633±0.055a	1.419±0.049b	1.667±0.045a	1.484±0.079b
total calcium (mmol/l)	3.18±0.19a	3.31±0.12a	3.15±0.17a	3.19±0.25a

Explanation
means with the same letter are significantely different at $p < 0.05$

Table ❶ **Changes in PTH in plasma (pg/ml), ionized calcium in whole blood (mmol/l) and plasma total calcium (mmol/l) during high- speed and prolonged low- speed exercise**

	first training bout		last training bout	
	Start	End	Start	End
High- speed exercise				
PTH(pg/ml)	11.4 ± 2.7a	30.4 ± 4.7b	9.2 ± 3.4a	31.2 ± 10.4b
Ca^{++}(mmol/l)	1.597±0.049a	1.416±0.096b	1.661±0.060a	1.473±0.076b
total calcium (mmol/l)	3.25±0.39a	3.16±0.16a	3.10±0.14a	3.03±0.10a
Prolonged low- speed exercise				
PTH(pg/ml)	11.8 ± 6.7a	8.8 ± 4.0a	12.3 ± 5.4a	13.5 ± 6.9b
Ca^{++}(mmol/l)	1.664±0.085a	1.662±0.049a	1.650±0.049a	1.646±0.054a
total calcium (mmol/l)	3.16±0.28a	3.14±0.16a	3.18±0.15a	3.20±0.27a

Explanation
means with the same letter are significantely different at $p < 0.05$

Discussion

The present study is the first one to describe the influence of different types of exercise and training on intact PTH in plasma under standardized conditions in young horses. The results demonstrated that intensive exercise was associated with a marked rise in plasma PTH concentration and a decrease in ionized calcium in blood in young horses. Lower intensity and training did not influence plasma PTH and ionized calcium levels in whole blood. On the one hand the main stimulus for PTH secretion is a low extracellular calcium concentration and on the other hand, adrenaline has been suggested as a possible factor of exercise-induced rise in PTH. It is widely accepted that the adrenergic system, which is strongly activated by high-intensity exercise (Coenen et al 2000), affects both calcium and PTH (Ljunghall et al 1984). The mechanisms responsible for the decrease in ionized calcium (corrected to pH 7.4) in whole blood are not fully understood. The reduction could depend on complex-binding to lactate and proteins, but a transport (i.e. into the muscle) cannot be excluded. PTH has been shown to have anabolic as well as catabolic effects on the bone turnover (Heersche et al 1994) and exercise is proposed as a preventive measure against loss of bone mass (i.e. osteoporosis), particularly in aging people (Zerath et al 1997). Continuous administration of PTH can induce bone loss, whereas intermittent administration has been found to increase bone volume (Dempster et al 1993).

The consequences of an increase in PTH and a decrease in ionized calcium during exercise in young horses are not clear. Young racehorses start their training when they are still in their growing stage, and the possibility of skeletal injury is enormous. At the onset of training a decrease in bone density and changes in bone markers like osteocalcin and ICTP are described (Hiney et al 1998). There might be a possibility of minimizing skeletal demineralisation by an improved calcium balance which reduces the effects of PTH to mobilize bone Ca^{++}. Further investigations are necessary about the hormonal regulation of calcium metabolism during exercise and about the effects of dietary manipulation (i.e. calcium supplementation) in calcium homeostasis in young exercising horses.

Tests to assess temperament in foals: individual consistency

Take home message

Foals display consistent individual responses when exposed to a novel object and when handled by humans. Our measures may be used to quantify and define a horse's temperament. Repeating these tests at older ages will reveal whether the consistent behavioural as well as physiological responses measured at an early age are consistent over a longer age interval, and hence will have a predicting value for certain aspects of the horse's temperament. This would be relevant in the selection of young foals for a specific purpose, be it leisure or sports.

Introduction

Temperament generally refers to relatively stable individual characteristics that show consistency over time and across situations. The interest in temperamental traits in animals has grown since we know that they are relevant for a better understanding of animal welfare. It places particular emphasis on the differences between individuals in how they react to environmental change and various stimuli. Behavioural tests are used to objectively assess these individual differences in response. Such tests have been widely performed in cows, pigs and rodents, but to a lesser extent in horses. Moreover, many of the horse studies used subjects differing in age, breed or husbandry conditions, and thus data are sometimes difficult to interpret.

The objective of this project was to study consistency in behavioural and physiological responses of horses of the same breed and age to behavioural tests.

Material and methods

Forty-one Dutch warm-blood (KWPN) horses were made familiar with testing equipment and testing environment. Two tests were developed and executed twice, at 9 and 10 months of age. In the Novel Object test the response to a novel object (unfolded umbrella) was recorded. The horse was left alone in a starting box, and after two minutes introduced into an arena adjacent to the starting box by opening a sliding door. After another two minutes it was an unfolded umbrella was lowered from the ceiling. In the Handling test the response of the horse to the presence of a human was recorded as well as the response of the horse to leading and making the horse cross a concrete 'bridge'. The horse was again left alone in the starting box. After three minutes a familiar human stood motionless in front of the starting box where the horse could see her, and after another three minutes the human entered the starting box.

After the horse had been attached to the rope the human stood next to the left shoulder petting the horse on the left shoulder. Following this three minute petting the horse was led out of the starting box through the arena approaching a concrete bridge (200x800x20cm). When the horse was standing in the starting box the human did not use the voice and later on, the human used neither voice nor force to make the horse cross the bridge. During both tests heart rate was measured continuously with Polar Horse trainer transmitters®, and behaviour was recorded with a real time video camera. Behaviour was analysed with the Observer system (Noldus Information Technology®). Statistical analysis (GenStat) was done using Spearman rank correlations.

Results

Horses showed considerable individual differences in response to the novel object, both behaviourally and physiologically. For many parameters individual differences proved consistent over time between 9 and 10 months of age. The innate reaction of a horse confronted unexpectedly with a novel object is to flee. Hence we measured the time spent running after the umbrella had been lowered. The range in this parameter was one to four minutes' running. Repeating this test at 10 months of age a wide variation in running between individuals was noticed again. However, using a Spearman rank correlation we found consistency of this parameter over time (R_{sp} 0.78, p<0.001). Horses also express uncertainty or fear with vocalisations. Snorting is an alarm call used in the wild to alert the herd for a possible threat. The frequency of snorting when confronted with the novel object was positively correlated over time (R_{sp} 0.47, p <0.005). At some point horses will overcome their fear and will approach or even investigate the novel object. The latency time to touch the umbrella proved not to be consistent over time (R_{sp} 0.25). The mean heart rate before the test, measured when standing in the home environment with conspecifics, was 53 (±SD 8) beats per minute at 9 months of age and 54 (±SD 13) beats per minute one month later. When the horse was alone in the arena the one minute before the introduction of the novel object this mean heart rate was 152 (±SD 47) and 154 (±SD 48) respectively at 9 and 10 months of age. The first minute after the umbrella had been lowered this mean heart rate increased to 193 (±SD 25) and 170 (±SD 35) respectively. The difference in heart rate as a result of the introduction of the novel object is the fourth parameter measured to quantify the horse's reaction. The difference in mean heart rate one minute after the umbrella had been lowered was compared with the one minute before it had been lowered. Twenty percent of the horses showed a slight decrease in heart rate whereas the other 80 percent showed an increase of up to 120 beats per minute. Also this parameter proved to be consistent over time (R_{sp} 0.58, p < 0.001).

During the Handling test we again noticed profound differences in behavioural as well as physiological responses between individual horses. When the human was standing in front of the starting box as well as when the human was standing in the starting box holding and petting the horse, the horses showed behaviour that could be interpreted as showing resistance towards the circumstances. For example, horses frequently stroked with their forelegs, reared, shook with their heads or tried to bite. The frequency of showing this type of resistance, measured by the behaviours mentioned above, showed a wide variety between individuals but also a positive correlation over time, while standing in front of the starting box (R_{sp} 0.63, p < 0.001) and while standing in the starting box (R_{sp} 0.75, p < 0.001). By measuring the latency to put its first foot on the 'bridge' (concrete plates) we aimed to measure the compliance and self-assurance to follow the human across the 'bridge'. This parameter proved to be consistent over time (R_{sp} 0.57, p < 0.001). Also, the number of attempts needed to cross the 'bridge' (maximum of three attempts) was consistent over time (R_{sp} 0.72, p<0.001). The mean heart rate within the home environment before the test was 54 (±SD 10) beats per minute at 9 months of age and 51 (±SD 6) at 10 months of age. Being left alone in the starting box caused the heart rate to increase to 115 (±SD 17) and 102 (±SD 20) respectively for 9 and 10 months of age. With a human standing motionless in front of the starting box the mean heart rate decreased to 97 (±SD 15) and 84 (±SD 15) respectively for both ages. A further decrease in mean heart rate was noticed when the human stood within the starting box petting the horse: 79 (±SD 11) at 9 months and 73 (±SD 13) at 10 months of age. Though these mean heart rate data showed profound differences between individuals it was significantly (p<0.001) consistent over ages R_{sp} 0.75 (standing alone), R_{sp} 0.72 (human in front), R_{sp} 0.70 (human in starting box).

Discussion

The behavioural and physiological parameters measured are suggested to reflect temperamental characteristics involving emotionality and reactivity to humans. Foals have been clearly shown to display consistent individual responses when exposed to a novel object and when handled by humans. This supports the idea that we have been able to assess stable individual temperamental traits and that our measures may be used to quantify and define a horse's temperament. Repeating these tests at older ages will reveal whether the consistent behavioural as well as physiological responses measured at an early age will still be consistent over a longer age interval, and hence will have a predicting value for certain aspects of the horse's temperament. Such a prediction is relevant in the selection of young foals for training and to help assess suitability of a foal for a specific purpose, be it leisure or sports.

Immunobiology of equine muscle healing

Take home message

With equine leukocytes and neutrophyles conditioned media promoted proliferation of equine myoblasts. Proliferation of myoblasts is a significant step in muscle fibers to keep adequate muscle mass and in muscle fiber regeneration.

Introduction

Strenuous exercise can cause acute myopathies with an accompanying inflammatory response. Associated with this inflammatory response are cellular infiltrates and rise in certain cytokines levels. Cells of the immune system, including neutrophils, monocytes, and lymphocytes, have been shown to be present in damaged muscle at various post exercise periods. As a consequence of soluble inflammatory mediators, these cells are also activated to produce cytokines. Cytokines have a role in muscle repair and regeneration and elevated levels of some cytokines are detectable follo-wing exercise. For example, in humans the level of plasma IL-6 has been shown to be elevated after eccentric exercise. IL-6 is produced by human myoblasts and stimulates their proliferation. Proliferated myobalsts either fuse into damaged muscle fibers (muscle hypertrophy) or fuse together for-ming a new myofiber (musle hyperplasia); therefore, induced myoblast proliferation is a necessary process to heal and regenerate damaged muscle fibers after strenuous training. In addition, myoblasts express neural cell adhesion molecule (N-CAM) and vascular cell adhesion molecule-1 (V-CAM1), and since revascularisation and reinnervation are necessary to heal muscle damage, these adhesion molecules may contribute to muscle regeneration by interaction with leukocytes. Furthermore, decreased myo-blast proliferation was seen in patients with Duchenne muscular dystro-phy in which proliferative capacity of myoblasts in patients is exhausted as a result of continuous regenerative demands of muscular dystrophy. Therefore, myoblast transplantation has been extensively studied as a potential therapy for Duchenne muscular dystrophy (DMD); and cytokines have a important role to improve survival rate of the injected myoblasts. This study was undertaken to investigate the effect of equine leukocytes on equine myoblasts in an effort to understand the immunobiology of equine muscle healing.

Materials and methods

Equine myoblasts were isolated from the biceps femoris muscle from a healthy horse and isolated into clonal populations using cloning rings. Equine myoblast clones were plated in Dulbecco's minimum essential medium (DMEM) with 5% fetal calf serum (FCS) and 1% penicillin/streptomysin on 0.1% pig skin gelatin coated 96-well plates at 2×10^4 cell/ml for 24 hours before adding conditioned media (CM) from leukocyte cultures. To produce CM, fresh blood was collected from a healthy horse. Total leukocytes were isolated from plasma by centrifugation followed by hypotonic lysis of erythrocytes. After centrifugation, leukocytes were resuspended in RPMI 1640 + 5% FCS at 1×10^7 cell/ml and incubated for 48 hours. To isolate different populations of leukocytes (neutrophils, monocytes and lymphocytes), cells were first centrifuged over a density gradient (Histopaque). Lymphocytes and monocytes were isolated from the interface and incubated in 5% FCS + RPMI 1640 for 2 hours. After 2 hours, unattached lymphocytes were removed and cultured for 48 hours. Monocytes remaining in the flask were incubated for 48 hours. Neutrophils and erythrocytes were collected from the pellet of the density gradient. Erythrocytes were lysed and neutrophils were incubated as described for leukocytes. Erythrocyte lysates (1×10^6 cell/ml) were added to isolated leukocyte cultures to control for exogenous stimulation. All leukocytes were incubated in RPMI 1640 + 5% FCS at 1×10^7 cell/ml for 48 hours. After 48 hours of incubation, CM was frozen at $-20°C$ overnight. This CM was applied to the equine myoblasts in DMEM with 0.5% FCS. No CM was added to control wells. Media was changed every 24 hours. After 144 hours (120 hours from adding CM), myoblasts were stained with methylene blue and the optical density was determined (620nm). All data were analyzed by one way ANOVA, and if necessary, pairwise Tukey test was used.

Results

The results indicated that myoblast proliferation was increased significantly in CM from leukocytes (242% increase compared to control) and neutrophils (163%). Therefore, leukocytes were subsequently stimulated with IFNγ, IL-2, LPS, latex beads (LB, 0.8μm) and formalin inactivated Staphylococcus aureus (SA) to examine the effect of CM on myoblast proliferation. The greatest myoblast proliferation was observed in cultures with CM from leukocytes stimulated by IFNγ (157%) and latex beads (157%). Proliferation was also observed in cultures with CM from leukocytes stimulated by IL-2 (148%) or SA (129%). However, there was no significant difference in myoblast proliferation with CM from leukocytes stimulated by LPS (108%).

Equine myoblasts were next co-cultured with stimulated leukocytes in 24-well plate inserts for 96 hours. Inserts physically separated leukocytes from myoblasts by a 0.4 μm pore membrane. Substances less than 2×10^3 kDa are able to cross the membrane, therefore, cytokines (8-80 kDa) produced by stimulated leukocytes could exert a paracrine effect on myoblasts. As controls, IFNγ and IL-2 were directly added to myoblasts to compare their effect to co-cultures with leukocytes stimulated by IFNγ and IL-2. The media was not changed during 96 hours incubation. After 96 hours, myoblasts were fixed and stained with Giemsa. The number of nuclei in 10 microscopic fields (0.16 mm^2) was counted and used to determine the total number of cells per well. Significant myoblast proliferation was seen in co-cultures stimulated by IFNγ (123%).

Human myoblasts are capable of expressing IL-6. This cytokine, which is also expressed by macrophages, is able to stimulate proliferation of myoblasts in an autocrine fashion. To determine the ability of equine myoblasts to express IL-6, the polymerase chain reaction (PCR) was used to amplify cDNA using primers specific for equine IL-6. RNA was isolated from equine myoblasts grown in DMEM with 10% FCS to approximately 80% confluency. Cells were scraped from the flasks, pelleted and resuspended in Trizol (Gibco BRL). RNA was harvested from the aqueous phase. As a control, equine leukocytes at 1×10^7 cells/ml were cultured overnight in media containing Concanavalin A (ConA 15μg/ml). RNA was isolated as with myoblasts. RNA was reverse transcribed to cDNA by Moloney murine leukemia virus reverse transcriptase using oligo dT primers. The resulting cDNA was used in a PCR reaction using primers designed from the known equine IL-6 sequence. Primers for ß-actin were also used to amplify cDNA from myoblasts and leukocytes. A plasmid containing the equine IL-6 gene (a gift from Dr. Dave Horohov) was also used as a control for the amplification product. A 550 base pair fragment was amplified from the plasmid containing the equine IL-6 gene, using the IL-6 primers. The same product was also amplified from equine myoblasts and leukocytes.

Myoblast proliferation was induced in cultures incubated with CM from leukocytes as well as co-cultures with stimulated leukocytes. This indicates that soluble factors expressed by equine leukocytes induce proliferation of equine myoblasts. Human myoblasts are stimulated to proliferate in response to both IL-6 and LIF and are capable of producing IL-6. Our PCR results demonstrate that equine myoblasts are also capable of expressing mRNA for equine IL-6. In strenuous exercise, cells of the immune system migrate into damaged muscle to initiate repair. Soluble factors released by these cells are capable of stimulating myoblast proliferation.

Proliferation of myoblasts is a significant step in muscle fibers to keep adequate muscle mass and also in muscle fiber regeneration in that it provides nuclei to damaged myofibers through myoblast fusion, resulting in either muscle hypertrophy or hyperplasia as well as muscle healing in trained muscles. This study demonstrates the overlapping contribution of leukocytes, cytokines, and myoblasts to the immunobiology of muscle.

2 INTERNAL MEDICINE

2.1 Articles

Incidence of hemosiderophages in bronchoalveolar lavage fluid of horses with chronic obstructive pulmonary disease (COPD)

Take home message

All COPD horses examined had hemosiderophages. Percentage of hemo-siderophages differed and did not depend on age and breed of horses or on COPD degree.

Introduction

Chronic obstructive pulmonary disease (COPD) is a debilitating disease in horses, often limiting their ability to perform in competitions. COPD is seen as an umbrella term for diseases with different etiologies, all resulting in lower airway obstruction. In race horses, exercise intolerance may be caused by exercise induced pulmonary hemorrhage (EIPH). It is diagnosed easily by clinical and endoscopic examination as long as frank blood is present in the upper airways and/or trachea. However, knowledge about the incidence of lower degrees of EIPH in horses and its clinical relevance is sparse. There has been widespread discussion about a possible relationship between small airway inflammatory disease and EIPH. To our knowledge, the occurrence of pulmonary hemorrhage in horses with a primary diagnosis of COPD has not yet been examined. Since obvious bleeding in horses which do not perform on high levels is rare, the presence of free iron in alveolar macrophages was used as a marker for pulmonary hemorrhage. An iron-laden macrophage is also termed hemosiderophage or siderophage (2). The aim of this study was primarily to survey the incidence of hemosiderophages in bronchoalveolar lavage fluid (BALF) of horses with COPD and without heavy loads of exercise and secondarily to check possible relationships with clinical and laboratory findings in these horses.

Material and Methods

48 horses with a history of chronic cough and diagnosed as suffering from COPD were included in the study. They underwent routine assessment of their pulmonary status, including clinical examination and endoscopy of upper airways and trachea, measurement of arterial blood gases, lung function parameters and cytology of BALF. Clinical and endoscopical findings were scored with a maximum of 10 resp. 13 points. The BALF was cytocentrifuged for 10 min at 400 g and cell preparations were stained with Wright-Giemsa and Prussian blue (HematoGnost Fe® Diagnostika Merck, Darmstadt, Germany). At least 400 cells were differentiated and 400 macrophages were searched for a positive prussian blue reaction. Results are given as percentages of the examined cells.

A classification as shown in Table 1 was used to assess the degree of COPD and horses were divided in 3 groups with low, intermediate and severe pulmonary disease.

Information of the owner (n=5) and course of the disease in inpatients (n=36) was used to estimate improvement of the condition with therapy. Seven cases were lost for follow-up. Furthermore, owners were asked about the use of the horse and the amount of daily exercise. According to this information, horses were classified as being breeding, leisure or competition horses.

Table ① Classification of COPD degree

Low	Intermediate	severe
PaO_2 13.3 ± 0.6 kPa* and	PaO_2 12.0 ± 0.6 kPa* or	PaO_2 11.3 kPa* or
$AaDO_2 < 1.3$ kPa* and	$AaDO_2 < 2$ kPa* or	$AaDO_2 > 12$ kPa* or
breaths/min. < 24 and	breaths/min. < 28 or	breaths/min. > 28 or
BALF neutrophils < 10 %	BALF neutrophils < 20 %	BALF neutrophils > 20 %
and total score < 10 and	and total score < 15	or total score > 15
R_{aw} 0.01-0.025 cmH$_2$O/l/min		
and Cdyn 2.3 ± 1.4 l/cmH$_2$O		

Explanations
* 1kPa = 7.5 mmHg

Results

Frank blood was not seen in any of the 48 horses by clinical or endoscopic examination. Macrophages with a positive prussian blue reaction were found in all BALF cytology preparations. However, the percentage of hemosiderophages differed considerably between horses: 0.4% to 53.8% of macrophages contained free ionic iron (mean 11.8% ± 13.1%). Thirty-three horses had hemosiderin in less than 10% of their macrophages, 6 horses were positive for hemosiderin in more than 10%-20% of their macrophages, and more than 20% of hemosiderophages were observed in 9 horses. These 9 animals were distributed equally (3 each) within the 3 groups of different COPD degrees (low degree: n=12, intermediate degree: n=13 and severe: n=23). No correlation was found between hemosidero-phage-percentage with breed, age, duration of coughing, clinical or endoscopy scores, neutrophil or macrophage content of BALF. Tables 2 and 3 give a synopsis of the relevant data.

Table ②   Results (mean values and standard deviations) of 48 patients with COPD according to percentage of hemosiderophages in BALF

Parameter / % hemosiderophages	<5 % (n=18)	5 – 10 % (n=15)	>10 % (n=15)	total (n=48)
Age [years]	13.1±5.5	10.3±5.0	13.3±4.0	11.9±4.9
Duration of cough [years]	1.5±1.3	1.1±0.9	1.2±1.7	1.3±1.3
Breaths [/min]	23.9±10.8	19.3 ±5.4	25.1±15.0	22.5±11.1
Clinical score (max. 10)	3.9±2.2	3.0±2.4	3.7±2.8	3.5±2.4
Endoscopical score (max.13)	7.6±2.6	7.0±3.7	6.3±2.9	6.9±3.0
PaO$_2$ [kPa*]	12.1±1.7	11.9±1.6	12.3±1.8	11.9±2.2
AaDO$_2$ [kPa*]	1.8±1.9	2.1±1.9	1.4±1.7	1.8±1.8
Neutrophiles [% in BALF]	12.3±9.0	12.7±10.2	13.0±7.8	12.6±8.7
Hemosiderophages [% of macrophages]	2.6±1.2	7.4 ±1.0	27.5±13.3	11.5±12.9

Table ③   **Breed, use of the horse, degree of disease and response to therapy in comparison to hemosiderophage percentage in BALF (number of horses)**

Parameter / % hemosiderophages		< 5 % (n=18)	5 – 10 % (n=15)	> 10 % (n=15)	total (n=48)
Breed	Warmblood	14	9	10	33
	Pony	2	3	3	8
	Quarter	1	2	-	3
	Thoroughbred	1	-	1	2
	Drafthorse	-	1	1	2
Use	Hobby	12	8	8	28
	Sport	4	4	6	14
	Breeding	2	3	1	6
Degree of COPD	Low	6	2	4	12
	Intermediate	5	4	4	13
	Severe	7	9	7	23
Response to therapy	Good	7	5	7	19
	Fair	4	5	2	11
	Frustrating	5	2	4	11
	No follow-up	2	3	2	7

Discussion

Pulmonary hemorrhage results in free erythrocytes in the alveoli. Alveolar macrophages are prone to clear the airways from large particulates by phagocytosis. They engulf red blood cells within hours and digest them within a few days (7). Hemosiderin is a degradation product, consisting mainly of ferritin and giving the typical, highly specific Prussian blue reaction with ferrocyanide stains. According to the manufacturer, the staining kit will detect up to $0.002\mu g$ of free iron. With this sensitive method, it was possible to observe siderophages in all 48 BALF cytopreparations examined. However, in 18 cases (37.5% of total horses), siderophage percentage was less than 5%. More than 20% of macrophages with a positive prussian blue reaction were seen in 9 (19% of total cases) horses. It has been shown that autologous erythrocytes in the airways impair airway resistence and dynamic compliance (1) and high hemosiderin content reduces the antibacterial effect of alveolar macrophages (4). On the other hand, EIPH can be detected in a high percentage of exercising horses (6;9), so there is a strong need for evaluation of its clinical relevance. BALF hemosiderophage content is helpful in estimating the degree of alveolar hemorrhage in human medicine (3;5;8).

All 48 horses were diagnosed as suffering from COPD. None of these horses was suspected to be a bleeder by history, clinical and endoscopic examination. There was no correlation between the degree of pulmonary disease or response to therapy and siderophage percentage in BALF. None of the horses had exercised severely before the study, so hemosiderophage percentages did not depend on exercise stress. The horses trained for starting in competitions were not more affected than leisure or breeding animals.

The high hemosiderophage incidence may be caused by accumulation of hemosiderin-storing macrophages over time and indicate an impaired clearance function of the airways. However, if this is the case, impaired clearance of neutrophils would be expected to occur concurrently. A correlation between neutrophil and hemosiderophage percentages in BALF was not seen.

To our knowledge, this is the first report about siderophage incidence and percentages in BALF of horse breeds different from racehorses and polo ponies. According to the distribution of patients in our clinic, mainly Warmbloods (n=33), followed by ponies (n=8), non-racing Quarter horses (n=3) and 2 retired thoroughbreds were examined, and siderophages were found even in 2 drafthorses.

Conclusion

The lack of relationship between percentage of hemosiderin-laden macrophages in BALF with the parameters examined here reveals, that some erythrocyte traffic into the airspaces of the lung occurs regularly in horses with COPD. Further studies are needed in healthy, not heavily exercising horses to check these findings and possibly to calculate a threshold value for hemosiderophage-percentage in BALF of horses.

Equine polysaccharide storage myopathy: differential diagnosis with unspecific exertional rhabdomyolysis

Take home message

Examination of muscle biopsies allows to distinguish between unspecific Recurrent Exertional Rhabdomyolysis (RER) and Equine Polisaccharid Storage Myopathy (EPMS)

Introduction

Disorders of skeletal muscle have long been recognised as a common cause of poor performance in athletic horses (Jeffcott et al 1982). Although there is an extensive etiological classification system for equine muscle disorders (see Bernard and Hopper 1998), most of the cases (70% approximately) suffer from a myopathy with the onset occurring during or after exercise (Freeston and Carlson 1992), a syndrome commonly referred to either as exercise-associated myopathy (Freeston and Carlson 1992), or as exertional myopathy (Snow and Valberg 1994). For a long time, there has been a tendency to consider most of these disorders under the broad heading 'tying-up syndrome' or exertional rhabdomyolysis. It has been implied or assumed that all horses that show evidence of muscle pain and cramping following exercise have the same disease. As a result, a great deal of controversy and confusion has developed regarding the cause and approach to treatment of exertional myopathies. Thus, exertional rhabdomyolysis likely represents a pathological description of a number of muscle diseases that have common clinical signs.

Specific exertional myopathies that have been identified in horses include (1) mitochondrial myopathy due to a deficiency in NADH CoQ reductase in an Arabian horse (Valberg et al 1994); (2) a defect in skeletal muscle excitation-contraction coupling resembling malignant hyperthermia in Thoroughbreds (Beech et al 1988); and (3) a polysaccharide storage myopathy in Quarter horses involving abnormal glycogen storage (Valberg et al 1992). Although the clinical signs in these patients were similar to those of horses with recurrent exertional rhabdomyolysis, histopathological findings of muscle biopsies were specific for these myopathies.

Equine polysaccharide storage myopathy (EPSM) is a metabolic disease that results in the accumulation of high muscle-glycogen concentrations and an abnormal polysaccharide in skeletal muscle (Valberg et al 1992 and 1997). This disease has been identified in Quarter horse-related breeds, Warmbloods and draught horses that exhibit the same clinical signs of exertional rhabdomyolysis (Valberg et al 1992; Valentine et al 1995). In this report, we describe the differential diagnosis between these two entities based on the identification of this abnormal polysaccharide in gluteus medius muscle biopsies from two horses with typical clinical signs of exercise-associated myopathies.

Horses

Two different horses with a history of low performance syndrome were presented for examination and diagnosis at the Clinic for Horses, School of Veterinary Medicine, Hannover (Germany). Horse A was a 6 year-old Quarter horse gelding with an intended use for dressage and with a massive loss of performance because of a previous history of associated respiratory problems 1.5 years ago. This animal had repeated episodes of rhabdomyolysis during and some time after exercise of low intensity and duration with the rider (muscle cramping, pain, intolerance to exercise and reluctance to move). Serum activities of muscle enzymes were, in general, higher than usual even after weeks of stall rest. Horse B was a 9 year-old Warmblood mare previously used for breeding purposes. A few months before this animal had started with an exercise-training program for dressage work. This horse showed some acute attacks of rhabdomyolysis associated with exercise: stiff gait, muscle cramping and severe intolerance to exercise. Activities of key muscle enzymes were also increased on serum. As both horses had repeated episodes of rhabdomyolysis that did not respond to rest, modification of the training schedule, and administration of electrolytes, vitamin E and selenium with the diet, it was decided to remove muscle biopsies to establish a definitive and differential diagnosis.

Percutaneous needle muscle biopsies

Two biopsies were obtained of each horse from the left and right gluteus medius muscles, according to the percutaneous needle biopsy technique described in detail by Lindholm and Piehl (1974). We used a needle biopsy with an outer diameter of 6 mm. The exact location of the sampling site for the gluteus medius muscle was fixed at the point located a third of the distance along a line running from the tuber coxae of the ilium to the head of the tail. Samples were removed at 80 mm of sampling depth in both horses. No complications occurred in any biopsed horses.

After collection, muscle specimens weighing 150 to 200 mg were divided into two parts, one for histochemical and histological analyses and the other for electron microscopy analysis. The samples for histochemical analyses were frozen by immersion for 30 seconds in isopentane cooled in liquid nitrogen. A small part of the muscle biopsy, designated for routine

electron microscopy, was fixed in glutaraldehyde buffered with cacodyla-
ted phosphate buffer (pH 7.3). Muscle samples were placed in plastic bags
on dry ice for shipments by overnight carrier to the Muscle Biology
Laboratory of the Faculty of Veterinary Sciences in Cordoba (Spain). On
arrival, samples were stored at −80 °C until analysed.

Methods

Once they were at the laboratory, biopsy specimens for histology and
histochemistry were transferred to a cryostat at −20 °C. Twenty successive 10 μm cryostat sections of each biopsy specimen were routinely placed
on 10 coverslips and then allowed to dry at room temperature for 20 to 30
minutes before staining. A battery of histological and histochemical stains
was applied to each muscle biopsy (Table 1). Specimens for electron
microscopic examination were prepared according to Tinling et al (1980).

Table ❶   Routine processing of cryostat sections for histology and histochemistry

Coverslip No.	Section No.	Histological stain or histochemical reaction	Purpose
1	1,2	Hematoxylin and eosin	Morphology of muscle fibres, nerves, blood vessels and connective tissue
2	3,4	Gomori's trichrome	Morphology of muscle fibres, nerves, blood vessels and connective tissue
3	5,6	Myofibrillar ATPase after preincubation at pH 10.4	Muscle fibre type identification (I, II)
4	7,8	Myofibrillar ATPase after preincubation at pH 4.2	Muscle fibre type identification (I, II)
5	9,10	Myofibrillar ATPase after preincubation at pH 4.45	Muscle fibre type identification −I, IIA and IIX (former IIB)−
6	11,12	NADH-tetrazolium reductase	Oxidative capacity of muscle fibres
7	13,14	Succinate dehydrogenase (SDH)	Oxidative capacity of muscle fibres
8	15,16	a-glycerophosphate dehydrogenase (GPDH)	Glycolytic capacity of muscle fibres
9	17,18	Periodic-acid Schiff (PAS)	Glycogen content of muscle fibres and presence of PAS-positive inclusions
10	19,20	alpha-amylase-PAS	Visualisation of capillaries and identification of abnormal polysaccharide

Observations

Histology and histochemistry

Figure 1

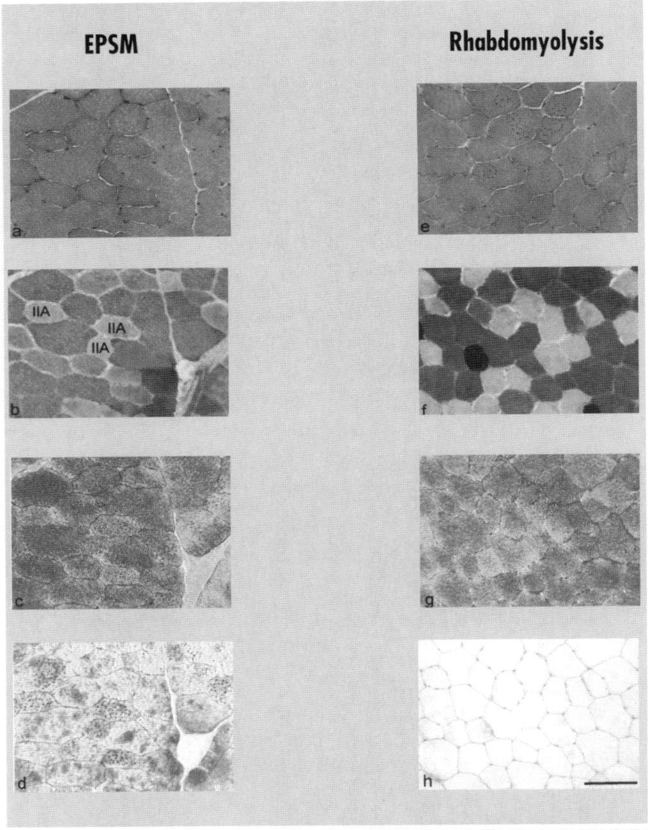

| EPSM | Rhabdomyolysis |

Horse A – Hematoxylin and eosin and Gomori's trichrome stains revealed very light unspecific myopathic changes in this horse, since most areas of the biopsy had a completely normal appearance (Fig. 1a). The very light myopathic changes seen in this horse (not shown) included increased variability in fibre size, light hypertrophy, hyper-contracted type II fibres and scattered fibres with internal nuclei. Some fibres were also observed with an increased number of basophilic (blue) inclusion bodies into the cytosol. Both muscle biopsies from this horse contained a very high percentage (more than 95 %) of type II fibres, particularly of type IIX (formerly designated IIB) fibres (Fig. 1b). There were a high number of fibres with very low oxidative capacity demonstrated by weak NADH-TR and SDH reactions (not shown), a feature typical of untrained horses. Type II fibres had a higher a-GPD reaction than type I, and although this was not quantified, within fast fibres glycolytic activity was higher in type IIX fibres than in type IIA fibres (not shown). The PAS stain revealed a high glycogen content in all fibre types and the presence of intensely PAS-positive inclusions in numerous type II fibres, particularly in type IIA fibres (Fig. 1c). These PAS-positive inclusions mostly resisted digestion with a-amylase and they were still present in the a-amylase-PAS reaction (Fig. 1d). These inclusions correspond to an abnormal polysaccharide accumulation.

Horse B – Histopathologic study of this horse revealed marked and characteristic myopathic changes: (1) multi-focal interstitial oedema with significant increase of intercellular spaces; (2) increased proportion of fibres with centrally-placed nuclei (25 % and 23 % in right and left muscles, respectively; see Fig. 1e); (3) focal presence of macrophages with rest of pigments (probably myoglobin) because of an old fibre degeneration; (4) splitting of some fibres; and (5) scattered hypercontracted type II fibres. Similarly to previous horse, Horse B had a very high percentage of type II fibres (more than 95 % of fibre composition), particularly of type IIX fibres (Fig. 1f). Also, the muscle profile of this horse was highly glycolytic and composed of a very high percentage of fibres with low oxidative capacity (around 50 % of the fibre population). The PAS reaction revealed a high intramuscular glycogen content, but lower than that seen in Horse A, and the presence of more intensely stained PAS-positive inclusions in type II fibres was not observed (Fig. 1g). In contrast to Horse A, myopathic changes seen in Horse B were not associated with abnormal accumulation of a-amylase-resistant complex polysaccharide since all glycogen content disappeared after digestion with a-amylase (Fig. 1g).

Electron microscopy

Electron microscopy revealed the presence of abundant ß-glycogen particles and filamentous material (Fig. 2 in Horse A). In some fibres the accumulation of this material was so extensive that it disrupted the normal arrangement of the myofibrils (Fig. 2a). Myopathic changes consisting of disruption of myofibrils with increased intermyofibrillar spaces, streaming of Z lines and degeneration of mitochondria were observed in addition (Fig. 2b). Electron microscopy could not be carried out in Horse B.

Figure ❷

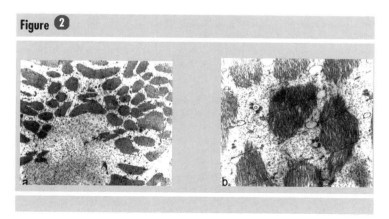

Discussion

Looking at the clinical side of the horses´ disease, no differentiation could be made between them: stiffness and muscle cramping after exercise, and elevated muscular enzymes after riding or at rest. The symptomatic diagnosis was Recurrent Exertional Rhabdomyolysis (RER). Horse A was in a regular training program. With or without training this horse showed elevated muscular enzymes and several episodes of RER with different severity. No treatment or training management seemed to improve the horses´ disease. Horse B was used as a breeding mare only for several years and was suddenly pushed into a daily training program for dressage purposes. The mare developed several episodes of RER. Most of them responded to treatment but without permanent success. Every new start with intensive training was followed by a new onset of RER in this horse.

Although both horses showed similar clinical symptoms there are great differences in the pathological understanding of the disorder "RER" or "myopathy".

Results of the present study explain why Horse A could not response to the usual treatment. Horses suffering from EPSM need a special diet that is low in carbohydrate and provide a high percentage of fat (Valentine et al 1997). To date, the precise cause of EPSM is unknown. Muscle-glycogen concentrations in horses with EPSM are 1.5 to 4 times higher than those reported for horses with unspecific exertional rhabdomyolysis (Valberg et al 1992). This fact, together with the abnormal polysaccharide present in skeletal muscle, classifies this disorder as a glycogen-storage disease, or a glycogenosis (Valberg et al 1997). These diseases can result from (1) impaired utilisation and breakdown of glycogen by tissues or (2) from abnormal increased glycogen synthesis (DiMauro et al 1994). Most glycogenoses identified to date in humans and animals are caused by inherited deficiencies in glycogenolytic, glycolytic, or lysosomal enzymes (see Valberg et al 1997 for a review). Several assays carried out of all glycogenolytic, glycolytic enzyme activities as well as the regulatory properties of phosphofructokinase (PFK) in Quarter horses with EPSM have failed to demonstrate significant enzyme deficiencies (Valberg et al 1997). Accumulation of glycogen and abnormal polysaccharide in skeletal muscle can then result from abnormal increased glycogen synthesis, but further research is necessary to confirm this hypothesis.

The histochemical and histological characteristics of the intramuscular polysaccharide found in Horse A of the present study were distinct from those of glycogen. However, several features of the storage material link it to glycogen metabolism and synthesis: (1) its exclusive presence in type II fibres which have the highest glycogen concentrations and the greatest activities of glycolytic enzymes; (2) the inter-myofibrillar distribution similar to that of normal glycogen; and (3) the ultrastructural features which are similar to unbranched glycogen (Valberg et al 1992).

This paper confirmed that the observations that storage of complex a-amylase-resistant polysaccharide and the abnormal accumulation of glycogen with intensely PAS-positive inclusions in numerous fibres, particularly in type II, are the basis for a definitive diagnosis of the equine polysaccharide storage myopathy.

In contrast to Horse A treatment of Horse B improved the mare's condition, but new episodes of the disease occurred when full training was performed. Depending on the fibre composition with more glycolytic metabolism in muscles and low oxidative capacity muscle fatigue was reached very fast in the mare. Obviously this horse needs a very careful training program which allows fibre composition to adjust to endurance work.

Prognosis, correct therapy and prophylaxis obviously need an assertive diagnosis. For example, approximately 50 % of human cases of Recurrent Exertional Rhabdomyolysis are due to errors of the skeletal muscle energy metabolism, and it is very probable that a similar situation might occur in the horse. If the muscle biopsy procedure is more commonly used for clinicians in the future and they adequately collaborate with muscular pathologists and researchers, the accurate diagnosis of exercise-associated myopathies in the horse would be significantly increased, and this is essential for prognosis and correct therapy. This paper showed that examination of muscle biopsies is the most important diagnostic test for the distinction between unspecific Recurrent Exertional Rhabdomyolysis and EPSM.

Transendoscopic laser surgery of the exercise-induced dorsal displacement of the softpalate (DDSP) in horses

Take home message

The presented laser surgical approach to the exercise induced DDSP offers important advantages, like shorter recoveries, combined with similar success rates as the two established procedures for treatment of DDSP (myectomy and staphylectomy).

Introduction

Dorsal displacement of the soft palate (DDSP) refers to intermittent or permanent malpositioning of the soft palate dorsal to the epiglottis during exercise. Intermittent DDSP is characterised by the patient being clinically and endoscopically normal at rest but transiently developing clinical signs on sustained very fast exercise, especially towards the end of a race. Horses suffering from persistent DDSP cannot replace the soft palate to a subepiglottic position, despite repeated spontaneous or induced swallowing attempts. Horses affected with permanent DDSP make continually very loud respiratory noises from the start of work, may cough frequently, especially when eating, and often have a bilateral nasal discharge that contains food. DDSP reduces the cross sectional area of the nasopharynx, thus increasing airflow resistance, and it also causes airflow turbulance which causes abnormal respiratory noise production by soft tissue vibrations. DDSP has been attributed to functional and anatomic abnormalities such as tongue movements due to swallowing, caudal retraction of the larynx, soft palate paralysis or paresis, epiglottic shortening, elongated soft palate, a lack of rigidity of the epiglottis and low negative pressure in the nasopharynx caused by other upper airway tract lesions, e.g. laryngeal paralysis. Transient and intermittent DDSP may be observed during any endoscopic examination, and this is insignificant if the history does not suggest DDSP. Conversely, failure to observe DDSP endoscopically does not rule out a diagnosis of DDSP. Theoretically, endoscopic examination of the exercising patient on a treadmill would give conclusive evidence of intermittent DDSP, but failure to observe DDSP during exercise does not rule out this problem. Because DDSP is difficult to reproduce in many horses outside racing conditions, an accurate history is frequently the most important diagnostic criterion.

Sternothyrohyoideus myectomy and staphylectomy have been recommended as treatments for DDSP, but the effect of these procedures has not been conclusively established. The mechanism by which each procedure results in alleviation of clinical signs is not fully understood. It has been proposed that the myectomy prevents caudal retraction of the larynx, which may be responsible for palatopharyngeal subluxation. There is also debate over whether staphylectomy stiffens the free edge of the soft palate, or whether the procedure simply increases the size of the pharyngeal ostium.

Material and methods

From 1995 to 1997 eleven racehorses, one Hanoverian and one Pony were presented to the Clinic for Horses of the School of Veterinary Medicine, Hannover with a suddenly appearing, very loud, gurgling expiratory respiratory noise. Considering the preliminary report and the clinical and endoscopical findings, an exercise induced intermittent DDSP was found to be the cause of the respiratory noise. The 13 horses were treated by transendoscopic coagulation of the caudal margin of the soft palate with a Neodym-YAG-Laser. For this transendoscopic correction the soft palate was permanent displaced above the epiglottis by intubation in general anaesthesia. Using a bare-fibre the tissue of about 5mm margin was coagulated (non-contact: 30 pulses, 4 sec, 40 W, or contact: 30 pulses, 4 sec, 20 W). This surgical intervention had to be repeated on four horses with unchanged symptoms.

Results

Eight of thirteen horses (62%) did not show any respiratory noises after the operation. By using race records, these horses were again successfully raced and ridden. Two horses (15%) improvement somewhat, while in 3 horses (23%) the respiratory noise was unchanged after surgery.

Discussion

The overall success rate reported in literature of the two established procedures for treatment of DDSP (myectomy and staphylectomy) is about 50% to 60%. Compared to previous therapies, the presented laser surgical approach to the exercise induced DDSP offers important advantages, like shorter recoveries, combined with similar success rates. Presumably, laser surgery stiffens the free edge of the soft palate, and the effect is comparable to the effect of staphylectomy.

Evaluation of career racetrack performance in 52 Thoroughbreds treated for laryngeal neuropathy with prosthetic laryngoplasty

Take home message

Aside from warning clients of the complications of prosthetic laryngoplasty surgery, it may be wise to provide a more guarded prognosis for full restoration of racing performance in older Thoroughbreds, unless they are especially talented individuals and are free of other racing related injuries/ problems.

Introduction

The goal of this study was to compare a detailed objective analysis of racing performance, before and after prosthetic laryngoplasty (PLP), to evaluate the outcome of this procedure in a group of 52 Thoroughbred racehorses affected with recurrent laryngeal neuropathy. Specifically, we were interested to determine: whether data from racing performances suggested the duration of left recurrent neuropathy prior to surgical intervention; if affected horses tended to race at shorter distances post-operatively; whether these horses were capable of running faster times after surgery at the same distances they competed prior to surgery; the racing longevity and success of these individuals after PLP.

Materials and methods

Fifty-two Thoroughbred racehorses were identified as having being diagnosed with laryngeal neuropathy and treated with PLP at Louisiana State University School of Veterinary Medicine from August 1981 to August 1989. Lifetime race records for these 52 Thoroughbreds were purchased, and organized for statistical analysis, using a previously developed and verified regression model published by our group. Details about the statistical analysis are found in Martin et al (1996) and Martin et al (1997). Individual race records and hospital records were also reviewed. Owners/ trainers were contacted when possible.

Results

Thirty-one "experienced" horses with an established baseline race record (4 or more race starts) before surgery demonstrated an obvious decline in performance as measured by performance index (see Table), earnings, earnings percentage (% of available 1st prize money earned per race), and mean prediction error (actual race finish time – predicted finish time from our regression model) within the 6 month period of presenting for PLP. As a group, these Thoroughbreds improved their performance level post-operatively relative to their 1-4 races immediately preceding surgery, but did not attain their previous baseline performance level. Factors identified that prevented horses from attaining previous baseline levels of performance included other racing related injuries/disorders (at least 17% of this population), major complications of surgery (15%), and that the study included a number of older racehorses.

Individually however, a number of horses had successful and long post-operative careers. Thirty-one of 52 horses (59.6%) won at least one race after surgery, and twelve of these horses (23%) won at least 3 races. The 31 horses with an established baseline record at the time of surgery competed in races of the same mean length (6.4 furlongs = 1300 meters) after surgery (total 586 races), as before (total 982 races). Fourteen of the 31 «experienced» Thoroughbreds achieved a best time at one or more race distances (range, 900-1700 meters) after PLP, relative to their times at those distances during their entire pre-surgical career. Horses 4 years of age or older, at the time of PLP, earned back less than 30% (median) of the total purse money they earned before surgery. This is probably due to there being less overall purse money available to older racehorses, and that some of these individuals were already in the twilight of their race careers for other reasons.

Fledgling Thoroughbreds (2 year olds) had statistically better post-operative career success rates, than older horses, as measured by prize money per race (P<0.0001), earnings (P=0.0057), earning percentage (P=0.0013), and prediction error (P<0.0001). There was however, no significant difference regarding performance index.

Table 1 **Career race records and Performance Index (in parenthesis) of 31 three year old or older Thoroughbred racehorses with 4 or more races before prosthetic larygoplasty (PLP).**

horse HID#	Age at Surgery	Baseline Race Record *(n: a,b,c)		** Last 4 Races Before PLP Surgery		Post-PLP surgery Race Record	
# 1	3 years	17: 1,4,2	(0.76)	4: 0,0,0	(0.00)	22: 4,0,1	(0.59)
# 2	5 years	53: 11,7,11	(1.09)	4: 0,0,1	(0.25)	6: 0,0,0	(0.00)
# 4	4 years	11: 1,2,2	(0.82)	4: 0,0,0	(0.00)	17: 0,0,2	(0.12)
# 5	6 years	48: 8,12,5	(1.10)	4: 0,0,0	(0.00)	10: 3,1,0	(1.10)
# 6	5 years	5: 0,0,0	(0.00)	4: 0,0,0	(0.00)	17: 1,1,2	(0.41)
# 7	5 years	38: 3,9,1	(0.74)	4: 0,0,0	(0.00)	2: 0,0,1	(0.50)
# 8	3 years	14: 3,1,1	(0.86)	4: 0,0,0	(0.00)	29: 5,5,0	(0.86)
# 9	4 years	45: 8,6,5	(0.91)	4: 0,0,1	(0.25)	21: 3,2,4	(0.81)
#10	6 years	59: 5,12,2	(0.69)	4: 0,0,0	(0.00)	47: 1,1,9	(0.30)
#13	4 years	7: 0,2,0	(0.57)	1: 0,0,0	(0.00)	17: 1,0,0	(0.18)
#15	3 years	1: 1,0,0	(3.00)	4: 2,0,0	(1.50)	1: 0,0,1	(1.00)
#16	3 years	9: 2,1,1	(1.00)	4: 0,0,0	(0.00)	62: 9,6,7	(0.74)
#18	7 years	53: 15,10,6	(1.34)	4: 0,2,0	(1.00)	12: 0,1,2	(0.33)
#19	4 years	10: 4,2,1	(1.70)	1: 0,0,0	(0.00)	13: 0,2,1	(0.38)
#21	6 years	35: 14,1,2	(1.31)	4: 0,0,2	(0.50)	38: 6,3,6	(0.79)
#22	3 years	4: 2,1,1	(2.25)	4: 0,0,1	(0.25)	8: 1,1,0	(0.63)
#24	9 years	104:19,18,13	(1.02)	4: 0,0,1	(0.25)	4: 0,0,1	(0.25)
#27	3 years	4: 0,1,0	(0.50)	2: 0,0,0	(0.00)	2: 0,0,0	(0.00)
#29	4 years	27: 6,2,5	(1.00)	4: 0,0,0	(0.00)	13: 1,0,1	(0.31)
#31	4 years	26: 3,2,5	(0.69)	4: 0,0,0	(0.00)	36: 4,3,3	(0.58)
#33	5 years	21: 1,3,1	(0.48)	4: 0,0,0	(0.00)	13: 1,0,1	(0.31)
#34	3 years	------	----	4: 1,2,0	(1.25)	4: 0,2,0	(1.00)
#36	5 years	28: 5,5,3	(1.00)	4: 0,1,1	(0.75)	2: 0,0,0	(0.00)
#38	4 years	41: 3,4,10	(0.66)	4: 0,0,1	(0.25)	6: 0,0,0	(0.00)
#39	5 years	40: 4,6,2	(0.65)	4: 0,0,0	(0.00)	42: 5,2,4	(0.55)
#40	6 years	62: 5,8,3	(0.55)	4: 0,0,0	(0.00)	9: 0,2,0	(0.44)
#44	5 years	37: 8,5,8	(1.14)	4: 2,1,0	(1.75)	43: 2,7,2	(0.51)
#47	3 years	3: 1,1,0	(1.67)	4: 0,0,1	(0.25)	26: 2,4,0	(0.54)
#48	4 years	14: 2,0,0	(0.43)	4: 0,0,0	(0.00)	40: 2,6,4	(0.55)
#50	4 years	12: 3,0,1	(0.83)	2: 0,1,0	(1.00)	11: 0,2,0	(0.36)
#51	5 years	40: 6,1,6	(0.65)	4: 0,0,1	(0.25)	13: 2,0,3	(0.69)
Number of Thoroughbreds		30		31		31	
Total number of races		868 .		114		586	
Mean Performance Index		$\mu = 0.90$		$\mu = 0.32$		$\mu = 0.54$	
Standard Error of the mean		0.010		0.046		0.009	

Performance Index Scoring: 1st place = 3 pts.; 2nd = 2 pts.; 3rd = 1 pt.; all other finish positions = 0 pts.; divided by the total # of races during that period.
* (n = total number of starts; a,b,c = total number of 1st, 2nd, & 3rd place finishes, respectively)
** number of consecutive races run during the 6 months preceding surgery up to a maximum of the final 4. This period does not include any races listed in the baseline period.

Discussion

This study indicates that prosthetic laryngoplasty improved racing performance in the group of "experienced" horses relative to the period of their careers when they were clinically affected by laryngeal neuropathy. Although a number of horses appeared to have their previous top racing form restored after PLP, complications of surgery, age at the time of PLP, and other racing related injuries/problems prevented others from attaining previous racing results.

Clearly, many factors influence a Thoroughbred's racing performance following prosthetic laryngoplasty. Post-operative complications related to the surgery are the initial factors that may diminish performance. It appears that horses affected and treated at a younger age respond with better performances post-operatively. This may be because younger horses adapt more easily to the laryngeal alterations associated with permanently abducting the arytenoid cartilage, or because their youth positions them earlier in their career, before age related decline in performance has occurred. On a practical basis it may be wise to provide a more guarded prognosis for full restoration of racing performance in older Thoroughbreds receiving prosthetic laryngoplasty, unless they are especially talented individuals and are free of musculoskeletal and other racing related problems.

3 ORTHOPEDICS

3.1 Overview articles

Alteration of locomotion in horses with vertebral lesions

1. Take Home Message

In vivo kinematic studies have demonstrated and quantified back flexibility in sound trotting horses. Under the same experimental conditions, horses presenting vertebral lesions showed a reduction of back passive flexibility at trot.

Under routine clinical conditions, alterations of back mobility at walk, trot and canter are interesting diagnostic criterias for decision-making in performing further investigations (radiography, ultrasonography) to assess vertebral lesions in equine patients. The purpose of this article is to present the locomotor parameters which can be altered in horses presenting back disorders as well as biomechanical studies demonstrating changes in the back mobility associated with vertebral injuries.

2. Introduction

Identification of the origin of locomotor problems presumably induced by back disorders represents the main cause of examination of referred horses in our veterinary school and centre (CIRALE, Normandy area). A definitive diagnosis of vertebral lesions is difficult in horses (Jeffcott 1975, Denoix 1998):
- the equine back is a large area covered by thick muscles; therefore, obser-

vation is limited during the physical examination;

- this large area presents little regional mobility, and alteration of movements is difficult to demonstrate in horses during the functional examination at gaits;
- because of the size of the area, imaging is difficult, and radiographic assessment of vertebral lesions requires special equipment.

The effect of an induced back pain on gait and performance has been investigated in trotting horses (Jeffcott et al 1982), and the consequences of back disorders on locomotion in sport horses have been presented (Denoix and Audigié 1999). Recently, several papers have been published on the functional anatomy and biomechanics of the equine back (Denoix 1999a, Denoix et al in press), and a review of the imaging assessment of vertebral lesions has been presented (Denoix 1998 and 1999b).

Although they are difficult, the physical examination and imaging modalities are essential in the diagnosis of back problems. Besides, the functional disorders need to be considered to establish the clinical significance of vertebral lesions.

The purpose of this article is to present our approach of the functional evaluation of horses suspected of vertebral lesions and the biomechanical support of our diagnostic criterias such as the restriction of passive flexibility at trot.

3. Functional evaluation of horses suspected of vertebral lesions

The functional evaluation takes place after a complete physical examination of the limbs and back. Physical examination of the thoracolumbar areas includes inspection, palpation of the back anatomical structures, pressure on bone structures, mobilisation (regional flexion, extension and lateroflexion), and in most horses transrectal palpation of the pelvis and sublumbar area.

Our routine functional evaluation of gaits of horses referred for back problems is presented in tables 1 to 5. These tables indicate the conditions of the patients´ examination (type of ground surface used, gaits) and the criteria taken into consideration as possible manifestations of back disorders. All the parameters listed in these tables can be affected by back pain and/or injuries.

Table ❶ **Chronology and conditions of the routine dynamic examination of horses presented for lameness or suspected of back problems**

Groun	Gait	Displacement
1-Hard	Walk	Straight line
	Trot	
	Walk	Alternate circle (3m diameter)
	Trot	Left hand (7m diameter) right hand
2-Soft	Trot	Right hand
	Canter	(10m diameter)
	Trot	Left hand
	Canter	(10m diameter)
3-Hard	Trot	Left hand (7m diameter)
		Right hand
		Straight line

Table ❷ **Chronology and conditions of the routine dynamic examination at the walk. Parameters used for evaluation of back disorders**

Groun	Gait	Displacement	Criteria
Hard (1)	Walk	Straight line	From behind •Symmetry of pelvis • Rotation (tuber coxae) • (lateroflexion) Caudolateral view • Relaxation • Active TL mobility • (lateroflexion) Lateral view: • Hindquarters attitude • Hindlimbs mobility (caudal phase/ cranial phase)
		Alternate circle (3m diameter)	• Lateroflexion •Hindquarters attitude • Hindlimbs mobility

Table ③ **Chronology and conditions of the routine dynamic examination during back up and trot. Parameters used for evaluation of back disorders.**

Groun	Gait	Displacement	Criteria
Hard (2)	Back up	Straight line	• Head positioning (neck attitude) • Lumbosacral flexion and contraction of abdominal muscles •Hindlimb mobility

	Trot	Straight line	From behind
			• Pelvis mobility
			  – rotation
			  – Lateroflexion (L/ R)
			• Lameness
			Lateral view:
			  – Hindquarters attitude
			  – Passive dorsoventral flexibility (TL+LS)
			  – Gait: stride parameters
			  – Suspension
			  – Lameness
			  – Surcingle test

		Left hand (7m diameter)
		Right hand
			• Lateroflexion: head position-incurvation
			  – passive DV flexibility
			  – Lameness

Table ④ **Chronology and conditions of the routine dynamic examination at trot and canter on soft ground. Parameters used for evaluation of back disorders**

Ground	Gait	Displacement	Criteria

Soft	Trot		• passive DV flexibility: TL (+LS)
			• Lateroflexion
			  – head position
			  – incurvation
			• Hindlimb propulsion
			• Lameness

	Canter	Right hand (10m diameter)	•Active flexion and extension: LS (+TL) movements • Hindlimb protraction/ Propulsion • Hindlimb placement (rotary canter) • Lateroflexion (incurvation) • Coordination (m. contract/ mvts) • Balance (elevation cranial part of body)
	Trot Canter	Left hand (10m diameter)	Idem Idem

Table ⑤ **Chronology and conditions of the routine dynamic examination at trot on hard ground. Parameters used for evaluation of back disorders**

Ground	Gait	Displacement	Criteria

Hard	Trot	Left hand (7 m diameter)	• Lateroflexion
			  – head position
			  – incurvation
			• (passive DV flexibility)
			Lameness (after exercise)

		Right hand (7m diameter)	Idem
		Straight line	Lateral view: • Passive DV flexibility (TL + LS) • Hinquarters attitude • Gaits: stride parameters • Suspension • Lameness (after exercise) From behind: • Rotation • Lateroflexion LR • Lameness (after exercise) Tests: • Surcingle test • Flexion test • Retraction test (LSI area)

3.1 Kinematic studies on sound horses

Recent in vivo studies have demonstrated and quantified the back flexibility in sound trotting horses (Audigié et al 1998, Pourcelot et al 1998). In these studies, horses were filmed at trot at 3 to 4 m/s on a hard rubber track with 2 video cameras placed on each side of the track. Image acquisition and analysis were performed using a special home-made 3D equine kinematic analysis system (EKAS, Pourcelot,1999).

The kinematic analysis took into account all joints of the 4 limbs and 3 joint angles of the back (Figure 1). This paper considers only the back angles. Two types of criteria were used for evaluation of back mobility, the regional angles and the dorsoventral displacements of the thoracolumbar vertebral column.

3.1.1 Regional vertebral angles

Five markers were placed in the following locations (Figure 1):
* on the top of the spinal process of the sixth and thirteenth thoracic vertebrae (T6 and T13),
* at the thoracolumbar junction,

Figure ❶ **Position of the markers (Mx) on the median plane of the equine back and regional angles taken into consideration in this sudy**

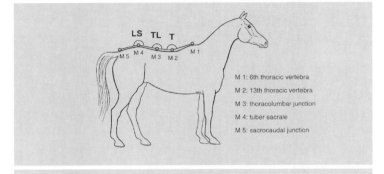

M 1: 6th thoracic vertebra
M 2: 13th thoracic vertebra
M 3: thoracolumbar junction
M 4: tuber sacrale
M 5: sacrocaudal junction

T : thoracic angle
TL : thoracolumbar angle
LS : lumbosacral angle

Figure ❷ **Sinusoidal variation of the regional angles in the back of a sound horse. Comparison between back flexion-extension movements and the electromyographic activity of 2 trunk muscles (Rectus abdominis and Longissimus muscles). The maximal extension (bottom of the curve) occurs during the mid-stance phase of each diagonal; the maximal flexion (top of the curve) occurs during the suspension phase.**

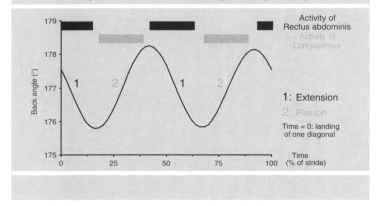

Activity of Rectus abdominis
Activity of Longissimus

1: Extension
2: Flexion

Time = 0: landing of one diagonal

• at the lumbosacral junction,
• at the sacrocaudal junction.

With these five markers 3 regional vertebral (thoracic, thoracolumbar and lumbosacral) angles were studied (Figure 1). In each location, the dorsal angle was considered for analysis (Audigié et al 1998, Pourcelot et al 1998). Therefore :
• a reduction of the angle indicates an extension movement,
• an increase of it is correlated with a vertebral flexion.

At trot, on sound horses, each vertebral angle describes a double sinusoidal oscillation during a complete stride (Figure 2) :
• maximal extension occurs during the mid-stance phase of each diagonal,
• a maximal flexion peak occurs during the suspension phase.

When comparison is made with the EMG activity of the trunk muscles, interesting findings are obtained :
• contraction of the rectus abdominis muscle

(flexor muscle) occurs during thoracolumbar vertebral extension;
• contraction of the longissimus muscle (extensor muscle) occurs
  during thoracolumbar vertebral flexion.
From these data, it can be considered that at trot the movements of the equine thoracolumbar vertebral column are passive movements induced by visceral (trunk) mass inertia, and that trunk muscle activity is dedicated to limit vertebral movement and stabilize the vertebral column.

The amount of flexion-extension movements of the regional vertebral angles has been quantified in 13 four year-old sound Selle-Français horses (Audigié et al 1998). It reaches approximately 4 degrees for the thoraco-lumbar and lumbosacral angles, and about 3 degrees for the thoracolumbar angle.

3.1.2 Dorsoventral displacements of vertebral interpolated points

A second complementary representation of back mobility closer to the clinical evaluation has been developed to approximate the displacement of each vertebra (between the sixth thoracic vertebra-T6 and the first sacral vertebra-S1).

The principle consisted of fitting the dorsal midline profile of the back. Based on the position of the 4 most cranial markers, the shape of the dorsal midline of the back was interpolated by a third degree polynomial (Audigié et al 1998, Pourcelot et al 1998) whose fixed origin was considered caudal, over the tuber sacrale (Figure 3).

The figure 4 represents the resultant polynomial during a complete stride. Because of the ventral bending of the dorsal midline curve, extension induces reduction of the cranio-caudal longitudinal distance between T6 and S1, and flexion increases this distance.

This curve was divided in 20 equidistant points, approximating the position of each intermediate vertebra

Figure ③ **Coordinates and landmarks used for fitting the dorsal midline of the equine back using a third degree polynomial**

S1   z   x   T6

Third degree polynomial

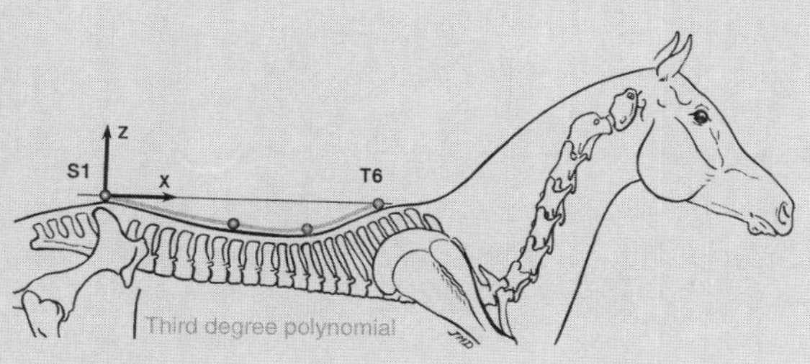

Figure ④ **Third degree polynomial reproducing flexion and extension movements of the dorsal profile of the back and displacements of the T6-S1 supraspinal interpolated points (with reference to the tuber sacrale considered as the fixed point) in a sound trotting horse.**

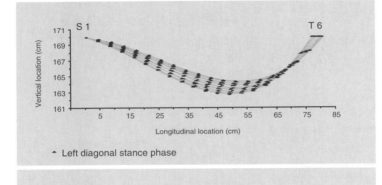

▲ Left diagonal stance phase

from T6 to S1 (Audigié et al 1998, Pourcelot et al 1998). The approximated displacement of the top of the spinal process of each of these vertebrae in a sound horse is also represented in figure 4.

3.2 Alterations of vertebral mobility in clinical cases

A symmetric reduction of dorsoventral passive thoracolumbar movements at trot (during both diagonal stance phase) was observed in horses with back lesions (Figure 5). This may be explained by two phenomena:

• an intrinsic one due to pain and/or mechanical limitation of intervertebral mobility (with ankylosis in some joints),

• an extrinsic one: reduced propulsion (similar to bilateral hindlimb lamenesses) is responsible for less active dorsoventral movements.

In order to clarify this data, a third type of representation of the back mobility was established. The amount of dorsoventral displace-

Figure ⑤ **Displacements of the T6-S1 supraspinal interpolated points in a trotting mare presenting extensive lesions of epiaxial synovial intervertebral osteoarthritis (involving the joints between the articular processes between T9 and T17).**

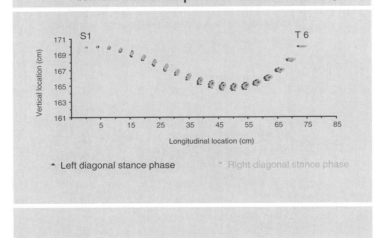

▲ Left diagonal stance phase   * Right diagonal stance phase

ments of each "vertebra" (interpolated point) between T6 and S1 has been represented and demonstrates the greater mobility of the mid-back area, near T14 (Figure 6). With this new representation, comparison of sound horses with horses presenting back problems underlines the reduction of dorsoventral displacements of the thoracolumbar spine in affected horses at trot (Figure 7).

Figure 6 Mean range of dorsoventral displacements of the T6-S1 supraspinal interpolated points (with reference to the tuber sacrale considered as the fixed point) in 13 sound trotting horses.

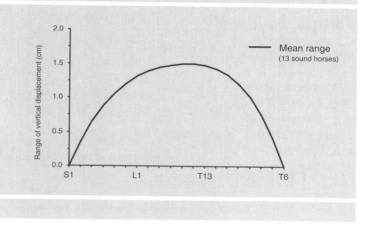

Figure 7 Range of dorsoventral displacements of the T6-S1 supraspinal interpolated points (with reference to the tuber sacrale considered as the fixed point) in a mare presenting extensive degenerative lesions of the epiaxial synovial intervertebral joints in comparison with 13 sound trotting horses.

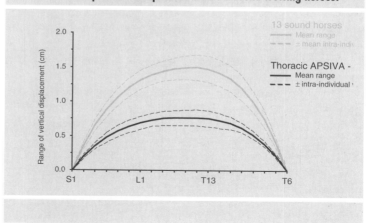

4. Conclusion

Kinematic studies provide objective parameters for evaluation of back mobility. A reduction of thoracolumbar dorsoventral displacements has been observed in horses with primary back lesions. Under routine clinical conditions this reduction of back motion at gaits can be assessed visually and helps in identifying horses with possible vertebral lesions (Tables 1 to 5). Complementary investigations with imaging modalities demonstrate that this reduction can be correlated with mechanical problems (partial or complete ankylosis) or pain (with the horse showing back rigidity to limit painful movements). As this can be observed in every area of the body, there is not always an absolute correlation between clinical signs of back disorders and vertebral lesions (Table 6).

Table ⑥   Complementary interpretation of functional abnormalities and lesions of equine back disorders

Functional abnormalities	Lesions (RX-US)	Interpretation
Reduction of mobility	Yes	• Patho- functional correlation (Clinical significance)
	No	• Soft tissue lesions or • Imaging limitations
Normal mobility	Yes	• Subclinical lesions • Good clinical tolerance, but sport incidence may be present
	No	• Clinically sound back

Lameness in the elite show jumper

1 Introduction

The athletic demands placed upon the elite show jumper are huge. It must be able to jump large fences with precision, accuracy and care, sometimes at speed. It must be supple and able to make sharp turns and jump from a virtual standstill, whilst also being able to jump almost from a gallop. It must have tremendous strength in the back and hindlimbs to be able to adjust stride length and jump from 'deep' and bascule, with the capacity to jump large spread fences.

The stresses place on the hindlimb suspensory apparatus on take off and the forelimb suspensory apparatus at landing are enormous. There is immense torque placed on joints when making quick turns. Thus there is the potential for sub-clinical lamenesses, causing low grade intermittent or continuous pain, to compromise performance without resulting in overt lameness. Nonetheless some horses are able to perform very successfully despite low grade overt lameness. Some problems that a horse can cope with adequately when performing at lower levels may become a problem when the horse is subjected to extreme demands on its athleticism.

Chronic lameness must be identified and controlled both to enable a horse to pass mandatory veterinary inspections and to optimise its performance. Acute onset lamenesses must be identified and treated rapidly to minimise the risk of the development of a chronic problem.

The elite show jumper generally has a heavy competition schedule with minimal time for recovery from injury before it is next expected to compete. It also has to withstand travelling long distances between competitions, and often confinement in relatively small stables, with little opportunity for turn out. Therefore exercise is restricted to ridden work and hand walking. The horse must be able to jump on a variety of surfaces, and when jumping outside will inevitably wear studs in all 4 shoes to improve traction and to avoid slipping. This will alter forces generated through the foot and distal limb. Since elite show jumpers travel so much, use of the same farrier becomes difficult, so the horse may be subjected to variable trimming and shoeing. Due to the intensity of competition early identification of any potential problem is crucial, and therefore regular, comprehensive monitoring of the musculoskeletal system is beneficial.

The majority of successful, modern elite show jumpers are naturally well balanced, loose moving athletes. They are relatively large horses, the majority being between 550 & 700 kg body weight. Unlike many other disciplines there is a reasonable balance of male (geldings and stallions) and mares, although there does not appear to be any difference in susceptibility to injury. Elite show jumpers vary in their conformation, but are generally well proportioned. The feet are a notable exception, in part related to natural conformation and in part due to the way in which they have been trimmed and shod. Greater attention to correct foot balance may help to prevent some lameness.

2 Clinical examination

Successful management of the elite show jumper requires knowledge of the individual, how it normally moves both in straight lines and in circles on both soft and hard surfaces and how it responds to a variety of manipulative tests. It is essential to have a good working relationship with not only the rider, but also the groom, who may have greatest knowledge of any subtle changes in the horse's action or behaviour.

Low grade problems may first be manifest as a change in performance rather than overt lameness. Manifestations of a musculoskeletal disorder may include:

- Not pushing evenly off both hind limbs, with the hindlimbs drifting to one side therefore not jumping squarely across a fence
- Reluctance to turn
- Refusing to land with one forelimb leading
- Difficulty in making the distance in a combination fence
- Difficulties in alteration of stride length
- Reluctance to get deep into a fence, or tendency to have rails down in such circumstances

Comprehensive clinical examination should include careful palpation of the limbs and back for detection of areas of heat, pain or swelling, and muscle tension. The development of synovial effusion not seen before, even in the absence of overt lameness, should be regarded with suspicion. Flexion and twisting of joints should be performed to assess both mobility and the presence of pain.

A significant number of elite show jumpers exhibit some degree of shivering type behaviour in one or both hindlimbs. Frequently this does not appear to be associated with any compromise in performance, but it does complicate the evaluation of the response to flexion of the hindlimbs.

The horse should be evaluated moving freely in hand on a hard surface, on the lunge on both left and right reins on both soft and hard surfaces. The response to distal and proximal limb flexion of each limb should be assessed. In some instances it is necessary to evaluate the horse ridden, and if necessary jumped in order to detect a problem. It may be necessary to rely on the feeling of the rider that the horse is 'not right'.

Perineural regional analgesia and intra-synovial analgesia are invaluable techniques for isolation of the site(s) of pain, either to alleviate overt lameness or to improve performance. It is sometimes necessary to medicate a suspicious joint on a diagnostic basis, since a better effect may be achieved. Nuclear scintigraphic examination can be invaluable in identifying areas with suspicious pathology in cases of low grade poor performance, but due to the large variation in scintigraphic appearance between clinically normal horses, it is usually necessary to desensitise the region to confirm that it is indeed a source of pain. Radiography and ultrasonography are essential components of the diagnostic armamentarium.

3 Management for optimal performance

The development of synovial effusion within a joint, pain on passive manipulation of a joint or inducement of lameness after flexion are all indicators of possibly significant pathology which merits treatment by judicious intra-articular medication. In the forelimb those most commonly affected are the distal interphalangeal (DIP), metacarpophalangeal, middle carpal and antebrachiocarpal joints. In the hindlimb the centrodistal and tarsometatarsal joints of the hock and the femoropatellar and femorotibial joints are most frequently affected.

The joint should be evaluated radiographically in order to determine the presence of pre-existing articular pathology, or, if a recurrent problem, progression of any previously identified pathological change. However not all radiographic abnormalities are necessarily of current clinical significance. For example small osteophytes on the dorsoproximal aspect of the third metatarsal bone are frequently present unassociated with any compromise in performance. Particularly in warmblood breeds modelling of the proximal articular margin of the middle phalanx in both forelimbs and hindlimbs is a common incidental finding.

The thoracolumbar region should be assessed carefully since the back is very prone to low grade muscular injury and bony abnormalities such as impingement of the summits of the dorsal spinous processes can cause recurrent low grade discomfort in elite athletes. However mild impingement can be present without associated clinical signs, therefore its significance should be assessed by clinical examination, response to local infusion of local anaesthetic solution and, if necessary, nuclear scintigraphy.

4 Acute onset lameness

There are many potential causes of acute onset lameness, which are not unique to the show jumper, elite or otherwise. There are however a number of conditions which seem to occur with higher frequency in elite level show jumpers, compared to horses performing at lower levels. These include:

- Desmitis of the accessory ligament of the deep digital flexor tendon (ALDDFT) in the forelimb
- Superficial digital flexor (SDF) tendonitis in the forelimb
- Deep digital flexor (DDF) tendonitis within the forelimb hoof capsule
- Proximal suspensory desmitis in the forelimb and less commonly the hindlimb
- Desmitis of the medial or lateral branch of the suspensory ligament (SL) in either the forelimb or hindlimb
- Tenosynovitis of the digital flexor tendon sheath (DFTS), either primary or secondary.

4.1 Desmitis of the accessory ligament of the deep digital flexor tendon

Lameness associated with desmitis of the ALDDFT is usually sudden in onset during work, often while jumping, with rapid development of swelling, heat and pain in the region of the AL. Very severe lameness and more extensive swelling may be the result of local haemorrhage, without structural damage to the ALDDFT. Differentiation is by ultrasonographic examination.

4.2 Superficial digital flexor tendonitis

Local heat and enlargement of the SDFT may develop prior to the recognition of lameness: if ignored the condition is likely to be progressive. In other horses lameness may be extremely acute and severe in onset, with no detectable preceding clinical signs. The condition is usually unilateral, unlike in three day event horses or racehorses, when commonly both forelimbs are affected. There is also a tendency for lesions to be restricted to the proximal third of the metacarpal region, which is more unusual in horses used for other disciplines. In some older elite show jumpers these lesions progress proximally to involve the SDFT within the carpal sheath, which merits a more guarded prognosis. Ultrasonography is invaluable for determining the extent of the lesion and response to treatment. Generally show jumpers are more tolerant of SDDFT injuries compared to horses from other disciplines and with judicious management can have a reasonable chance of return to full athletic function despite persistence of ultrasonographic abnormalities, but some cases do present recurrent problems. Each case must be treated and monitored individually. Progression of ultrasonographic abnormalities or development of concurrent desmitis of the ALDDFT are poor prognostic indicators.

4.3 Deep digital flexor tendonitis within the hoof capsule

Until relatively recently primary lesions of the DDFT within the hoof capsule have been largely overlooked, but with the development of nuclear
scintigraphy, computerised tomography and arthroscopic evaluation of the
navicular bursa, this condition is becoming better recognised. Lesions may
occur within the tendon proximal to the navicular bone, or further distally
involving its insertion. Lameness is usually acute in onset, although may be
insidiously progressive. There are usually no detectable palpable abnormalities, unless the lesion extends proximally into the pastern region. Unlike
lameness associated with navicular disease, lameness is often worse when
the horse is turning on a soft surface. Lameness may be improved by perineural analgesia of the palmar digital nerves, but perineural analgesia of
the palmar nerves at the level of the proximal sesamoid bones is often
necessary to resolve the lameness fully. Intra-articular analgesia of the DIP
joint rapidly improves lameness in some horses, but in others there is no
response. Analgesia of the navicular bursa often improves lameness, but
does not alleviate it fully.

Radiographic examination is often negative, although occasionally ent-
heseous new bone is identified in a lateromedial projection on the facia
flexoria of the distal phalanx, which may correspond to a region of increased uptake of bone seeking radioisotope if examined using nuclear scintigraphy. Nuclear scintigraphic evaluation using lateral pool phase images
and both lateral and solar bone phase images has been most useful in identifying lesions. Superimposition of a lateral radiograph over a lateral scintigraphic image is invaluable for accurate anatomical identification of the
region of increased uptake of the radiopharmaceutical. Definitive diagnosis
requires computerised tomography, magnetic resonance imaging or arthroscopy.

Figure **1** CT scan of an elite show jumper with a core lesion in one lobe of the DDFT

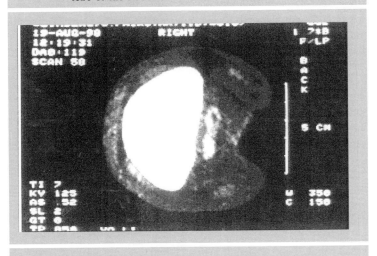

Figure **2** MRI scan of an elite show jumper with a core lesion in the DDFT

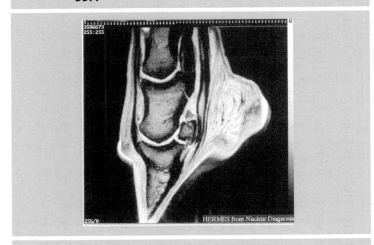

4.4 Proximal suspensory desmitis

Proximal suspensory desmitis results in acute onset mild to severe lameness. In the acute phase there may be slight oedema in the proximal metacarpal region or slight enlargement of the medial palmar vein, with pain on firm pressure applied to the proximal aspect of the SL, but in some horses there are no palpable abnormalities. Lameness is usually worst on a circle on a soft surface, with the affected limb on the outside. Lameness is usually substantially improved by perineural analgesia of either the lateral palmar nerve at the level of the accessorio-ulnar ligament, or the palmar metacarpal nerves. Diagnosis is confirmed ultrasonographically. Abnormalities include enlargement of the SL, poor definition of one or more of the borders, especially the dorsal border, areas of diffuse reduction in echogenicity or a central hypoechoic region and a disruption in fibre pattern in longitudinal images.

4.5 Suspensory ligament branch injuries

Injuries to the medial or lateral branch of the suspensory ligament usually result in mild to moderate lameness associated with enlargement of the damaged ligament, periligamentous oedema, localised heat and pain on palpation. There may be concurrent effusion in the metacarpophalangeal joint and pain on distal limb flexion. Intra-articular analgesia of the metacarpophalangeal joint may need to be performed to exclude the joint as an additional source of pain. Diagnosis is confirmed ultrasonographically. Abnormalities include enlargement of the branch, poor definition of its margins, diffuse reduction in echogenicity or focal hypoechoic regions, and disruption of fibre pattern. There may be periligamentous oedema or echodense material subcutaneously. Lesions at the insertion should be evaluated carefully to identify any concurrent osseous pathology.

4.6 Tenosynovitis of the digital flexor tendon sheath

Sudden onset lameness associated with distension of the DFTS may be due to a primary tenosynovitis or be secondary due to desmitis of the palmar annular ligament (PAL) or lesions of the enclosed digital flexor tendons, especially the DDFT. There is usually localised heat and pain on passive manipulation of the fetlock. Careful palpation is required to identify any other soft tissue abnormality. Lameness is accentuated by distal limb flexion. If there was pre-existing enlargement of the DFTS it may be necessary to perform local analgesic techniques to confirm the source of pain. Lameness is improved by intra-thecal analgesia, but may not be alleviated fully. A better response may be seen after perineural analgesia of the palmar (plantar) and palmar metacarpal (plantar metatarsal) nerves. Careful ultrasonographic evaluation is essential to determine whether the condition is primary or secondary. In the presence of synovial effusion care must be taken not to confuse the normal synovial plicae with adhesions. The size and shape, echogenicity and definition of the margins of the SDFT, DDFT and PAL should all be carefully assessed.

4.7 Desmitis of the middle patellar ligament

Desmitis of the middle patellar ligament has only been identified in show jumpers by the author. In acute cases there may be slight oedema around the middle patellar ligament, but in chronic cases there are no palpable abnormalities. Lameness varies from mild to moderate. Lameness may be partially improved by intra-articular analgesia of the femoropatellar joint in some, but not all, affected horses. There are usually no detectable radiological abnormalities. Nuclear scintigraphic evaluation reveals a region of increased uptake of the radiopharmaceutical in the cranioproximal aspect of the tibia, and sometimes also involving the patella.

Figure ❸   Desmitis of the middle patellar ligament

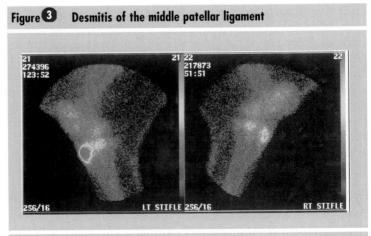

Explanations
Grand prix show jumper with left hindlimb lameness associated with insertional desmopathy of the middle patellar ligament. Note the intense increased uptake of the radiopharmaceutical on the cranioproximal aspect of the tibia

Diagnosis is by ultrasonographic examination. Lesions occur most commonly at the distal insertion and are characterised by hypoechoic areas and disruption of fibre pattern.

4.8 Subchondral bone injury

Acute onset moderate to severe lameness may be the result of subchondral bone injury in a variety of locations e.g. the distal condyles of the third metacarpal bone. Synovial effusion is often not present, but there may be pain on manipulation of the joint Lameness may be accentuated by flexion of the affected joint. The response to intra-articular analgesia is usually less than that achieved by desensitisation of the region by perineural analgesia. There is usually no detectable radiological abnormality. Diagnosis requires nuclear scintigraphy. A marked focal increase in uptake of the radiophar-maceutical is identified in the subchondral bone.

Figure ❹ Subchondral bone injury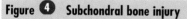

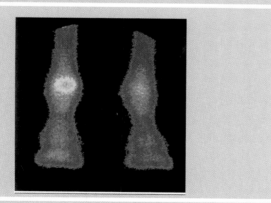

Explanations

Dorsopalmar scintigraphic images of the distal forelimbs of a grand Prix show jumper with acute onset right forelimb lameness, accentuated by distal limb flexion. There is marked increased upta-ke of the radiopharmaceutical in the distal aspect of the third metacarpal bone of the right forelimb, reflecting a stress reaction in the subchondral bone. Intra-articular analgesia produced only a partial improvement in lameness, which was alleviated by perineural analgesia of the fetlock region. The horse made a complete recovery.

5 Conclusions

The elite show jumper is a highly specialised athlete on which are placed some unique demands. Elite show jumpers tend to be older than eight years of age, and some are between 15 and 20 years of age, therefore some injuries may be a cumulative effect of degenerative ageing changes and the stresses imposed by the sport. Diseases or injuries which may be secondary to poor conformation, or which have a heritable basis may have already been manifest prior to the horse reaching elite status. Thus many of the injuries are a genuine reflection of the stresses imposed by the sport. Careful monitoring is essential to minimise risks of serious injury and to manage low grade problems that may compromise performance. With the development of magnetic resonance imaging, further advances in diagnosis will unquestionably be made, particularly related to more specific diagnosis of foot lameness.

Benefits of non-focalised CO_2 laser in horses

Take Home Message

Using non-focalised CO_2 laser as a complement to conventional intra-articular treatment of acute synovitis of fetlock joints is beneficial.

Introduction

The fast technical development in veterinary medicine has continously created new possibilities for clinical examination, diagnostics and treatments. Regarding lameness and joint disease, the methods of treating acute traumatic arthritis have not changed much during the last 20 years. Even if the veterinary surgeons have become more skilled in diagnosing and treating lamenesses, the use of new methods of treatment such as laser therapy has not yet been approved among equine surgeons. It is however very important to obtain practical knowledge about how and when to use laser therapy especially on joint disease.

In Sweden soft lasers have been used for many years by trainers, horse owners, and by so-called equi therapeutists among others. The target for treatment has mainly been joint disease and muscle soreness. There has been and still is a lot of scepticism among equine surgeons about the use of laser therapy in veterinary medicine. This may be due to the lack of scientific studies in horses and no or little practical experience. However, research on the biological effect of different lasers has matured, and the question is no longer whether therapeutic lasers have biological effects, but rather how they work and how best to use them (In: Tunér and Hode, 1999). A scientific investigation of the biological effect of CO_2 laser therapy of fetlock joints is presently being performed at the Department of Clinical Sciences, Faculty of Veterinary Medicine, Swedish University of Agricultural Sciences, Uppsala, Sweden. Results of it have not yet been published. Surgical lasers are used in both human and veterinary medicine and are used in the fields of ophthalmology, urology, gynecology, dentistry, gastroenterology and general surgery, especially of the upper respiratory tract, as well. Surgery with CO_2 laser in the upper respiratory tract is described by Ohnesorge and Deegen in this book.

In order to contribute to the advancement of science and technology related to CO_2 laser and its application, we have been examining the clinical effect of non-focalised CO_2 laser on traumatic arthritis in our equine hospital during the last 6 years. Thus in in this paper I will focus on the use of CO_2 laser treatment of traumatic arthritis but will also discuss the application in other pathologies. In addition to CO_2 laser treatment, the use of Nd:YAG lasers and so called soft lasers will be discussed as well.

What is a laser?

The name LASER is the short form for Light Amplification by Stimulated Emission of Radiation. The first described laser was a rubidium laser (Maiman, 1960) and during the years after, several lasers of different wave lengths were developed. Patel (1960) was the first to develop a CO_2 laser, and by 1972 Jako was using laser surgery of vocal cords in dogs. Today more than a thousand different laser mediums are available. Quite early the laser was tested as a surgical instrument for cutting, coagulation and steaming. A laser produces electromagnetic radiation which is a flow of energy appearing with a certain wave length, and there is a flow of particles, so-called photons, that deliver the energy. The photon energy is proportional to the mass and speed of the photon according to the formula by Einstein $E = m \times c^2$.

The energy of the photon is reversibly proportional to the wave length; the bigger the wave length the smaller the energy. Depending on the wave length the laser has different effect on the body. The CO_2 laser beam is absorbed in water and thus can not penetrate very deep into the tissue, only less than 1 cm, whereas the Nd:YAG laser is absorbed in tissue such as muscle and connective tissue and can penetrate deeper in the tissue compared to the CO_2 laser.

The laser beam is coherent, i.e. all light waves are in phase and they are also parallel. The laser beam is not spread out like ordinary light. All lasers have wave lengths located in the spectrum between infrared and ultraviolet light.

Table ❶   The most common laser types in medicine and surgery

Laser name	Wavelength	Pulsed or continous	Use in medicine
Crystalline laser medium			
Ruby	694 nm	p	tattoo and hair removal
Alexandrite	755 nm	p	bone cut, hair removal
Nd:YAG	1,064 nm	p	coagulation of tumours
Ho:YAG	2,130 nm	p	surgery, dentistry
Er:YAG	2,940 nm	p	dental drill, laser peeling
Semiconductor lasers			
GaAlAs	780, 820, 870nm	c	biostimulation, surgery
GaAs	904, 905 nm	p	biostimulation
Gas lasers			
Excimer	193, 248, 308 nm	p	eye, vascular surgery
Argon	350, 514 nm	c	dermatology, eye
HeNe	633, 3390 nm	c	biostimulation
CO_2	10600 nm	c/p	dermatology, surgery

Explanation
(for reference see: Tunér and Hode, 1999)

Surgical lasers

Nd:YAG and CO_2 lasers are the most common ones in use for treatment of horses. The Nd:YAG laser has been used for trans-endoscopic surgery of the upper respiratory paths for many years. This technique is applied on the standing horse as well as under general anaesthesia on many different pathologies of the pharynx. The light of this laser is in the invisible near-infrared spectrum at a wavelength of 1,064 nm and therefore a Helium Neon aiming beam is used as a guide for the surgeon to direct the laser beam.

The Nd:YAG light is absorbed in tissue protein and not by water or blood which makes this specific laser better for use in the upper respiratory paths. The endoscope should be about 70 cm in length with a biopsy channel of 2.3 mm in diameter to allow the laser fibre to fit in the biopsy channel. Special glasses are necessary to look through the endoscope, or a safer way is to look through a laser-compatible videoendoscope. It is also important to think about the safety of the horse, for instance evacuation of smoke from the upper respiratory paths, and to use a endotracheal tube with a cuff. The effect of the Nd:YAG laser is to coagulate and vaporise tissue. Different probes are used depending on expected effect.

We have been testing the Nd:YAG laser on sore back muscles. After 3-5 treatments the stiffness and pain is reduced or has disappeared. Of course a complete lameness examination is always performed to diagnose the exact origin of the lameness which most often is the underlying cause of muscle soreness of the back. In man the Nd:YAG laser is used to treat ligament and tendon inflammation and tear as well as muscle soreness. Also inflammation of tendon sheaths has been treated with success. The results of thousands of treatments in man will be published shortly.

The non-focalised CO_2 laser (Electro-Engineering, Florens, Italy) was tested on horses for the first time at our clinic 6 years ago. The reason for me to start testing CO_2 laser on horses was that my epicondylitis (tennis elbow) was treated twice with non-focalised CO_2 laser therapy with great success and the pain completely disappeared. After this little personal test we started to use a non-focalised CO_2 laser on joint and leg problems in many horses.

The surgical CO_2 laser used has 25 W. Each fetlock joint is treated once a day, or once every other day, during 12 minutes, thereby accumulating the energy of about 60 J/cm^2 per treatment. Horses with a heavy fur coat are clipped around the joint before treatment. For this type of laser a helium neon beam is used as a guide to direct the laser beam. We started testing this treatment prescription on many pathological conditions such as acute synovitis, chronic synovitis, synovitis caused by POF and OCD and arthritis. We also tested the effect of laser treatment on wound healing and acute tendinitis and any kind of acute swellings of the legs.

After one year of testing we believed in our positive results with laser therapy and we know what to treat and what to avoid treating. We studied the literature to try to understand the biological effect of this laser. We assume that a CO_2 laser has an anti-inflammatory effect on tissues and increases blood flow. It probably also has an analgesic effect and seems to stimulate intracellular components. Laser treatment is non-toxic and has not shown negative side-effects.

Wound healing is accelerated. Also edemas around tendons and tendon sheaths or bruises from kicks on the legs often seem to disappear fast after three to four treatments. However, the effect on tendinitis is poor. In spite of the fact that up to 10 treatments were performed on acute tendinitis of the superficial flexor tendon or suspensory ligament, clinically, the result was not different than in horses given rest for several months.

Traumatic arthritis

The most interesting target for CO_2 laser treatment is traumatic arthritis. The best results were obtained after treatment of traumatic arthritis of fetlock joints. These can be divided into five categories: Acute synovitis and/or capsulitis, chronic synovitis, distorsion, fetlock joints with bone changes such as fragments of the posterior border (POF) and arthrosis.

The positive effect on chronic synovitis, POF and arthrosis of the fetlock joint lasts only for about one week. Sometimes there is no effect at all. A thorough clinical examination is therefore very important because the result of treatment depends on the pathology involved.

Longing the horses or working them at higher speeds on a treadmill is initially performed at our clinic. Flexion tests, intra-articular anaesthesias and radiographs are important tests to do in order to obtain as good and correct diagnoses as possible. Acute synovitis/capsulitis of fetlock joints is the best target for non-focalised CO_2 laser treatment.

Some time ago I presented the results of treatment of 333 cases with acute synovitis in fetlock joints (169 horses of 5 different breeds) treated with either non-focalised CO_2 laser or with conventional intra-articular treatment with hyaluronan and corticosteroids. This presentation was in Reno, USA at the American Laser Society in Surgery and Medicine. All horses had had a lameness examination prior to treatment, and the affected joints were anaesthetised. Most of the horses were radiographed. The results were evaluated either as fully recovered or not recovered 3-4 weeks and 8-10 weeks after treatment. A slight improvement was evaluated as not recovered. The results showed 75% fully recovered fetlock joints for both types of treatment, and there was no significant difference between the two groups.

We have also performed a blind test in which one fetlock joint was either treated intra-articularly on one occasion or with non-focalised CO_2 laser three times, once every other day. Also this test showed a good affect of the CO_2 laser treatment. We have not observed any systemic effect when one of two fetlocks with acute synovitis was treated with CO_2 laser. The horses are always checked for lameness after treatment and remain in a small paddock for one week after treatment. Thereafter they return to normal training. The positive result after treatment can already be seen on the day of the last treatment.

Horses treated intra-articularly with hyaluronan and betamethason received box rest for 4 days and were then kept in a small paddock for two weeks. Two weeks after intraarticular treatment training was allowed to begin. Thus convalescence time after laser treatment was one week and after intraarticular treatment 2 weeks.

Conclusions

The use of non-focalised CO_2 laser therapy on acute synovitis/capsulitis of fetlock joints (metacarpo-phalangeal or metatarso-phalangeal joints) has been proved to have a positive therapeutic effect, equal to traditional intraarticular treatment.

- A correct diagnosis of the lameness cause is important for good results of treatment, and acute synovitis seems to be the joint disease that responds best to non-focalised CO_2 laser therapy.
- The convalescent time after laser treatment seems to be shorter with the same positive results as compared with intra-articular treatment with hyaluronan and corticosteroids.
- No biological side-effects have been noticed after CO_2 laser treatment.
- Non-focalised CO_2 laser treatment seems to be a good alternative in the treatment of acute synovitis of fetlock joints in horses.

Hyonate® i.v. Now joints may be treated with hyaluronic acid intra-articularly or intravenously.

Hyonate® Solution for Injection 2 ml. For intraarticular and intravenous injection. 1 ml contains: Natr. hyaluron, 10 mg. Natr. chlorid 8,5 mg. Dinatr. phosph. anhydr., 0,2 mg. Natr. dihydrogen. phosph. monohydr., 40 µg et aq. ad inject. q. s. Keep cold (+2–+8 °C).

www.bayer-animal-health.com

Joint repair in the equine athlete

1. Introduction

Traumatic joint disease (which includes synovitis, capsulitis, articular cartilage and bone fragmentation, ligamentous tearing and osteoarthritis) is a significant problem in horses. The long term consequence of inflammation to the soft tissue or acute damage to articular cartilage and bone is osteoarthritis (OA) and correct and aggressive treatment is indicated to prevent the development of OA as well as treat the immediate discomfort and inflammation. Despite the best care, articular cartilage loss does occur and is a permanent situation. Methods currently used to try to augment the repair process will also be discussed.

When the author discusses repair, the therapeutic strategies can be divided into 1) minimization of all deleterious processes such as degradation of articular cartilage matrix in association with cytokines and metalloproteinases, and 2) augmentation of synthetic processes by growth factor augmentation (either protein administration or gene therapy) and other surgical techniques designed to augment healing.

2. Relevant pathobiology

When considering a traumatically injured joint, two basic pathobiologic processes should be considered: 1) inflammation of the synovial membrane and fibrous joint capsule (synovitis and capsulitis), and 2) physical or biochemical damage to the articular cartilage and bone. Acute synovitis and capsulitis can cause significant clinical compromise and may also contribute to the degenerative process by the release of enzymes, inflammatory mediators and cytokines.[22,24] These processes are outlined in Figures 1 and 2.

Figure ❶ Factors involved in articular cartilage degradation in the horse. Many of the pathways involve soft tissue compromise.

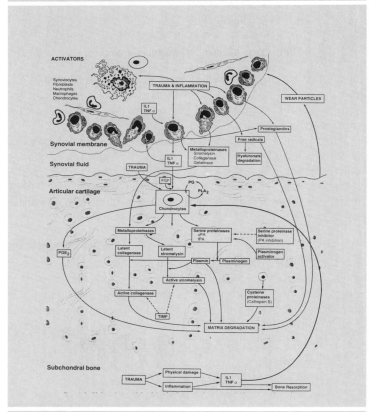

Explanations

(Adapted from McIlwraith CW, Trotter GW [eds]: Joint Disease in the Horse. Philadelphia, WB Saunders, Company, 1996.)

Figure ❷ **Possible factors in enzymatic degradation of cartilage matrix. Factors associated with synovitis are illustrated in the upper part of the diagram. IL1, interleukin 1; TNFß, tumor necrosis factor ß; FGF, fibroblast growth factor; PG, prostaglandin; PLA2, phospholipase A2, uPA, urokinase plasminogen activator; tPA, tissue plasminogen activator; TIMP, tissue inhibitors of metalloproteinases.**

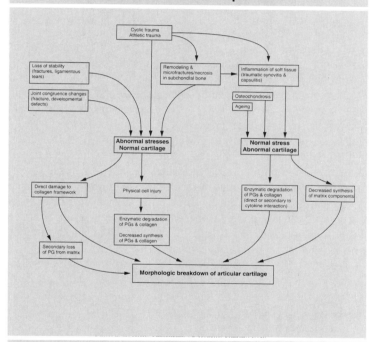

Explanations

(Adapted from McIlwraith CW, Trotter GW [eds]: Joint Disease in the Horse, Philadelphia, WB Saunders Co, 1996.)

In addition to direct injury that may occur to the synovial membrane, the reaction of synovial membrane to articular cartilage damage or other mechanical destruction of intra-articular tissues is well recognized. The presence of cartilaginous wear particles incites synovitis and increases the cellular production of various mediators.[22]

There has been considerable in vitro and some in vivo work to characterize the important mediators in joint disease in various species but it has been only recently that the mediators in the horse have been characterized. Metalloproteinases (MMPs) suggested to be of significance include collagenases 1, 2 and 3 or MMPs 1, 8 and 13 (which cleave all three chains of the alpha (1) chain of collagen types I, II, and III), stromelysin (that has a wide variety of substrates including the proteoglycans aggrecan, decorin, and fibromodulin, as well as link protein, types IV, V, VII, IX and XI collagen and type II collagen in nonhelical sites and gelatin-degrading proteinases (gelatinases-MMPs 2 & 9) that degrade denatured type II collagen. Metalloproteinases are inhibited by two tissue inhibitors of metalloproteinase known commonly as TIMP (TIMP-1 and TIMP-2). In addition to the metalloproteinase stromelysin, another proteinase has been shown to be involved in proteoglycan degradation and given the name "aggrecanase".[27] More recently there has been evidence provided in nonequine species that stromelysin is not the only enzyme that can degrade aggregating proteoglycan (aggrecan). Another enzyme (aggrecanase) appears to be the main agent causing direct degradation of proteoglycan in osteoarthritis whereas stromelysin plays a more important role in normal turnover.

Recent work in our laboratory at CSU has confirmed that in clinical cases of equine joint disease, most of the MMPs purported to cause cartilage degradation are indeed present in equine joints in increased amounts and the presence of increased amounts of the two cytokines IL-1 and TNF-alpha has also been demonstrated.

Synovitis can also produce plasminogen activators (serine proteinases) that cleave plasminogen to active plasmin and this cascade plays a role in activating metalloproteinases and cysteine proteinases (cathepsin-B and cathepsin-L are best known), which are also considered of importance in cartilage degradation. Prostaglandins (primarily the E group) are produced in inflamed equine joints[11] and can be released from synovial cells and chondrocytes in response to IL-1. Actions of PGE_2 include proteoglycan depletion from cartilage (by both degradation and inhibition of synthesis) as well as enhancing pain perception. Oxygen-derived free radicals, including superoxide anion, hydroxyl radicals and hydrogen peroxide may be released from injured joints. Studies have demonstrated cleavage of hyaluronic acid, proteoglycans and the alpha chains of collagen by free radicals.[22]

The synthesis and activity of metalloproteinases appears to be induced by cytokines. Cytokines are defined as soluble peptides produced by one cell affecting the activity of other cell types. Studies of cytokines in joint tissues suggest that IL-1 and tumor necrosis factor (TNF-alpha) modulate the synthesis of metalloproteinases by both chondrocytes and synovial cells and are important mediators in joint disease.[22] Normal turnover of the extracellular matrix of the articular cartilage is also regulated by the chondrocytes under the control and influence of cytokines and mechanical stimuli.[22] Articular cartilage degradation in association with disease represents an exacerbation of these normal processes. The recent isolation of the genes for equine IL-1-alpha and IL-1-beta should help characterize its importance in the horse.[19]

3. Treatment of synovitis

Treatment of synovitis (and capsulitis), particularly the acute form, is indicated to:

- Alleviate the immediate compromising effects of inflammation including pain and reduced function.
- Prevent the development of permanent fibrosis in the joint capsule which in turn will cause decreased motion and compromised shock absorption capabilities in that joint.
- Prevent or minimize the development of osteoarthritis (OA).

As implied above, medications used in joint disease can potentially act in a number of ways: 1) by decreasing pain which in turn provides comfort to the patient as well as allowing better usage of the joint; 2) by their anti-inflammatory effects, with varying activities against the proteinases and deleterious substances previously described, and 3) chondroprotection. The term chondroprotection has been used frequently in promotional materials for hyaluronan and polysulfated glycosaminoglycan. The term chondroprotection was originally coined by Annefeld and Fassbender to describe the protective effects of some nonsteroidal anti-inflammatory drugs in preventing ultrastructural changes in chondrocytes from young rats caused by massive doses of corticosteroids.[1] A chondroprotective agent was later defined as one capable of sustaining chondrocyte metabolic activity while suppressing the degradative actions of mediators on articular cartilage.[4] The most common mechanisms of evaluating cartilage metabolism have been measuring glycosaminoglycan synthesis with $^{35}SO_4$ uptake and measuring the total glycosaminoglycan content of the articular cartilage using the dimethyl methylene blue assay. With such methods, all the commonly used medications have been shown as chondroprotective in some experiments. Chondroprotection is a property that can be endowed via several pathways. Improved clinical function is not necessarily an index of chondroprotection. On the other hand, chondroprotection may not be the most critical need of our patients. Reduction of pain (if the level of harmful mediators is also reduced) may be beneficial long term as well as short term.

The following is discussion of therapies that are commonly used in the treatment of synovitis and capsulitis. All of these decrease the production of inflammatory mediators. Some cause no deleterious effects to the articular cartilage, whereas others appear to and this will be delineated in the discussion. When there is evidence of chondroprotective properties as defined in the previous section, these will be documented as well.

3.1 Nonsteroidal anti-inflammatory drugs

There are various nonsteroidal anti-inflammatory drugs available for and used in the treatment of joint disease in the horse. The most common drug is phenylbutazone. Nonsteroidal anti-inflammatory drugs (NSAIDs) are substances other than steroids that suppress one or more components of the inflammatory response. Such a broad definition would include both phenylbutazone-type drugs and the new intra-articular preparations such as HA, PSGAG and pentosan sulfate. The term NSAID tends to be used more restrictively to describe anti-inflammatory agents that inhibit some component of the enzyme system that converts arachidonic acid into prostaglandins and thromboxanes.[21] As defined above, all NSAIDs inhibit cyclooxygenase activity to some degree. A recent advance that should greatly increase our understanding of variations in the activity of different NSAIDs, as well as offering enhanced therapeutic usefulness, is the discovery of constitutive (COX-1) and inducible (COX-2) forms of cyclooxygenase.[21] It is suggested that COX-1 is responsible for the production of PGs involved in normal physiologic functions, whereas COX-2 is responsible for the production of PGs produced by bacterial lipopolysaccharide and cytokines and that would appear to have a role in inflammation. It has been suggested that drugs such as aspirin and indomethacin, which are more effective inhibitors of COX-1 than COX-2, are more likely to produce mucosal damage and ulceration in the gastrointestinal tract than such agents as naproxen, carprofen and meloxicam, which are relatively more effective against COX-2. It may be possible to reduce the toxicity of NSAIDs by choosing individual agents that are specifically active against the inflammation-associated isoenzyme COX-2 and leave the "physiologic" isoenzyme COX-1 unaffected to perform its homeostatic role.

There have been various criticisms of aspirin with regard to deleterious effects on the articular cartilage when used in human osteoarthritis. Most of this research data is based on rabbits. Although there have been no in vivo studies, there have been in vitro studies evaluating the effect of phenylbutazone on articular cartilage and it has been demonstrated that phenylbutazone does not have harmful effects on articular cartilage and can decrease the degradation induced by IL-1 on cartilage explants.

3.2 Intra-articular hyaloronan (Hyaloronate)

Under physiologic conditions, hyaluronate is anionic and associated with monovalent cations. It has been suggested that when the cation or polysaccharide is undetermined the compound is properly referred to as hyaluronan (HA).[18] Synthesis and function of endogenous hyaluronan has been described in a number of articles and has recently been reviewed.[18]

Beneficial effects after intra-articular administration of HA have been reported in a number of equine studies[2,18,26] as well as in other animals and man. The mechanism through which beneficial effects have been achieved remains controversial and may include supplementation of the actions of depleted or depolymerized endogenous HA, or result from other properties that have been ascribed to HA based on experimental work. It has not been determined what concentration or degree of polymerization of HA is necessary for effective intra-articular soft tissue lubrication. HA also plays a role in articular cartilage lubrication. The relationship between effects and presence of HA in the joint is somewhat confusing. The half-life of exogenous intra-articular HA injected into normal equine joints has been estimated to be 96 hours.[17] The half-life of exogenously administered HA is reduced in diseased joints. In a sheep experimental model the half-life was reduced from 20.8 hours in normal joints to 11.5 hours in arthritic joints. It has, however, been shown that although most exogenously administered HA is rapidly cleared from the joint, a proportion remains associated with synovial tissues. It has been suggested that some of the exogenous HA and its breakdown products localize in the intercellular space surrounding the synoviocytes, influencing the metabolic activity of these cells. The mechanism by which exogenous HA produces clinical benefit beyond its presence in the joint is of great interest. Effects include inhibition of chemotaxis of granulocytes, macrophages and migration of lymphocytes, as well as reduction of phagocytosis by granulocytes and macrophages.[18] It has been suggested that the anti-inflammatory effect of HA is the result of reduced interaction of enzymes, antigens or cytokines with target cells through steric hindrance.[18]

It has been repeatedly stated that the injection of HA into a pathologic joint results in increased synthesis of high molecular weight endogenous HA by the synoviocytes. Many of these authors reached the conclusion, based on a hypothesis by Asheim and Lindblad in 1976.[2] In a later in vitro study it was demonstrated that HA of molecular weight greater than 5 x 105 daltons stimulated the synthesis of HA in a concentration-dependent manner.[29] However, HA preparations of molecular weight less than 5 x 105 daltons had little or no effect except at high concentrations where HA synthesis was depressed. Whether these in vitro effects occur in vivo have not been clearly demonstrated. It is also possible that normalization of synovial fluid HA concentration and molecular weight may occur secondarily as a result of other benefits derived from the exogenous sodium hyaluronate therapy rather than through direct pharmacologic effects. There have been no demonstrated direct effects on intact articular cartilage. However, in vitro studies have demonstrated that high concentrations of HA suppress IL-1-alpha and TNF-alpha induced release of $^{35}SO_4$ proteoglycans from chondrocytes in culture.

The first report of the clinical use of HA for intra-articular treatment of equine joint disease was published in 1970[26] in which cases of traumatic degenerative equine arthritis were treated with methylprednisolone acetate versus an HA/methylprednisolone acetate combination in 20 racing Thoroughbreds and Standardbreds. The investigators concluded that the combination of HA and methylprednisolone acetate resulted in better and more lasting improvement than the corticosteroid alone. In 1976, Asheim and Lindblad provided the first report of treatment of equine traumatic arthritis with intra-articular HA alone in 54 joints of 45 racehorses previously treated unsuccessfully by conventional means.[2] Through a one year observation period, 38 of 45 horses were free of lameness and 32 returned to the racetrack after treatment. Since these early reports, numerous clinical and experimental studies have been conducted to evaluate the efficacy of HA in the treatment of equine joint disease. Most studies include response to intra-articular anesthesia as a criterion for case selection, which helps in localizing the problem but provides little information about the specific diagnosis.

Controversy exists concerning the relationship between molecular weight of exogenous HA and the clinical efficacy of treatment in equine joint disease. Although many of the in vitro effects of HA have been shown to be enhanced with higher molecular weight HA (including inhibition of fibroblast proliferation, inhibition of phagocytosis, enhanced synthesis of HA by cultured synoviocytes and inhibition of PGE_2 production by IL-1 stimulated chondrocytes, the correlation between molecular weight and clinical effect are less clear. Also, recent studies with intravenous HA make the situation more confusing.

3.3 Intravenous Hyaluronan

A formulation of HA for intravenous administration has been developed. The drug is marketed as Legend in the United States and Hyonate elsewhere. It is administered intravenously as a 40 mg dose. Anecdotal information from personal communication with veterinarians and personal experience suggests efficacy and efficacy has been demonstrated in a controlled study.[20] Osteochondral fragments were created unilaterally on the distal aspect of the radial carpal bone of 12 horses and the horses were subjected to a controlled program of exercise using a high speed treadmill. Six horses were treated with 40 mg HA intravenously on day 13, 20 and 27 after osteochondral fragmentation and six control horses were similarly treated with physiologic saline. Seventy-two days after surgery joints subjected to osteochondral fragmentation had increased synovial fluid total protein, glycosaminoglycan and prostaglandin E2 levels compared to contralateral joints without osteochondral fragments, as well as increased synovial membrane vascularity and cellular infiltration. With treatment with intravenous HA there was a reduced degree of lameness as well as significantly reduced levels of synovial fluid total protein and prostaglandin E2 compared to joints in nontreated horses, as well as reduced synovial membrane cellular infiltration and vascularity. The mechanism by which intravenously administered HA achieves therapeutic levels intra-articularly is undetermined but we hypothesize that it is associated with alteration at the level of the HA receptor. There are three types of receptors to HA but the most common one is the CD-44 receptor and we have shown expression of these receptors on equine synoviocytes as well as equine neutrophils and lymphocytes.

3.4 Polysulfated glycosaminoglycan (Adequan®)

Polysulfated glycosaminoglycan (PSGAG) belongs to a group of polysulfated polysaccharides that includes, in addition to Adequan, pentosan polysulfate (Cartrophen®) and glycosaminoglycan peptide complex (Rumalon®). This group has often been referred to as having chondroprotective properties (previously discussed) and because of this, PSGAG has been traditionally used where cartilage damage is considered to be present rather than in the treatment of acute synovitis.[32] PSGAG has been shown to inhibit the effects of various mediators associated with cartilage degradation, including collagenase and stromelysin, serine proteinases, and PGE2 synthesis.[32] Some other work in which PSGAG reduced proteoglycan breakdown associated with conditioned synovial membrane suggests an anti-IL-1 effect.[32] In addition to anti-degradative effects, PSGAG has been shown to stimulate the synthesis of HA in the horse.[33]

There have been three in vitro studies on the effects of PSGAG on equine cartilage and the results are somewhat contradictory. Initially it was reported that PSGAG caused increased collagen and glycosaminoglycan synthesis in both articular cartilage explants and cell cultures from normal and osteoarthritic equine articular cartilage and that collagen and glycosaminoglycan degradation was inhibited by PSGAG.[13] However, another investigator using smaller doses of PSGAG (50 and 200 µg/ml vs 25 to 50 mg/ml and normal equine articular cartilage explants) found a dose-dependent inhibition of proteoglycan synthesis, little effect on proteoglycan degradation and no effect on proteoglycan monomer size.[5] In a further study using osteoarthritic equine articular cartilage explants and small (0.025 mg/ml) and large (25 mg/ml) doses of PSGAG, the same investigator found a decrease in proteoglycan synthesis, little effect on proteoglycan degradation, no change in the size of the proteoglycan monomer and no change in the aggregability of the monomer.[6]

The first in vivo investigation in the horse involved 250 mg injections of PSGAG intra-articularly twice weekly for three weeks and then once weekly for the next three weeks in horses having joint swelling and lameness.[30] A significant improvement in synovial fluid protein concentration and synovial fluid viscosity was reported as well as an overall impression of decreased clinical signs (lameness, swelling and effusion), as well as increased flexion. Intra-articular PSGAG was then tested using a Freund's adjuvant-induced model in the carpus of 30 horses.[16] This study concluded that the clinical signs of arthritis were reduced in treated animals. The latter investigators, in a clinical trial in 109 horses, also felt that PSGAG improved clinical signs more frequently than horses not treated.[16]

PSGAG was then tested on chemically-induced, as well as physically-induced lesions in the horse in our laboratory. Treatment with intra-articular injections of 250 mg PSGAG once weekly for five weeks in carpal joints injected with sodium monoiodoacetate revealed less articular cartilage fibrillation and erosion, less chondrocyte death and markedly improved safranin-0 staining but did not have any effect on physically induced lesions (partial and full thickness). A second study using intramuscular PSGAG (500 mg every four days for seven treatments) showed relatively insignificant effects with treatment. The effects were limited to slightly improved safranin-0 staining in sodium monoiodoacetate-injected joints when PSGAG was used. More recent studies have evaluated the effects of intramuscular PSGAG with or without exercise on the repair of articular cartilage defects as well as the development of osteoarthritis in the carpus of ponies. The authors concluded that PSGAG was beneficial in ameliorating the clinical, radiographic and scintigraphic signs of joint disease. Some research has demonstrated that intra-articular PSGAG may have greater potential to cause iatrogenic infection than other drugs but that this infection could be prevented by the simultaneous administration of 125 mg amikacin.[14,15] At the time this data was reported, intramuscular PSGAG was developed and is now the main way the drug is used. There is minimal objective data supporting effectiveness for intramuscular Adequan in the horse but the drug is widely used and anecdotal reports support its value. The issue of absorption after intramuscular injection was addressed by Burba et al.[3] In this study, PSGAG was labeled with tritium and scintillation was done on synovial fluid as well as joint tissues. It was felt that levels of drug consistent with that seen in other non-equine studies were obtained and it was concluded that therapy every four days was effective in maintaining anti-inflammatory levels in the joint.

3.5 Oral glycosaminglycans

Oral glycosaminoglycan products available for horses include a purified chondroitin sulfate product from bovine trachea (Flex-Free®) and a complex of glycosaminoglycans and other nutrients from the sea mussel Perna canaliculus (Syno-Flex®). More recently, a combination of glucosamine hydrochloride, chondroitin sulfate and what is described as a mixture of other PSGAGs has been marketed as a "nutraceutical" (Cosequin®). The oral administration of glucosamine sulfate has been associated with decreased pain and improved range of motion compared to placebo in a controlled clinical trial in humans.[25] In another controlled study, glucosamine sulfate was as effective as ibuprofen at relieving symptoms of osteoarthritis in people. In vitro studies using glucosamine sulfate have demonstrated increased glycosaminoglycan and proteoglycan synthesis and in vivo studies have demonstrated anti-inflammatory activity through inhibition of lysosomal enzyme activity and free radical production. There was also some evidence for oral bioavailability of glucosamine sulfate and tropism for articular cartilage after oral administration. There is conflicting evidence regarding the enteral absorption of orally administered glycosaminoglycans. Cosequin has been evaluated using the Freund's adjuvant model of inflammatory joint disease in horses.[34] The oral supplement was used at the recommended dose beginning 10 days prior to arthritis induction and continuing for a further 26 days. No benefit was demonstrated based on clinical (lameness, stride length, carpal circumference, carpal flexion) and synovial fluid (protein) parameters.

There is now a wide range of oral glycosaminoglycans/glucosamine products available for the horse. There is still a lack of good controlled data but nonequine literature continues to demonstrate certain value with osteoarthritis. The mechanism of action of these products is still unknown but is probably more than simply anti-inflammatory.

3.6 Intra-articular corticosteroids

Although it has been implied by some that intra-articular corticosteroids have been replaced by HA and PSGAG, many clinicians have returned to or persisted in the use of corticosteroids.[23] The untoward effects of intra-articular corticosteroids in horses have been repeatedly documented in the veterinary literature and more recently in the lay press. Several investigators have attempted to critically evaluate the effects of corticosteroids in equine joints[31] and these results are helping identify a more definitive role for these agents in the management of joint disease. Much new information has been gained recently and it is clear many previous generalizations are wrong and that there are many differences with regard to the type and dose of corticosteroid used, as well as the reaction of individual tissues.

The effects of corticosteroids have been reviewed recently.[31] Corticosteroid effects are exerted through an interaction with steroid-specific receptors in the cellular cytoplasm of steroid-responsive tissues. Due to this interaction, transcription of genes is modulated, and mRNA coding for proteins produces the hormonal effect.

Traditionally, the primary anti-inflammatory effect of corticosteroids has been related to stabilization of lysosomal membranes with a concomitant decrease in the release of lysosomal enzymes. However, the anti-inflammatory effects are considerably more complex than this.[31] Glucocorticoid receptors have been demonstrated in neutrophils, lymphocytes and eosinophils and it is possible that all glucocorticoid anti-inflammatory effects are exerted through receptor-mediated mechanisms. A major effect of corticosteroids is their inhibition of movement of inflammatory cells (including neutrophils and monocyte-macrophages) into a site of inflammation.[31] Corticosteroids also affect neutrophil function but to a lesser extent than movement and the effect on neutrophil function seems to be dose-dependent. Corticosteroids affect the humoral aspects of inflammation, predominantly by inhibition of prostaglandin production. This action is considered to be largely due to the inhibition of phospholipase A2 by the steroid-inducible group of proteins called lipocortins.

A number of equine studies have evaluated the effects of methylprednisolone acetate injected into normal equine joints. Studies by Chunekamrai et al[7] and Trotter et al[35] showed that some regressive changes occurred to normal equine cartilage when 6-alpha-methylprednisolone acetate was used. Questions still remain with MPA regarding what is the minimally effective dose and what effects these doses have on an experimental equine model under exercise.

Relatively recent work (now published in the Equine Veterinary Journal) using our experimental osteoarthritis model has demonstrated a mixture of positive and negative effects. Although we showed a significant decrease with MPA treatment in inflammatory parameters such as protein and PGE_2 levels, we did not show a significant reduction in lameness. In addition, we did show deleterious effects in the articular cartilage, including a decreased amount of safranin-0 staining for glycosaminoglycan as well as an increased pathologic score. Although many veterinarians feel they get their best and longest results with this product, another choice of corticosteroid is ideal for long term joint health.

The effects of betamethasone (Betavet Soluspan®) were investigated using an arthroscopic model of carpal fragmentation.[9] Osteochondral fragments were created arthroscopically on the distal aspect of both radial carpal bones in 12 horses to evaluate the effects of intra-articular betamethasone with and without exercise. One intercarpal joint of each horse was injected with betamethasone (2.5 ml) at 14 days after surgery and the procedure was repeated at 35 days. The opposite joint was injected with saline, 2.5 ml, as a control. Six of the horses were maintained in box stalls throughout the study as nonexercised controls and six were exercised five days per week on a high speed treadmill with a regimen of two minutes trot, two minutes gallop, two minutes trot. Three weeks after the second injection, horses were clinically examined for lameness and synovial effusion, radiographs were taken and the horses were euthanized. The results of histologic, histochemical and biochemical examination of the articular cartilage did not show any consistent detrimental effects of betamethasone with or without exercise. The exercised horses also had similar levels of glycosaminoglycans in treated vs control joints. The use of betamethasone in this carpal chip model did not show any consistent detrimental effects in either rested or exercised horses.

The results of recent work in our laboratory at CSU suggest that triamcinolone acetonide may indeed be chondroprotective in the horse.[11] In this study 18 horses were trained on a high speed treadmill and then had an osteochondral fragment created at the distal aspect of the radial carpal bone of one randomly chosen intercarpal joint. Six horses were treated with intra-articular injection of polyionic fluid in both intercarpal joints (group 1), six horses were treated with 12 mg triamcinolone acetonide intra-articularly in the intercarpal joint without an osteochondral fragment (the opposite intercarpal joint was treated IA with a similar volume of poly-ionic fluid)(group 2), six horses were treated with 12 mg triamcinolone acetonide in the joint that contained the osteochondral fragment (the opposite midcarpal joint was treated IA with a similar volume of polyionic fluid) (group 3). Triamcinolone and placebo treatments were given twice at days 14 and 28 after surgery and treadmill exercise proceeded five days per week, beginning on day 15 and ending on day 72. Horses that were treated intra-articularly with triamcinolone in a joint containing a fragment (Group 3) were less lame than horses in groups 1 and 2. Synovial membrane from groups 2 and 3 joints had less inflammatory cell infiltration, intimal hyperplasia and subintimal fibrosis. Analysis of articular cartilage morphologic parameters evaluated using a standardized scoring system were significantly better from groups 2 and 3 irrespective of which joint received triamcinolone (TA). There was less staining with SOFG in group 2 compared to group 3 and group 1, although the GAG synthetic rate was elevated in group 2 as compared to groups 1 and 3. Increased HA concentrations were observed in TA treated joints, which also suggests a favorable corticosteroid effect on synoviocyte metabolism. This work supports a chondroprotective effect of corticosteroids in a controlled model of osteoarthritis and is in marked contrast to the detrimental effects of corticosteroids seen in in vivo osteochondral fragment models where methylprednisolone was used.

Although harmful effects may result from extensive use of some corticosteroids, the protective effects and possibly even anabolic effects of certain of these agents, when given in a more physiologic dose, lay open to question the generalized enunciation of corticosteroids as harmful drugs. We need to define what dose of corticosteroid is necessary to achieve therapeutic effects and then look more closely at the effect of these dosages in vivo. Corticosteroids are very effective for a number of traumatic and degenerative processes and before we can eliminate them from our armamentarium we need to have either a) better or more effective drug, and/or b) scientific data on both the effectiveness and deficiencies of presently available corticosteroids.

3.7 Combination therapy

The most common combination used in intra-articular therapy is that of HA and a corticosteroid. Effects on synovial fluid production and the increased concentrations of HA and decreased proteoglycans in synovial fluid (considered to be a marker of cartilage degeneration) was demonstrated when a combination of intra-articular corticosteroid and HA was injected into normal joints.[36] This combination therapy is logical because hyaluronan alone will not always provide sufficient resolution of the clinical problem but the steroid-HA combination often does and the dose rate of cortico-steroids can generally be lower. Although other combinations are possible, they have yet to be critically evaluated in controlled studies.

Recent in vitro work in our laboratory has shown that the overall ana-bolic effects as well as degradation of articular cartilage by interleukin-1 can be ameliorated by a triamcinolone acetonide and IGF-1 combination compared to triamcinolone acetonide alone. If these in vitro data could be translated into in vivo data, it may be a very useful combination for a medi-cation such as methyl prednisolone acetate that has degradative effects on its own.

4 New horizons

4.1 Metalloproteinase Inhibitors and Gene Therapy Techniques

Direct inhibition of metalloproteinases by specific inhibitors offer potential as therapeutic agents. There are a number of generations of MMP inhibi-tors. We are currently working in our laboratory on a third generation MMP inhibitor and we have shown in vitro that there is significant reduc-tion of the important MMPs and the presence of this MMP inhibitor will significantly reduce degradation caused by interleukin-1 (Billinghurst and McIlwraith, 1999). Obviously such products need to be analyzed carefully in vivo with particular attention paid to possible side effects. Metalloproteinases are involved in tissue remodeling procedures and the-refore their use may be contraindicated in the young patient.

Gene therapy offers some exciting potential at administering specific therapeutic agents and we have recently completed a major project in our laboratory using gene therapy with interleukin-1 receptor antagonist. Interleukin-1 receptor antagonist (IRAP) is the normal antidote for IL-1 and competes for the IL-1 receptor with IL-1-alpha and -beta (there are two iso-forms). There are two possible routes of administration of IRAP: 1) as the protein, 2) via gene therapy. The principles of gene therapy are to take the gene sequence for equine IRAP (a sequence previously isolated in our lab by Dr. Rick Howard) and using a viral vector (in our case an adenovirus that does not cause any gross pathologic change) and inoculate it into the joint. Work headed by Dr. Dave Frisbie has demonstrated that good levels of pro-tein expression are achieved with a single inoculation of IRAP-adenovirus combination and this has been followed by work with our experimentally induced equine OA model in which we showed significant decrease in lameness as well as significant decrease in articular cartilage degradation. This was with a single injection.

The potential exists for administration of degradative cytokines as well as anabolic growth factors. We are presently working on a project looking at the combination of IRAP and IGF-1 administered by gene therapy as a treatment for cartilage erosion.

4.2 Augmentation of Articular Cartilage Healing

As implied in the introduction, there is still considerable frustration at our relative inability to heal articular cartilage defects. However, there are a number of promising experimental methods that have been developed to facilitate repair of articular cartilage, including the use of medications that may alter the course of osteoarthrosis (previously discussed), the removal of molecules that interfere with repair of cartilage (interleukin-1 would be a good example) and the use of cytokines (such as IGF-1, TGF-beta, BMP-2, CTGF) and cell transplants to stimulate replacement of damaged cartilage. We have been doing work on articular cartilage repair on horses over the past 15 years. We have evaluated the use of subchondral drilling, periosteal grafting, autogenous sternal cartilage grafting, and all of these have not demonstrated an ability to improve healing significantly long term. More recently we have worked with subchondral microfracture and demonstrated that there is an increased amount of repair tissue in the defects. We now use subchondral microfracture as a technique when we have an intact and/or sclerotic subchondral bone plate. In the meantime, the quest for better methods of healing in our laboratory include 1) evaluation of the potential for growth factor administration via gene therapy, and 2) the use of tissue engineering. In our case, in collaboration with Neocyte Joint Venture (Advanced Tissue Sciences and Smith & Nephew Dyonics) we are evaluating the use of cultured chondrocytes within artificial matrices.

3.2 Articles

The oral bioavailability of chondroitin sulphate in horses – a pilot study

Take home message

There is no evidence of increased serum levels of GAG following oral administration of chondroitin sulphate containing compounds at, and four times above, the manufacturer's recommended feeding rate.

Introduction

Chondroitin sulphate containing products are commonly administered to horses to treat or prevent joint disease (White 1989). There is evidence of in vitro anti-inflammatory activity (Ronca et al 1998), and human clinical trials have shown clinical efficacy (Uebelhart et al 1998). No large or controlled, blinded clinical trials have been performed in horses (Reid Hansen 1996). White et al (1994) failed to demonstrate beneficial activity in an induced carpitis model in horses. The oral bioavailability of chondroitin sulphate has been studied in humans, rats and dogs (Palmieri et al 1990; Conte et al 1991; Ronca et al 1998), but no trials have been performed in horses. The aim of this pilot study was to determine whether oral absorption of chondroitin sulphate could be demonstrated in horses.

Materials and methods

Five mature Thoroughbred cross horses with diagnosed low grade, chronic osteoarthrosis were used in this study. Four different commercially available feed supplements were used in the study ("Flexfree", Vitaflex; "Cortaflex Solution", Equine America; "Superflex", Natural Animal Feeds and "Chondroitin sulphate powder", Natural Animal Feeds). Three were powder presentations and one was a solution. The "Cortaflex" and "Superflex" also contained glucosamine. They were fed at manufacturer's recommended dose rates (0.8-7 mg/kg), and in two horses the dose was repeated one week later at 4 times the manufacturer's recommended dose rate (3.2-25.6 mg/kg). Venous blood samples were obtained before feeding and at 1, 2, 3, 4, 5, 6, 8 and 24 hours after administration. Negative control samples were also obtained from four untreated horses. The serum was separated and stored at -70°C.

The glycosaminoglycan (GAG) content of the serum samples was assayed using a modified dimethylene blue (DMB) assay (Farndale, Buttle and Barrett 1986; Alwan et al 1991). After dilution with phosphate buffered saline, protein digestion was performed with papain, and then inactivated with iodoacetic acid. The DMB reagent was added and the absorbance at 525 nM was read after 15-20 seconds in a spectrophotometer. All assays were performed in triplicate and calibrated against reagent blanks and known concentrations of chondroitin sulphate.

Results

The control and initial chondroitin sulphate concentrations ranged from 0.1 to 0.25 µg/ml. No significant elevation in the serum GAG concentrations above baseline was evident in the post-administration samples. None of the averaged samples demonstrated serum levels above 0.5 µg/ml at any stage.

Discussion

There was no evidence of increased serum levels of GAG following oral administration of chondroitin sulphate containing compounds at, and four times above, the manufacturer's recommended feeding rate. Despite manufacturer's claims to the contrary, there was no evidence of improved absorption of the liquid preparation. The DMB assay is specific for polymeric GAGs, and it is possible that there is absorption of monomers or degradation products. However the anti-inflammatory activity of chondroitin sulphate refers to the intact polymer, not breakdown products. The serum levels of GAGs in this study were lower than previously published results from horses with osteoarthrosis (Alwan et al 1991), which may reflect the low grade of osteoarthrosis in the selected horses. The low levels of GAGs meant that the results were not in the most linear portion of the chondro-itin sulphate calibration curve, but any significant absorption would have come into this region.

On the basis of these results, and the published literature, there seems to be little justification for the oral administration of chondroitin sulphate in the treatment of equine lameness.

Dr. Stelzer
Instrumentarium für Pferdezahn-Behandlung

Instruments for Dental Treatment of Horses

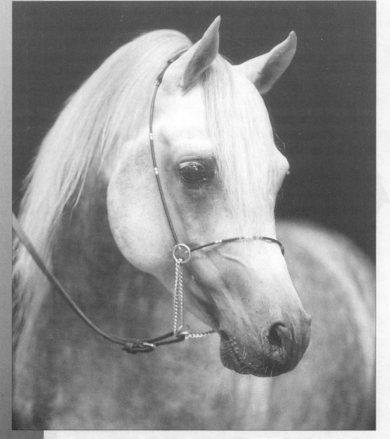

erbrich - instrumente GmbH
Eugenstr. 33 · D-78532 Tuttlingen
Tel.: +49 74 61 / 96 57 30
Fax: +49 74 61 / 96 57 320
E-mail: erbrich-instruments@t-online.d

Clinical and ultrasonographic findings of sport horses afflicted with injuries of tendons and ligaments after treatment with extracorporeal shock waves (ESW)

Take home message

In the great majority of cases included in this study, treatment with ESW had a positive effect with perfect re-alignment of tendon fibres. It was ultrasonographically documented and resulted in a disappearance of the disorder.

Introduction

Extracorporeal shock waves (ESW) passed through a watery substance are the underlying principle of lythotripsy, a method used in the human field as early as 1980 to crush renal, biliary and salivary stones. From the early nineties on, this technology has been adopted in the treatment of certain bone pathologies in man (faulty consolidation after fracture, pseudo-arthrosis), while the use of ESW was later extended to injuries of the muscle and tendon system (insertional tendinitis, periarthritis of the shoulder, epicondilitis, bursitis, heel spurs). The high percentage of success in the human field (from 70 to 85%, according to the cases treated) gave rise to an extension of the application of this technology to the pathology of bones in the veterinary field. At the beginning of 1998 we established a work group to schedule suitable treatment protocols using ESW in the most frequent injuries of the locomotor system in sport horses. Our experience is described in this paper.

Material and methods

Since 1998 158 sport horses (racehorses, show jumpers, three-day eventers) were given therapy with ESW for acute and chronic tendinitis or ligament disorders: lesions of the superficial flexor tendon in the acute (n=55) and chronic (n=35) phases; lesions of the deep flexor tendon in both acute (n=7) and chronic (n=13) phases; lesions of the carpal bridle (n=8; two of them in the acute phase); lesions of the suspensory ligament of fetlock to the proximal insertion, both of the fore and hind limbs (n=19, four of them in the acute phase); and lesions in the chronic phase of the central part of the suspensory ligament and its branches (n=21).

Of the 68 horses with lesions in the acute phase, 57 had had no other treatment before ESW. Eleven horses with lesions of the flexor tendon in the acute phase had had intra-tendon infiltrations of hyaluronic acid and/or cortison or sarapinaceal infiltration immediately after the trauma. Of the 90 horses with lesions in the chronic phase, 6 had undergone infiltration, 35 had been treated with revulsives and 2 had been cauterized.

A therapeutic unit with an electromagnetic-type shock wave generator was used. It had a cylindrical coil and parabolic reflector (Minilith SL1-Storz Medical, Kreuzlingen, CH).

A 7.5 MHz ultrasonographic probe was placed in the centre of the generator, coaxial to the EWS source, to pin down the focal area precisely during treatment: the generator, which is mounted on an articulated arm so that it can be rotated on several axes and hence easily placed against the skin, produces power ("peak of pressure") ranging from 80 to 800 bars such that the density of power can be regulated between 0.005 and 0.5 mJ/mm^2. The ESW are propagated (interposed with echography gel) through a buffer of water of varying volume placed in the head which contains the electromagnetic source. The fact of being able to vary the focal depths, under constant echographic control, ensures localization of the part to be treated, with penetration ranging from 0.4 to 5 cm.

Each horse was sedated, the pathological area shaved, and diagnostic ultrasonography performed in standing position. At every therapeutic session, which lasted from 15-20 minutes, 1,500-2,500 shocks were administered (240 bits/minute frequency), the levels of power being suitably regulated (according to the extent of the lesion and the characteristics of the horse) between 0.03 and 0.11 mJ/mm^2. The number of treatments varied, with fortnightly intervals, according to the disorder (acute or chronic) and the constitutional characteristics of the horse.

The horses did not need to be hospitalised after therapeutic treatment and were given free for transportation 30 minutes after ESW treatment. Complete rest for 2-3 days was generally prescribed after treatments; subsequently, a complete return to normal activity was allowed one month after the last treatment. Echographic check-up was generally carried out by the horse's customary veterinary surgeon 30-40 days after the last therapeutic session.

Results

The average follow-up of the cases presented was 18 months. All in all 87% of the horses treated with ESW therapy recovered completely.

In 97% of the cases with acute ailment there was a definite improvement, with a reduction of intratendon edema, 7 days after the first therapeutic session. A further clinical improvement was observed after the second ESW application, in general so pronounced that it was considered unnecessary to give the horses more treatment. The ultrasound scan carried out 30-40 days later was found to be negative.

A positive response was observed in 94 % of the cases with chronic disease which had undergone three ESW therapy sessions. In 50% of the cases a temporary increase in edema was observed after the first ESW treatment, as had been foreseen by the treatment protocol. Complete recovery was generally achieved 30-60 days after the last application.

A relapse of the tendon lesion was observed in 5 out of 11 cases (in the acute phase) which had been submitted to infiltration before ESW therapy. In two cases (one of them had had no previous treatment before ESW) there was no response to treatment at all.

In every instance when a horse returned to full sporting activity, echographic check-ups were carried out 60-80 days after the last application; they demonstrated the complete "restitutio ad integrum" of the tendon, the fibres being perfectly re-aligned.

Only four of the 57 horses treated in the acute pathological phase which had taken part in competitions again suffered relapses. One of these was given a further ESW session and has not suffered a relapse six months after returning to sporting activity.

Of the 90 horses treated for chronic pathologies, 61 returned to sporting activity: four of them suffered a relapse after competing.

Conclusions

In the great majority of cases included in this study, treatment with ESW had a positive effect with perfect re-alignment of the tendon fibres, ultrasonographically documented and with disappearance of the disorder. In only 10 horses with lesions of the superficial tendons in the acute phase, which had undergone infiltration immediately after the trauma, did we fail to obtain a high percentage of recovery (with 5 relapses and one failure to respond to treatment). We have found that horses given traditional treatment (cauterization, vesicants) for analogous disorders, still do not have a complete re-alignment of the tendon fibres after considerable time, and in any case recovery takes considerably longer than after ESW therapy.

With ESW therapy it may be unnecessary to administer pharmaceutical products (analgesics, anti-inflammatory substances, corticosteroids, etc.).

The high cost of ESW therapy is ammortized by the reduced time during which the horse is unable to compete. Furthermore, the absence of marks or scars on the skin due to treatment does not affect the animal's market value.

"If only I'd used Farrier's Formula when I first saw the problem"

Sometimes, people try to do without Farrier's Formula® until the situation has become desperate, perhaps because they think that it will be expensive.

But of course, it is only expensive because the situation is desperate! It is only then that you have to feed Farrier's Formula® at the full level and therefore use it up more quickly. The maintenance level lasts twice as long.

So the time to use Farrier's Formula® is when you first see the problem developing. Flaking, cracking, crumbling: just a little… at the edges. Then you can put it right - quickly.

If you wait until he can't keep a shoe on, it's going to cost you a fortune on the shoeing, six months wasted and another precious season down the drain.

Now that's expensive!

Epidemiological survey of tarsus alterations in horses

Take home message

Osteoarthritis was the most frequent radiologically-diagnosed alteration found in patients from the Clinical Hospital of the Faculty of Veterinary of Córdoba examined between 1995 and 1999. However, the clinical implications of this condition were low. Few cases of articular degenerative processes of tarsocrural and talocalcaneal joints were observed, but the incidence of tarsus osteochondrosis was high (22.4%).

Introduction

The tarsus represents the most frequent affected site of the locomotive alterations of horses. Most studies were reported on Thoroughbred, Standarbred and Warmbloods, all considered as high-activity horses. In this region, most horses perform a mild activity mainly as saddle horses, and only few racecourse animals are found.

The aim of this study was to determine the radiological incidence and clinical implications of the tarsus alterations in horses from the southern region of Spain (Andalucía).

Material and methods

A prospective study was performed on a sample of 388 horses (79.9 % males; 20.1 % mares) from the Clinical Hospital of the Faculty of Veterinary of Córdoba in the last 4 years (May 1995 - May 1999). Animals included required radiological studies and, occasionally, ecographical ones of the tarsus.

Several breeds were represented: Andalusian horses (N=222; 57.2 %); Angloarabians (N=37; 9.5 %); Thoroughbred (N=11; 2.8 %); Warmbloods (N=34; 8.8 %); crossbreds (N=78; 20.1 %); and other breeds (N=6; 1.6 %). Class distribution by age was: < 3 years (N=112; 28.9%), 4 to 12 years (N=217; 55.9%) and > 12 years (N=59; 15.2%).

Horse activities included free grazing, breeding, saddle, training, dressage and others. Horses routinely active were grouped relating to the work intensity as follows: moderate to high (jumping, endurance, dressage) 82 (21.3%), light (saddle, training) 205 (52.8), and free grazing, 101 (26%).

Both healthy and clinically tarsus-affected horses were included. Tarsus alterations consisted of tarsocrural effusion, altered gait, lameness, positive forced flexion test, positive anaesthetic blockage, etc. At least two of the specific radiographical views for tarsus examination were performed in all horses.

Results

Three hundred and eighty eight horses were assessed with 111 out of 388 (28.6%) considered as normal. The remaining 277 animals (71.4%) showed different clinical or radiological findings: osteoarthritis (N=114; 41.2%); osteochondrosis (N=62; 22.4%); fractures and luxations (N=28; 10.1%); infectious arthritis-osteomyelitis (N=27; 9.7%); ossification defects (N=10; 3.2%) and focal conditions and/or soft tissue lesions (N=96; 35%). Percentages were related to the total number of sick horses.

Osteoarthritis (OA) were detected in 114 horses (67 Andalusians and 47 of other breeds). Lameness was seen in only 24 horses out of the 114 (21.1%), (9 Andalusian horses and 15 other breeds). A bilateral implication was observed in 43% of horses, mainly involving the tarsometatarsal and centrodistal articulations (figure 1).

Figure ❶

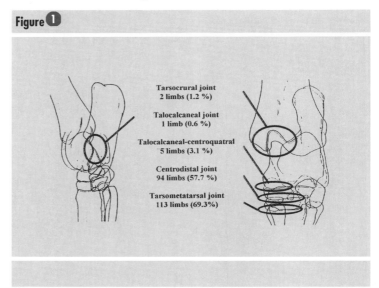

Tarsocrural joint
2 limbs (1.2 %)

Talocalcaneal joint
1 limb (0.6 %)

Talocalcaneal-centroquatral
5 limbs (3.1 %)

Centrodistal joint
94 limbs (57.7 %)

Tarsometatarsal joint
113 limbs (69.3 %)

Osteochondrosis (OCD) was observed in 62 horses. Clinically, animals showed a more or less distended tarsocrural joint (41 horses, 66,1%). Lameness could only be seen in a few horses (N=14, 22.6%) with lesions in several sites or in the lateral throclea of talus.

Osteochondrosis was characterized by the presence of one or more osteochondral fragments attached to their original site or free in the tarsocrural joint, and by a flattened ridge of bone surface. These signs were bilateral in 22 horses (52.4 %). Osteochondrosis was mainly described on the intermediate ridge of the distal tibia, the lateral throclear ridge of talus, the medial throclear ridge of talus and lateral malleolus of tibia. Multiple affected sites were seen in some horses (figure 2).

Figure ❷ Affected sites of tarsus osteochondrosis

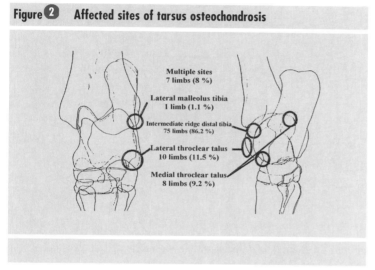

Multiple sites
7 limbs (8 %)

Lateral malleolus tibia
1 limb (1.1 %)

Intermediate ridge distal tibia
75 limbs (86.2 %)

Lateral throclear talus
10 limbs (11.5 %)

Medial throclear talus
8 limbs (9.2 %)

The incidence of infectious processes was 9.7%, with specific radiological signs only occuring in alterations longer than 15 days. Osteomyelitis of the hock tuberosity showed radiological differing considerably animal to animal.

Fractures and luxations were detected in 28 animals (10.1%). Fractures mainly affected the talus and hock, whereas luxations could be detected in the talocalcaneal-centroquatral and tarsometatarsian articulations (figure 3).

Soft tissue alterations included: bog spavin (34), thoroughpin (2), desmitis, (13), tendinitis (23), enthesiopathy (23), calcaneal bursitis (8), cuneanan bursitis (26) and others (26).

Figure ③   Fractures Sites

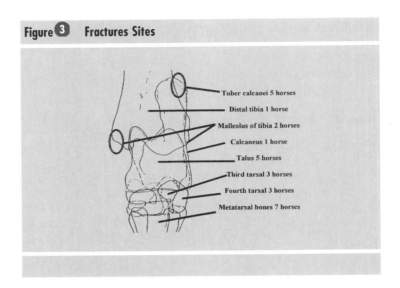

Tuber calcanei 5 horses
Distal tibia 1 horse
Malleolus of tibia 2 horses
Calcaneus 1 horse
Talus 5 horses
Third tarsal 3 horses
Fourth tarsal 3 horses
Metatarsal bones 7 horses

Discussion

Osteoarthritis could be considered the most frequent radiologically-diagnosed alteration (114 animals) with few clinical implications (lameness in only 24 horses, 21.1%). Thus, radiological signs can only be considered in association with clinical signs (Storgaard et al 1997). Mainly in <4 year-old horses, radiological images consisted of periarticular osteophytes or enthesiophytes on the dorsal tarsometatarsus ligament insertion in the dorsoproximal metatarsus III bone, both with doubtful clinical meaning (Widmer and Blevins 1994). Some authors considered these signs as the beginning of an articular degenerative process, whereas others proposed a physiological or radiological variation of the normal tarsus of young horses (Hartung et al 1983), mainly due to a bad conformation (Pools 1996) frequently seen in Andalusian horses with cow and sickle hocks.

In this study, articular degenerative processes of tarsocrural and talocalcaneal joints were observed in fewer cases as previously described (Phillips 1986; May 1996). The talocalcaneal joint showed lysis and sclerosis of the subchondral bone as described in tarsus joints with less movement. The tarsocrural degenerative processes were mainly proliferative with periarticular osteophytes and enthesiophytes.

In this study the incidence of tarsus osteochondrosis was high (22.4%) with 18.9% in Andalusian horses and 4-20% in other breeds (Alvarado et al 1989; Storgaard 1997).

No clear relationship but only a low tendency could be found between the degree of clinical signs and location and extension of the osteochondral lesions (McIlwraith 1993); thus, more severe effusions were seen when alterations of lateral throclea of talus, OCD in several locations or other hock diseases. Similar tendencies were observed with lameness or gait alteration but less constantly (McIlwraith 1993).

In this study, OCD was mainly observed on the intermedial ridge of the tibial cochlea (86.2 %), and on the lateral throclea of talus (11.5 %), as described in other breeds. Incidence in other locations was similar to that previously reported (Alvarado et al 1989; McIlwraith 1993; Canonici et al 1996; Jeffcott 1997).

Some studies in Standardbred trotters (Storgaard et al 1997) showed no significant association between OCD on the tarsus and the subsequent performance and longevity of horses affected with the disease. Radiological changes should, therefore, not be overemphazised (Alvarado et al 1989). However, as McIlwraith (1993) pointed out, the problem is different in nonraced horses. In Andalusian horses as a saddle breed, functional complains (lameness) are less important than aesthetic implications (tarsocrural effusion), which determine their economic value.

Radiological and clinical signs in infectious processes have been widely described (Firth et al 1985). However, in a small number of horses, infection in the calcaneal tuberosity was associated with a variety of radiological images (McDonald et al 1989). In these cases a dorsoplantar (flexed) view proved useful to assess lesions.

Horses that were mainly less than 4 years-old showed distension of the tarsocrural joint (bog spavin) not associated with radiological signs. Such associations with osteochondral processes may only be observed by arthroscopy (McIlwraith 1993).

Inflammation and deformation were detected in a considerable number of animals mostly with no radiological implications. Bone proliferation in soft tissue insertion sites (enthesiophytes) or dystrophic mineralization were seen only in chronic cases (Dik and Keg 1990) (figures 4 & 5). Although an ecographical study is the best method to detect these alterations in the first stages, radiographical exploration results are useful to rule out the presence of bone lesions (Verschooten and Schramme 1994).

Figure 4   **Lateromedial view**

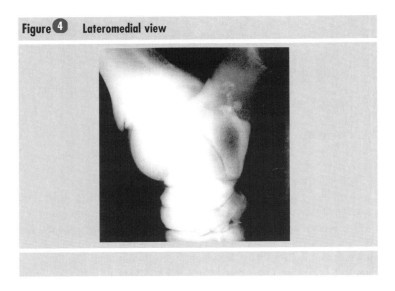

Figure 5   **Dorsoplantar flexed view**

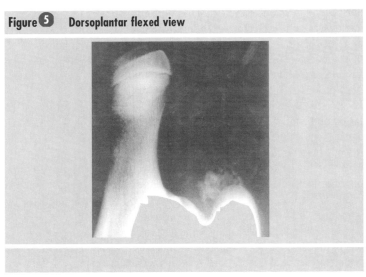

Figures 4 & 5. Dystrophic mineralization near the sustentaculum tali of the calcaneus. It is really a calcinosis circumscripta in the medialplantar pouche of tarsocrural joint. This figure could be considered as a "false thoroughpin".

Page 13 — Barrey E and Langlois B

INRA, Station de Génétique Quantitative et Appliquée, Groupe cheval.
F-78352 Jouy-en-Josas Cedex, France.

Barrey E and Valette JP (1993)
Exercise-related parameters of horses competing in show jumping events ranging from a regional to an international level. Ann Zootech 42: 89-98.

Barrey E, Blanchard G and Orange F (1993)
Analyse cinématique du saut d'obstacle chez le cheval de concours hippique: influence du niveau d'épreuve, de l'âge, du sexe, de la race et de l'origine paternelle. Rec Méd Vet 169: 37-43.

Barrey E and Galloux P (1997)
Analysis of the equine jumping technique by accelerometry. Equine Vet J Suppl 23: 45-49.

Barrey E, Valette JP, Jouglin M, Blouin C and Langlois B (1999)
Heritability of percentage of fast myosin heavy chain in skeletal muscles and relationships with the performances. Proceedings of the Fifth International Conference on Equine Exercise Physiology, Jeffcott LB (Ed). Equine Vet J Suppl 30: 289-292.

Bruns E, Rauls B and Bade B (1985)
Die Entwicklung von Selektionskriterien für die Reitpferdezucht. Züchtungskunde 57: 172-182.

Clayton HM, Colborne GR, Burns TE (1995)
Kinematic analysis of successful and unsuccessful attempts to clear a water jump. Equine Vet J Suppl 18: 166-169.

Deuel N and Park J (1990)
Kinematics analysis of jumping sequences of Olympic show jumping horses. In Equine Exercise Physiology 3. Eds: SGB Persson, A Thornton, LB Jeffcott. ICEEP publications, Davis, California. 158-166.

Galloux P and Barrey E (1997)
Components of the total kinetic moment in jumping horse. Equine Vet J Suppl 23: 41-44.

Langlois B (1975)
Interpretation statistique et génétique des gains des chevaux dans les compétitions équestres françaises. Livest Prod Sci 2: 191-204.

Leach DH, Ormrod K, Clayton HM (1984)
Stride characteristics of horses competing in Grand prix jumping. Am J Vet Res 45: 888-892.

Merkens HW, Schamhardt HC, Van Oscht GJVM, van den Bogert AJ G (1991)
Ground reaction force analysis of Dutch Warmblood horses at canter and jumping. In Equine Exercise Physiology 3. Eds: SGB Persson, A Thornton, LB Jeffcott. ICEEP publications, Davis, California. 128-135.

Preuschoft H (1989)
The external forces and internal stresses in the feet of dressage and jumping horses. Zts Säugetierkunde 54: 172-190.

Schamhardt HC, Merkens HW, Vogel V and Willekens C (1993)
External loads on the limbs of jumping horses at take-off and landing. Am J Vet Res 54: 675-680.

Tavernier A (1990)
Estimation of breeding value of jumping horses from their ranks. Livest Prod Sci 26: 277-290.

Van den Bogert AJ, Jansen MO and Deuel NR (1993)
Kinematics of the hind limb push-off in elite show jumping horses. Equine Vet J Suppl 17: 80-86.

Page 25   Harris PA

MA, PhD, VetMB, MRCVS Equine Studies Group Waltham Centre for Pet Nutrition Waltham-on-the-Wolds,
Leistershire LE14 4RT England

1 Balsom PD, Ekblom B, Söderlund K, Sjödin B and Hultman E (1993a)
Creatine uptake and dynamic high intensity exercise. Scand J Med Sci Sports 3: 143-149.

2 Birch R, Noble D and Greenhaff P L (1994)
The influence of dietary creatine supplementation on performance during repeated bouts of maximal isokinetic cycling in man. Eur J appl Physiol 69: 268-270.

3 Clarke LL, Roberts MC, Argenzio RA. 1990.
Feeding and digestive problems in horses: Physiologic responses to a con-centrated meal. Vet Clin North Am Equine Pract 6: 433-50.

4 Covalesky Me, Russoniello CR and Malinowski K (1992)
Effects of showjumping performance stress on plasma cortisol and lactate concentration and heart rate and behaviour in horses. J Equine Vet Sci 12: 244 –251.

5 Cuddeford D (1996)
Equine Nutrition. Crowood Press ISBN 1-85223-852-6.

6 Duren SE Pagan JD Harris PA and Crandell K (1999)
Time if feeding and fat supplementation affect plasma concentrations of insulin and metabolites during exercise. Equine Vet J Suppl 30: 479 – 484

7 Earnest C P, Snell P G, Rodriquez R, Almada A L and Mitchell T L (1995)
The effect of creatine monohydrate ingestion on anaerobic power indices, muscular strength and body composition. Acta Physiol Scand 153: 207-209.

8 Eaton M D, Hodgson D R, Evans D L, Bryden W L and Rose R J (1995)
Effect of a diet containing supplementary fat on the capacity for high inten-sity exercise Equine Exercise Physiology 4. Equine vet J Suppl 18: 353-356.

9 Fassbender HM, Bach GL, Haase W, Rovati LC, and Setnikar I (1994)
Glucosamine sulphate compared to ibuprofen in osteoarthritis of the knee. Osteoarthritis and cartilage 2: 61-69.

10 Fenton J I , Chlebek-Brown, K A., Caron J.P and Orth M.W (1999a)
Glucosamine inhibits cartilage degradation in equine articular cartilage explants. Proceedings of the Equine Nutrition and Physiology Society: 52 –53.

11 Fenton J I , Chlebek-Brown, K A., Nielsen B D, Corn C D , Waite K S and Caron J.P (1999b)
Effect of longeing and glucosamine supplementation on serum markers of

bone and joint metabolism in yearling quarter horses. Can J Vet Res 63: 288-91

12 Frape DL (1998)
Equine Nutrition and Feeding.2nd edition Blackwell Scence ISBN 0-632-04105-6

13 Frape DL. 1994.
Diet and exercise performance in the horse. Proc Nutr Soc 53: 189-206.

14 Freeman D Potter G Schelling G and Krieder J (1988)
Nitrogen metabolism in mature horses at varying levels of work. J Anim Sci 66: 407.

15 Gallagher K, Leech J and Stowe H (1992a)
Protein energy and dry matter consumption by racing thoroughbreds : a field survey. J equine vet Sci 12: 43

16 Gallagher K, Leech J and Stowe H (1992b)
Protein energy and dry matter consumption by racing standardbreds : a field survey. J equine vet Sci 12: 382

17 Graham Thiers P M , Kronfeld DS and Kline KA (1999)
Dietary protein influences acid base responses to repeated sprints. Equine Vet J Suppl 30: 463 – 467.

18 Greenhaff P L, Bodin K, Söderlund K and Hultman E (1994)
The effect of oral creatine supplementation on skeletal muscle phosphocreatine resynthesis. Am J Physiol 266: E725-E730.

19 Greenhaff P L, Casey A, Short A H, Harris R C, Söderlund K and Hultman E (1993)
The influence of oral creatine supplementation on muscle torque during repeated bouts of maximal voluntary exercise in man. Clin Sci 84: 565-571.

20 Hanson RR Smalley LR, Huff GK, White S and Hammad TA (1997)
Oral treatment with a glucosamine-chondroitin sulfate compound for degenerative joint disease in horses: 25 cases. Equine Practice 19: 16-22

21 Harris RC, Marlin DJ, Snow DH. (1991)

Lactate kinetics, plasma ammonia and performance following repeated bouts of maximal exercise. In: Equine Exercise Physiology III Persson SGB, Lindholm A, Jeffcott LB (Eds) Davis, California. ICEEP Publications: 173-178.

22 Harris RC, Söderlund K and Hultman E (1992)

Elevation of creatine in resting and exercised muscle in normal subjects by creatine supplementation. Clin Sci 83: 367-374

23 Harris RC, Viru M G, Greenhaff PL and Hultman E (1993)

The effect of oral creatine supplementation on running performance during short term exercise in man. J Physiol 467: 74P.

24 Harris RC (1994)

Naturally occurring substances. In: Proc 10th Intl Conference Racing Analysts and Veterinarians, Stockholm, Sweden. Kallings P, Bondesson U and Houghton E (eds) R & W Publications, Newmarket: 79 - 84.

25 Harris PA, Frape DL, Jeffcott LB, Lucas DM Meyer H and Savage CJ (1995)

Equine Nutrition and Metabolic Diseases. In: Equine Manual Higgins AJ & Wright I M (eds) WB Saunders London.

26 Harris PA (1997)

Energy sources and requirements of the exercising horse Ann Rev Nutr 17: 185 - 210.

27 Harris PA and Harris R (1998)

Nutritional ergogenic aids in the horse - uses and abuses. In: Proc of the Conf on Equ Sports Med and Sci. Lindner A (ed) Wageningen Press. The Netherlands: 203–218.

28 Holland et al (1996)

Behaviour of horses is affected by soy lecithin and corn oil in the diet. J Anim Sci 74: 1252 – 1255.

29 Hughes SL, Potter GD, Greene LW, Odom TW and Murray-Gerzik M (1995)

Adaptation of Thoroughbred horses in training to a fat supplemented diet. Equine vet J Suppl 18: 349-352.

30 Kienzle E, Radicke S, Wilke S, Landes E, Meyer H (1992)
Praeileale Stärkeverdauung in Abhängigkeit von Stärkeart und -zuberei-
tung (Pre-ileal starch digestion in relation to source and preparation of
starch). 2. Europäische Konferenz über die Ernährung des Pferdes,
Hannover: 103-106.

31 Kronfeld DS and Harris PA (1997)
Feeding the Equine Athlete for Competition. In: The Veterinarians Practical
Reference to Equine Nutrition, American Association of Equine
Practitioners

32 Kronfeld DS (1996)
Dietary fat affects heat production and other variables of equine performance under hot and humid conditions. Equine Vet J Suppl 22: 24 - 35.

33 Lawrence LM Soderholm LV Roberts AM and Hintz HF (1993)
Feeding status affects glucose metabolism in exercising horses. J Nutr
1123: 2151-2157.

34 Lawrence LM, Hintz HF, Soderholm LV, Williams J and Roberts AM (1995)
Effect of time of feeding on metabolic responses to exercise. Equine Vet J
Suppl 18: 392-395.

35 McIlwraith W (1999)
What is new in medical treatment of joint disease. 3rd Maastricht
International congress on Equine Medicine.

36 McMiken DF (1983)
An energetic basis of equine performance. Equine Vet J 15: 123- 125.

37 Meyer H, Ahlswede L and Reinhardt HJ (1975)
Untersuchungen über Fressdauer;„Kaufrequenz und Futterzerkleinerung
beim Pferd. Deutsche Tierärztliche Wochenschrift 82: 49- 96.

38 Meyer H (1987)
Nutrition of the Equine Athlete. Equine Exercise Physiology 2: 645 – 673.

39 Meyer H., Radicke A., Kienzle E., Wilke S and Kleffken D (1993)
Investigations of Preileal digestion of oats, corn and barley Starch in relati-
on to grain processing. Proc 13th Equine Nutr Physiol Symp Gainesville,
Florida: 92

40 Meyers MC, Potter GD, Evans JW, Greene LW and Crouse SF (1989)
Physiologic and metabolic responses of exercising horses fed added dietary fat. J Equine vet Sci 9: 218-223.

41 National Research Council (1989)
Nutrient requirements of horses. 5th edition, Washington DC National Academy press.

42 Orme CE, Harris RC, Marlin DJ and Hurley JS (1997)
Metabolic adaptation to a fat supplemented diet in the thoroughbred horse. Br J Nutr 78: 443-458.

43 Pagan JD (1998)
Proceedings of Alltechs first Annual Equine School.

44 Pagan JD (1999)
Vitamins, trace elements and electrolytes for the performance horse. Proc of the BEVA specialist day on Equine Nutrition: 63 -66

45 Pagan JD and Harris PA (1999)
The effects of timing and amount of forage and grain on exercise response in Thoroughbred horses. Equine Vet J Suppl 30: 451-457.

46 Potter GD, Hughes SL, Julen TR, Swinney DDL (1992)
A review of research on digestion and utilisation of fat by the equine. Pferdeheilkunde: 119 -123.

47 Rodiek A, Bonvicin S, Stull C and Arana M (1991)
Glycaemic and endocrine responses to corn or alfafla fed prior to exercise . Equine exercise Physiology 3 Persson SGV, Lindholm A, and Jeffcott LB (Eds), ICEEP publications, Davis, California: 323-330.

48 Scott BD, Potter GD, Greene LW, Hargis PS and Anderson JG (1992)
Efficacy of a fat-supplemented diet on muscle glycogen concentration in exercising Thoroughbred horses maintained in varying body conditions. J Equine vet Sci 12: 109-113.

49 Sewell DA and Harris RC (1995)
Effect of creatine supplementation in the Thoroughbred horse. Equine vet J Suppl 18: 239-242.

50 Theodasakis J, Adderly B and Fox B (1997)
The Arthritis Cure. St Martins Press New York.

51 Vandenberghe K, Goris M, Van Hecke P, Van Leemputte M, Vangerven L and Hespel P (1997)
Long-term creatine intake is beneficial to muscle performance during training. J Appl Physiol 83: 2055-2063.

52 Wright I (1999)
Can Supplements help heal joint injuries. Horse and Hound Nov 18th: 69.

Page 45   Mikael Holmström

Horse Evaluation System AB
Brorslundsvägen 19c, SE 236 34 Höllviken, Sweden

Boldt H (1978)
Das Dressurpherd. H Haberbeck and HR Haberbeck, Verlagsgesellschaft GmbH. Lage-Lippe. 60-71 (ISBN 3-921879-03-5).

Bourgelat C (1750)
Elémens d'Hippiatique au Nouveaux Principes sur la Connaissance et sur la Médicine de Chevaux. T 1, Lyon.

Ehrengranat A (1818)
Om hästens rörelser i deras samband med ridkonsten. [In Swedish] Lund.

Holmström M, Magnusson LE and Philipsson J (1990)
Variation in conformation of Swedish Warmblood horses and conformational characteristics of elite sport horses. Equine vet J 22: 186-193.

Holmström M and Philipsson J (1993)
Relationship between conformation, performance and health in 4-year old Swedish Warmblood Riding Horses. Livestock Prod Sci, 33: 293-312.

Hörman J (1837)
Hästens exteriör. Hästen både naturhistoriskt och tekniskt betraktad. [In Swedish] Skara. 39-122.

Magnusson LE (1985)
Studies on the conformation and related traits of Standardbred trotters in

Sweden. I. An objective method for measuring the equine conformation. Thesis. SLU, Skara (ISBN 91-576-2315-5).

Page 57 Lopez Rivero JL[1] and Islas Letelier A[2]

[1] Laboratory of Muscular Biopathology, Department of Comparative Anatomy and Pathological Anatomy, Faculty of Veterinary Sciences, University of Córdoba,
Córdoba, Spain; Phone: Int + 34 957 21 81 43; Fax: Int + 34 957 21 88 47; email: an1lorij@uco.es
[2] Department of Clinical Sciences, Faculty of Veterinary Medicine, University of Concepción,
Chillán, Chile

Andrews FM, Reed SM and Johnson GC (1993)
Muscle biopsy in the horse: its indications, techniques and complications. Vet Med US - Equine Pract 3: 293-322.

Barrey E (1997)
Locomotion variables. In: Performance diagnosis of horses. A Lindner (Ed). Wageningen Pers, Wageningen, The Netherlands: 72-96.

Barrey E and Galloux P (1997)
Analysis of the equine jumping technique by accelerometry. Equine Vet J Suppl 23: 45-49.

Clayton HM (1990)
Conditioning for dressage and jumping horses. In: Proceedings of the International Conference on Equine Sports Medicine. P Kallings (Ed). Almqvist & Wiksell Tryckeri, Uppsala: 51-53.

Clayton HM (1994)
Training show jumpers. In: The Equine Athlete. DR Hodgson and RJ Rose (Eds). WB Saunders Company, Philadelphia: 429–438.

Clayton HM, Colborne GR and Burns TE (1995)
Kinematic analysis of successful and unsuccessful attempts to clear a water jump. Equine Vet J Suppl 18: 166-169.

Covalesky ME, Russoniello CR and Malinowski K (1992)
Effects of show-jumping performance stress on plasma cortisol and lactate concentrations and heart rate and behaviour in horses. J Equine Vet Sci 12: 244.

Divers TJ, Valentine BA, Jackson CA, VanMetre DC and Mohammed HO (1996)
Simple practical muscle biopsy test for motor neuron disease. Proc Am Assoc Equine Pract 42: 180-181.

Huxley HE (1969)
The mechanism of muscular contraction. Science 164: 1335-1346.

Islas A, Bernal A, Rivero JLL, Quezada M, Merino V, Mora G, Briones M, Escalona C, Espinoza A and Marín L (1997)
Histochemistry and biochemistry characteristics of gluteus medius muscle fibers in inactive jumping horses. In: Proc Assoc Eq Sports Med: 4-7.

Islas A, Rivero, JLL, Quezada M, Merino V, Mora G and Bernales A (1998)
Muscular adaptations of young Chilean horses in training for jumping competition. In: Conf on Eq Sport Med Sci. (CESMAS). A Lindner (Ed), Wageningen Pers, Wageningen: 242-244.

Jeffcott LB, Rossdale PD, Freeston J, Frank CJ and Towers-Clark PF (1982)
An assessment of wastage in Thoroughbred racing from conception to 4 yrs of age. Equine Vet J 14: 185-198.

Lindholm A and Piehl K (1974)
Fibre composition, enzyme activity and concentrations of metabolites and electrolytes in muscles of standarbred horses. Acta Vet Scand 15: 325-339.

Lindholm A (1998)
Relationship between back problems and muscle disorders: possibilities of prevention and therapy. In: Conf Eq Sports Med Sci (CESMAS). A Lindner (Ed), Wageningen Pers, Wageningen: 140-145

López Rivero JL, Agüera E, Morales-López JL, Galisteo AM and Vivo J (1990)
Muscle fibre size in horses. Equine Ath 3: 1-11.

López-Rivero JL, Serrano AL, Diz AM and Galisteo AM (1992)
Variability of muscle fibre composition and fibre size in the horse gluteus medius: an enzyme-histochemical and morphometric study. J Anat 181: 1-10.

Merkens HW, Schamhardt HC, van Oscht GJVM and van den Bogert AJ (1991)
Ground reaction force analysis of Dutch Warmblood horses at canter and jumping. In: Eq Exer Phys 3. SGB Persson, A Thornton and LB Jeffcott (Eds). ICEEP Publications, Davis, California: 128-135.

Morris E, Seeherman HJ and O'Callaghan MW (1991)
Scintigraphyc identification of skeletal muscle damage in horses 24 hours after strenuous exercise. Equine Vet J 23: 347.

Rivero JLL, Serrano AL, Henckel P and Agüera E (1993a)
Muscle fibre type composition and fibre size in successfully and unsuccesfully endurance-raced horses. J Appl Physiol 75: 1758-1766.

Rivero JLL, Serrano AL, Diz AM and Morales JL (1993b)
Changes in cross-sectional area and capillary supply of the muscle fibre population in equine gluteus medius muscle as a function of sampling depth. Am J Vet Res 54: 32-37.

Rivero JLL, Talmadge RJ and Edgerton VR (1996a)
Myosin heavy chain isoforms in adult equine skeletal muscle: an immunohistochemical and electrophoretic study. Anat Rec 246: 185-194.

Rivero JLL, Islas A, Quezada M, Mora G, Briones M, López J, Aguirre G and Marín L (1996b)
Histochemical properties and enzyme activities of skeletal muscle in Chilean draught horses. Pferderheilkunde 12: 514-517.

Rivero JLL (1999)
Muscle biopsy as an aid in the diagnosis of muscle disorders related with low performance syndrome in the horse. In: SISVet Ann Meet Sel Abs 1: 13-20.

Rivero JLL and Serrano AL (1999)
Skeletal myosin heavy chain composition and carriage training. Equine Vet J Suppl 30: 318-323.

Rivero JLL, Talmadge RJ and Edgerton VR (1999)
Interrelationships of myofibrillar ATPase activity and metabolic properties of myosin heavy chain-based fibre types in rat skeletal muscle. Histochem Cell Biol 111: 277-287.

Rivero JLL and Glitz F (2000)
Polysaccharide storage myopathy in horses: differential diagnosis with unspecific exertional rhabdomyolysis. In: "The Elite Show Jumper". A Lindner (Ed), Arbeitsgruppe Pferd, Essen, Germany.

Serrano AL, Miró F, Rivero JLLL y Galisteo AM (1996a)
Parámetros cinemáticas del paso y el trote en caballos Españoles jóvenes entrenados y no entrenados y relación con las características musculares. En: Características musculares y análisis de la locomoción del caballo: Adaptaciones con el entrenamiento y correlación con el rendimiento deportivo. AL Serrano, Tesis Doctoral, University of Córdoba, Spain: 71-85.

Serrano AL, Petrie JL, Rivero JLL and Hermanson JW (1996b)
Myosin isoforms and muscle fibre characteristics in equine gluteus medius muscle. Anat Rec 244: 444-451.

Snow DH and Valberg SJ (1994)
Muscle anatomy, physiology, and adaptations to exercise and training. In: The Equine Athlete. DR Hodgson and RJ Rose (Eds) WB Saunders Company, Philadelphia: 144–179.

Valberg SJ, Macleay JM and Mickelson JR (1997)
Exertional rhabdomyolysis and polysaccharide storage myopathy. Comp Cont Educ Pract Vet 19: 1077.

Valentine B (1996)
Muscle biopsy diagnosis of equine motor neuron disease (EMND) and equine polysaccharide storage myopathy (PSSM). Vet Pathol 33: 389.

van den Bogert AJ, Jansen MO and Deuel NR (1994)
Kinematics of the hind limb push-off in elite show jumping horses. Equine Vet J Suppl 17: 80-86.

Willian RS and Neufer PD (1996)
Regulation of gene expression in skeletal muscle by contractile activity. In: Handbook of physiology: integration of motor, circulatory, respiratory and metabolic control during exercise. LB Rowell and JT Shepherd (Eds), American Physiological Society, Bethesda, MD: 1124-1150.

Page 79   Powers P and Harrison D

Department of Physical Education and Sport Sciences
University of Limerick Ireland

Alexander R Mc N and Bennett-Clarke HC (1977)
Storage of elastic strain energy in muscle and other tissues. Nature 265: 114-117.

Blignault K (1997)
Successful Schooling. Train your horse with empathy. London: JA Allen & Company Limited.

Clayton HM (1997)
Effect of added weight on landing kinematics in jumping horses. Eq Vet J Supplement 23: 50-53.

Clayton HM (1990)
Kinematics of equine jumping. Equine Athlete 3: 17-20.

Clayton HM (1989)
Terminology for the description of equine jumping kinematics. J Eq Vet Sci 9: 341-348.

Clayton HM and Barlow DA (1991)
Stride Characteristics of Four Grand Prix Jumping Horses. In: Equine Exercise Physiology 3. SGB Persson, A Lindholm and LB Jeffcott (Eds). Davis, California: ICEEP Publications. Pp 151-157.

Clayton HM and Barlow DA (1989)
The effect of fence height and width on the limb placements of showjumping horses. J Eq Vet Sci 9: 179-185.

Clayton HM, Colborne GR and Burns TE (1995)
Kinematic analysis of successful and unsuccessful attempts to clear a water jump. Eq Vet J Supplement 18: 166-169.

Clayton HM, Colborne GR, Lanovaz J and Burns TE (1996)
Linear kinematics of water jumping in Olympic showjumpers. Pferdheilkunde 12: 657-660.

Colborne GR, Clayton HM and Lanovaz J (1995)
Factors that influence vertical velocity during take off over a water jump. Eq Vet J Supplement 18: 138–140.

Deuel NR and Park J (1991)
Kinematic analysis of jumping sequences of Olympic show jumping horses. In: Equine Exercise Physiology 3. SGB Persson, A Lindholm and LB Jeffcott (Eds). Davis, California: ICEEP Publications. Pp 158-166.

Galloux P and Barrey E (1997)
Components of the total kinetic moment in jumping horses. Eq Vet J Supplement 23: 41–44.

Hadley S (1987)
Training the Showjumper. London: Threshold Books.

Hall SJ (1995)
Basic Biomechanics, 2nd ed St. Louis, MO: Mosby-Year Book, Inc.

Hartley Edwards E (1994)
The Encyclopaedia of the Horse. London: Dorling Kindersley Limited.

Hay JG (1985)
The Biomechanics of Sports Techniques, 3rd ed. Englewood Cliffs, New Jersey: Prentice Hall.

Hay JG (1986)
The biomechanics of the long jump. Exercise and Sports Science Review 14: 401-446.

Klimke R (1989)
Basic training of the young horse. London: JA Allen & Company Limited.

Komi PV and Bosco C (1978)
Utilization of Stored Elastic Energy in leg extensor muscles by men and women. Med Sci Sports 10: 261-265.

Leach DH and Dagg AJ (1983)
A review of research on equine locomotion and biomechanics. Eq Vet J 15: 93-102.

Leach DH, Ormrod K and Clayton HM (1984)
Stride characteristics of horses competing in Grand Prix jumping. Am J Vet Res 45: 888-892.

Meyer H (1996)
Zum Zusammenhang von Halshaltung, Rückentätigkeit und Bewegungsablauf beim Pferd. Pferdeheilkunde 12: 807-822.

Powers PNR (2000)
Performance Evaluation of the Sport Horse. PhD Thesis, University of Limerick.

Powers PNR and Harrison AJ (1999)
Models for biomechanical analysis of jumping horses. J Eq Vet Sci 19: 799-806.

Powers, PNR., Harrison AJ and Storey NB (1999)
Kinematic analysis of take off parameters during loose jumping in young untrained horses. In: Proceedings of the XVII International Symposium on Biomechanics in Sports. Sanders RH and Gibson BJ (Eds). Perth, Western Australia: School of Biomedical and Sports Science: 101-104.

Serio T (1992)
Perfecting form over fences. Practical Horseman, March, pp 34–35.

Page 91   Aguilera-Tejero E, Estepa JC, López I, Bas S, Garfia B and Rodríguez M*

Dpt. Medicina y Cirugía Animal, Universidad de Córdoba, Campus Universitario de Rabanales, Ctra Madrid-Cádiz km 396, 14014 Córdoba, Spain and
***Unidad de Investigación**
Hospital Universitario Reina Sofía de Córdoba, Spain.

Aguilera-Tejero E, Garfia B, Estepa JC, López I, Mayer-Valor R and Rodríguez M (1998)
Effects of exercise and EDTA administration on blood ionized calcium and parathyroid hormone concentrations in horses. Am J Vet Res 12: 1605-1607.

Estepa JC, Aguilera-Tejero E, Mayer-Valor R, Almadén Y, Felsenfeld AJ and Rodríguez M (1998)
Measurement of parathyroid hormone in horses. Equine vet J 30: 476-481.

Geiser DR, Andrews FM, Rohrbach BW, White SL, Maykuth PL, Green EM and Provenza MK (1995)
Blood ionized calcium concentrations in horses before and after the cross-country phase of three-day event competition. Am J Vet Res 56: 1502-1505.

Hodgson DR (1993)
Exercise-associated myopathy: is calcium the culprit? Equine vet J 25: 1-3.

Lindinger MI and Ecker GL (1995)
Ion and water losses from body fluids during a 163 km endurance ride. Equine vet J Suppl 18: 314-322.

Snow DH, Kerr MG, Nimmo MA and Abbott EM (1982)
Alterations in blood, sweat, urine and muscle composition during prolonged exercise in the horse. Vet Rec 110: 377-384.

Page 95   Cassiat G[1], Degueurce C[1], Pourcelot P[1], Tavernier L[2], Geiger D[3], Denoix JM[1]

[1] **UMR INRA-DGER Biomécanique du Cheval,**
Ecole Nationale Vétérinaire d'Alfort, 94704 Maisons-Alfort cedex;
[2] **Section hippique du CEZ de Rambouillet,** 78000 Rambouillet;
[3] **Laboratoire de Mécanique Physique,**
CNRS UPRES-A 7052, Université Paris XII Val de Marne, 94000 Créteil;
All France

1. Abdel-Aziz H, Karara H (1971)
Direct linear transformation from comparator coordinates in object-space coordinates in close-range photogrammetry, Proc Congress Am Soc Photogrammetry, Urbana, Illinois: 1-18.

2. Clayton HM, Barlow DA (1989)
The effect of fence height and width on the limb placements of show jumping horses. J Eq Vet Sci 9: 179-185.

3. Clayton HM, Barlow DA (1991)
Stride characteristics of four Grand Prix jumping horses. Equine Exerc Physiol 3. Eds: SGB Persson, A Lindholm, LB Jeffcott. ICEEP Publications, Davis, California: 151-157.

4. Clayton HM, Colborne GR, Burns TE (1995)
Kinematic analysis of successful and unsuccessful attempts to clear a water jump. Equine Vet J Suppl 18: 166-169.

5. Clayton HM, Colborne GR, Lanovaz J, Burns TE (1996)
Linear kinematics of water jumping in olympic show jumpers. Pferdeheilkunde 12: 657-660.

6. Colborne GR, Clayton HM, Lanovaz J (1995)
Factors that influence vertical velocity during take off over a water jump. Equine Vet J Suppl 18: 138-140.

7. Deuel NR, Park J (1991)
inematic analysis of Jumping Sequences of olympic show jumping horses. Equine Exerc Physiol 3. Eds : SGB Persson, A Lindholm, LB Jeffcott, ICEEP Publications, Davis, California: 158-166.

8. Dufosset JM, Langlois B (1984)
Analyse statistique du geste à l'obstacle de 122 chevaux de selle français et intérêt du jugement du saut en liberté. CEREOPA Compte-rendu de 10e journée d'étude: 2-26.

9. Leach DH, Ormrod K (1984)
The technique of jumping a steeplechase fence by competing event-horses. Appl Anim Behav Sci 12: 15-24.

10. Leach DH, Ormrod K, Clayton HM (1984)
Stride characteristics of horses competing in Grand Prix jumping. Am J Vet Res, 45: 888-892.

11. Pourcelot P, Audigié F, Degueurce C, Denoix JM (1997)
- EKAS: An equine kinematic analysis system for clinical gait analysis (conférence). 5th Congress of the World Equine Veterinary Association, Padova, abstract publié dans Rivista Sidi, 3: 55.

12. Van den Bogert A J, Jansen MO, Deuel NR (1994)
Kinematics of the hind limb push-off in elite show jumping. Equine Vet J Suppl 17: 80-86.

Page 103   **Coenen M[1], Vervuert I[1], Harmeyer J[2], Wedemeyer U[1], Chobrock C[2] and Sporleder HP[2]**

Department of Animal Nutrition[1] and Department of Physiology[2]
School of Veterinary Medicine Hannover, Bischofsholer Damm 15, D-30173 Hannover

Desmecht D, Linden A, Amory H, Art T and Lekeux P (1996)
Relationship of plasma lactate production to cortisol release following completion of different types of sporting events in horses. Vet Res Comm 20: 371-379.

Dybdal NO, Gribble D, Madigan JE and Stabenfeldt GH (1980)
Alterations in plasma corticosteroids, insulin and selected metabolites in horses used in endurance rides. Equine vet J 3: 137-140.

González O, González E, Sánchez C, Pinto J, González I, Enríquez O, Martínez R, Filgueira G and White A (1998)
Effect of exercise on erythrocyte ß-adrenergic receptors and plasma concentrations of catecholamines and thyroid hormones in Thoroughbred horses. Equine vet J 30: 72-78.

Greiwe J, Hickner RC, Shah S, Cryer P and Holloszy JO (1999)
Norepinephrine responses to exercise at the same relative intensity before and after endurance exercise training. J Appl Physiol 86: 531-535.

Kurosawa M, Nagata S, Takeda F, Mima K, Hiraga A, Kai M and Taya K (1998)
Plasma catecholamine, adrenocorticotropin and cortisol responses to exhaustive incremental treadmill exercise of the Thoroughbred horse. J Equine Sci 9: 9-18.

Lehmann M, Dickhuth HH, Schmid P, Porzig H and Keul J (1984)
Plasma catecholamines, beta-adrenergic receptors and isoproterenol sensitivity in endurance trained and non-endurance trained volunteers. Eur J Appl Physiol 52: 362-369.

Mazzeo RS and Marshall P (1989)
Influence of plasma catecholamines on the lactate threshold during graded exercise. J Appl Physiol 67: 1319-1322.

Snow DH and Rose RJ (1981)
Hormonal changes associated with long distance exercise. Equine vet J 13: 195-197.

Snow DH, Harris RC, MacDonald A, Forster CD and Marlin DJ (1992)
Effects of high-intensity exercise on plasma catecholamines in the Thoroughbred horses. Equine vet J 24: 462-467.

Page 113   Fazio E, Alberghina D, Aronica V, Medica P and Ferlazzo A

Institute of Veterinary Physiology,
University of Messina, Italy

Clayton HM (1989)
J Equine Vet Sci 9: 341.

Ferlazzo A, Fazio E, Iannelli N, Murania C, Panzera M and Piccione G (1993)
Atti Soc it di Ippol 11: 25-28.

Ferlazzo A, Fazio E, Aronica V, Di Majo R, Medica P and Grasso L (1998)
Proc 2nd Conference on Equine Sports Medicine and Science: 53-56.

Foreman JH and Ferlazzo A (1996)
Pferdeheilkunde 12: 401-404.
Lekeux P, Art T, Desmecht D and Amory H (1991)
Equine Exercise Physiol 3: 385-390.

Linden A, Art T, Amory H, Desmecht D and Lekeux P (1991)
Equine Exercise Physiol 3: 391-396.

McCarthy RN, Jeffcott LB, Funder JW, Fullertone M and Clarke IJ (1991)
Austr Vet J 68: 359-361.

Page 117

Giovagnoli G[1], Reitano M[2] and Silvestrelli M[1]

[1] **Centro di Studio del Cavallo Sportivo - Università di Perugia,**
Italia.
[2] **Ispettorato Logistico Esercito Italiano,**
Dipartimento Sanità e Veterinaria, Roma, Italia.

Giovagnoli G, Pieramati C, Castellano G, Reitano M, Silvestrelli M (1998)
Analysis of neck muscle (splenius) activity during jumping by surface video-electromyography technique. Proc Conf on Equ Sports Med and Sci (CESMAS) Cordoba, Spain, Arno Lindner (Ed): 57-60.

Grillner S (1985)
Neurobiological bases of rhythmic motor acts in vertebrates. Science 228: 143-149.

Robert TDM (1967)
Neurophysiology, Butterworth, London, UK: 354.

Page 127

Goldberger N and Martinez A

Physiology Sciences Department,
College of Veterinary Medicine, Central University of Venezuela, Maracay, Aragua, Venezuela.

Holesch H (1993)
Praxis der Hämatogenen Oxydations-Therapie (HOT) und der Ultraviolett-Bestrahlung des Blutes. UVB Verlag, München. Pp 27.

Stadtlaender H (1980)
Hämatogene Oxidationstherapie-HOT (Fotobiologische Oxydationstherapie). Kurzgefaßte Fibel. Theoritische und Praktische Einführung mit Anleitung für die Therapie mit dem HOT-Great. UV-med-S Verlag Königstein Taurus. Pp 93.

Steel RGD and Torrie JH (1992)
Bioestadística principios y procedimientos. 2Da Edicion (1era en español) Mcgraw-Hill. Interamericana. Mexico. Pp 526-528.

Turowski A, Paulistchke M and Wack R (1991)

Die Behandlung chronischer Leberkrankungen mit der hämatogenen oxy-dationstherapie (HOT). Ärztezeitschr Naturheilverf 32: 12-19.

Page 131   Gondim F, Silveira LR, Pereira-da-Silva L, Macedo DV

Lab de Bioquímica do Exercício,

Depto Bioquímica, IB/UNICAMP, Campinas, SP, Brasil
gondim@obelix.unicamp.br

(1) Viru A (1984)

The mechanism of training effects: A hypothesis. International Journal Sports Medicine 5: 219-227.

(2) Kuipers H (1997)

Training and overtraining: NA introduction. Medicine and Science in Sports and Exercise 30: 1137-1139.

(3) Davies KJ, Quintanilha AT, Brooks GA. and Packer L (1982)

Free radicals and tissue damage produced by exercise. Biochemical Biophysical Research Communication 107: 1198-1205.

(4) Imlay JA and Linn S (1988)

DNA damage and oxygen radical toxicity. Science 240: 1302.

(5) Fitts RH (1994)

Cellular mechanisms of muscle fatigue. Physiological Review 74: 49-94.

(6) Yagi K (1976)

A simple fluorimetric assay for lipoperoxide in blood plasma. Biochemical Medicine 15: 212-216.

(7) Levine RL, Garland D and Oliver CN

Determination of carbonyl content in oxidatively modified proteins. Methods Enzymology 186: 464-478.

(8) Smith IK, Vierheller TL and Thorne CA. (1988)
Assay of glutathione reductase in crude tissue homogenates using 5,5(-dithiobis(2-nitrobenzoic acid). Analytical Biochemistry 175: 408-413.

(9) Aebi H (1984)
Catalase. Methods in Enzymology 105: 121-126.

Page 137   **Hanzawa K, Kubo K [1], Kai M [2], Hiraga A [2] and Watanabe S**

Laboratory of Animal Physiology, Tokyo University of Agriculture,
1-1, Sakuragaoka 1 chome, Setagaya-ku Tokyo, 156-8502;
[1]**Japan Livestock Technology Association,**
9-20 Yushima 3 chome, Bunkyo-ku, Tokyo, 113-0034;
[2]**Equine Research Institute, Japan Racing Association,**
321-4, Togami-cho, Utsunomiya, Tochigi, 320-0856; all Japan.

Hanzawa K, Kubo K, Kai M, Hiraga A and Watanabe S (1995)
Effects of exercise on erythrocytes in normal and splenectomized Thoroughbred horses. Equine vet J Suppl 18: 439-442

Hanzawa K, Kubo K, Kai M, Hiraga A and Watanabe S (1998)
Effects of the spleen on osmotic fragility of circulating red cells in Thoroughbred horses during exercise. In; The book of 1st conference on Equine Sports Medicine and Science (CESMAS), Cordoba, Spain: 65-68

Hanzawa K, Orihara K, Kubo K, Yamanobe A, Hiraga A and Watanabe S (1992)
Changes of plasma amino acid and inorganic ion concentrations with maximum exercises in Thoroughbred young horses. Jpn J Equine Sci 3: 157-162.

Kent JE and Goodall J (1991)
Assessment of an immunoturbidimetric method for measuring equine serum haptoglobin concentrations. Equine Vet J 23: 59-66.

Mills PC, Auer DE, Kramer H, Barry D and Ng JC (1998)
Effects of inflammation-associated acute-phase response on hepatic and renal indices in the horse. Aust Vet J 76: 187-194.

Putnum FW (1975)
Haptoglobin. The plasma proteins: Structure, function, and genetic control. 2nd ed. (Putnum FW eds.) Academic Press, New York: 2-50

Page 141   Hyyppä S

Agricultural Research Centre,
Equine Research, FIN-32100 Ypäjä, Finland

Fregin GF and Thomas DP (1983)
Cardiovascular response to exercise in the horse. A review. Snow DH, Persson SGB, Rose RJ (eds): Equine Exercise Physiology, Granta Editions, Cambridge: 76.

Hyyppä S and Pösö AR (1996)
Interval training at anaerobic threshold in Standardbred trotters. Pferdeheilkunde 12: 706.

Marlin DJ, Harris RC, Harman JC and Snow DH (1987)
Influence of post-exercise activity on rates of muscle and blood lactate disappearance in the Thorougbred horse. In: Gillespie JR and Robinson NE (eds) Equine Exercise Physiology 2, ICEEP Publications, Davis, CA: 321.

Marlin DJ, Harris RC and Snow DH (1991)
Rates of Blood Lactate disappearance following exercise of different intensities. In: Persson SGB, Lindholm A, Jefcott LB (eds) Equine Exercise Physiology 3, ICEEP Publications, Uppsala, Sweden: 188.

Persson SGB (1983)
Evaluation of exercise tolerance and fitness in the performance horse. In: Snow DH, Persson SGB, Rose RJ (eds) Equine Exercise Physiology, Granta Editions, Cambridge: 441.

Poole RC and Halestrap AP (1993)
Transport of lactate and other monocarboxylates across mammalian plasma membranes. Am J Physiol 264: C 761.

Väihkönen LK, Hyyppä S and Pösö AR (1999)
Factors affecting accumulation of lactate in red blood cells. Equine vet J Suppl 30: 443.

Page 149   **Lightowler CH** [1]**, Pidal G** [1]**, Mercado MC** [1] **and Cattaneo ML** [2]

[1] **Department of Medicine and** [2] **Department of Preventive Medicine and Public Health School of Veterinary Sciences.**
University of Buenos Aires. Chorroarín 280 (1427) Buenos Aires. Argentina

1 Devereux MD et al (1977)
Echocardiographic determination of left ventricular mass in man. Circulation 55: 613.

2 Hodgson DR et al (1994)
Evaluation of performance potential. In Hodgson D and Rose R. Principles and practice of Equine Sport Medicine. The Athletic Horse. WB Saunders: 238.

3 Kline H et al (1991)
Heart and spleen weights as a function of breed and somatotype. In Persson SGB, Lindholm A, Jeffcott LB (eds). Equine Exercise Physiology 3. Davis, Califorina ICEEP Publications: 17.

4 Kubo K et al (1974)
Relationship between training and heart in the thorough-bred racehorse. Exp Rep Equine Health Lab 11: 87.

5 O'Callagham MW (1985)
Comparison of echocardiography and autopsy measurements of cardiac dimensions in the horse. Equine Vet J 17: 361.

6 Reichek N (1987)
Standardization in the Measurement of Left Ventricular Wall mass. M-mode Echocardiography. Hypertension 9[Suppl II]: II-27-II-29

7 Rose RJ et al (1990)
Clinical exercise testing in the normal thoroughbred racehorse. Aust Vet J 67: 345.

8 Shan DJ et al (1978)
The committee on M-mode standardization of the American Society of Echocardiography. Recommendations regarding quantitation in M-mode echocardiographic methods. Circulation 58:1052.

9 Steel JD (1963)
Studies on electrocardiogram of the racehorse. Australasian Medical Publishing Co Ltd Sydney.

10 Steel JD et al (1974)
Electrocardiography of the horse and potential performance ability. J Sth Afr Vet Ass 45: 263-268.

11 Steel JD et al (1977)
The inheritance of heart score in racehorse. Aust Vet J 53: 306.

Page 157   Nielsen BD[1], Waite KL[1], Bell RA[1] and Rosenstein DS[2]

[1] Department of Animal Science and [2] Department of Large Animal Clinical Science,
Michigan State University, East Lansing, MI 48824-1225, USA

Bell RA, Nielsen BD, Waite K, Heleski C, Rosenstein D and Orth M (2000)
Influence of housing on the third metacarpus and markers of bone and cartilage metabolism in Arabian weanlings. J Anim Sci (submitted).

Hoekstra KE, Nielsen BD, Orth MW, Rosenstein DS, Schott HC and Shelle JE (2000)
Comparison of bone mineral content and biochemical markers of bone metabolism in stall- versus pasture-reared horses. Equine Vet J (in press).

Kimmel DB (1993)
A paradigm for skeletal strength homeostasis. J Bone Miner Res 8: S515.

Jee WSS(1988)
The skeletal tissues. Weiss L (Ed) Histology, Cell and Tissue Biology, Elsevier Biomedical, New York: 207.

Maenpaa PH, Pirskanen A and Koskinen E (1988)
Biochemical indicators of bone formation in foals after transfer from pasture to stables for the winter months. Am J Vet Res 49:1990.

Meakim DW, Ott EA, Asquith RL and Feaster JP (1981)
Estimation of mineral content of the equine third metacarpal by radiographic photometry. J Anim Sci 53: 1019.

Nielsen BD and Potter GD (1997)
Accounting for volumetric differences in estimates of bone mineral content from radiographic densitometry. Proc 15th Equine Nutr Phys Symp: 367.

Norwood GL (1978)
The Bucked-Shin Complex in Thoroughbreds. Proc 24th Am Assoc Equine Pract: 319.

Nunamaker DM, Butterweck DM and Provost MT (1990)
Fatigue fractures in Thoroughbred racehorses: relationships with age, peak bone strain, and training. J Orth Res 8: 604-611.

Raub RH, Jackson SG and Baker JP (1989)
The effect of exercise on bone growth and development in weanling horses. J Anim Sci 67: 2508-2514.

SAS (1997)
SAS System for Mixed Models. SAS Institute Inc, Cary, NC

Page 161   Piccione G, Fazio F, Giudice E*

Istituto di Fisiologia Veterinaria;
***Dipartimento di Medicina e Farmacologia Veterinaria**
Università degli Studi di Messina, Italy

Beckner GL, Winsor T (1954)
Cardiovascular adaptations to prolonged physical effort. Circulation 9: 835.

McKrichnie JK, Leary WP, Joubert SM (1967)
Some electrocardiographic and biochemical changes recorded in marathon runners. J S Afr Med 41: 722.

Nakamoto K (1969)

Electrocardiograms of 25 marathon runner before and after 100 meters dash. Jap Circ J 33: 105.

Nielsen K, Vibe-Petersen G (1980)
Relationship between QRS duration (heart score) and racing performance in trotters. Equine Vet J 12: 81.

Physick-Sheard PW, Hendron CM (1982)
Heart score: physiological basis and confounding variables. In Snow DH, Persson SGB, Rose RJ (Eds) Equine Exercise Physiology. Cambridge, Granata Editions: 121.

Rose R (1997)
Valutazione dell'apparato cardiovascolare a riposo e durante l'esercizio fisico. Atti 3% Congresso Annuale S I V E Medicina Sportiva del Cavallo: 120-130.

Steel JD, Hall MC, Stewart GA (1976)
Cardiac monitoring during exercise test in the horse. 3. Changes in the electrocardiogram during and after exercise. Aust Vet J 52: 6-10.

Steel JD and Stewart GA (1978)
L'elettrocardiografia e le prestazioni agonistiche. In Zannetti G, Del Bue M (1980): Trattato di Medicina e Chirurgia del Cavallo 2, Edizioni Medico Scientifiche, Torino: 1335-1343.

Page 165   Tedeschi D[1], Baragli P[1], Pellegrini Masini A[1], Casini L[2], Ducci M[1], Martelli F[1], Sighieri C[1]

[1]Dipartimento di Anatomia Biochimica e Fisiologia Veterinaria, and
[2]Dipartimento di Produzioni Animali,
Viale delle Piagge 2, Università di Pisa, Italy

Berthoud HR, Laughton WB, Powley TL (1986)
A method for large volume blood sampling and transfusion in rats. Am J Physiol 250: E331-7.

Davies CTM and Few JD (1973)
Effects of exercise on adrenocortical function. J Appl Physiol 35: 887-91.

Desmecht D, Linden A, Amory H, Art T, Lekeux P (1996)
Relationship of plasma lactate production to cortisol release following completion of different types of sporting events in horses. Vet Res Comm 20: 371-9.

Ferlazzo A and Fazio E (1997)
Endocrinological variables in blood and plasma. In: Performance diagnosis of horses (ed Lindner A). Wageningen press: 30-43.

Linden A, Art T, Amory H, Massart AM, Burvenich C, Lekeux P (1991)
Quantitative buffy coat analysis related to adrenocortical function in horses during a three-day event competition. Zentralbl Veterinarmed 38: 376-82.

Martin SM, Bauce LG, Malkinson TJ, Cooper KE (1993)
A method for continuous blood sampling during cold water immersion. Life Sci 53: 611-3.

Tedeschi D, Baragli P, Ducci M, Gatta D, Sighieri C, Martelli F (1998)
A dyalitic system for continuous blood drawing during treadmill exercise. Proceedings 17th AESM meeting: pp 72-73.

Thornton JR (1985)
Hormonal responses to exercise and training. Vet Clin North Am: pp 477-96.

Page 169   Vervuert I[1], Coenen M[1], Harmeyer J[2], Wedemeyer U[1], Chobrock C[2] and Sporleder HP[2]

Department of Animal Nutrition[1] and Department of Physiology[2],
School of Veterinary Medicine Hannover, Bischofsholer Damm 15, D-30173 Hannover

Aguilera-Tejero E, Garfia B, Estepa J, López I, Mayer-Valor R and Rodriguez M (1998)
Effects of exercise and EDTA administration on blood ionized calcium and parathyroid hormone in horses. Am J Vet Res 59: 1605-1607.

Coenen M, Vervuert I, Harmeyer J, Wedemeyer U, Chobrock C and Sporleder HP (2000)
Effects of different types of exercise and training on plasma catecholamines in young horses. CESMAS 2000 (in press).

Dempster D, Cosman W, Parisien M, Shen V and Lindsay R (1993)
Anabolic actions of parathyroid hormone on bone. Endocr Rev 14: 690-709.

Estepa JC, Aguilera-Tejero E, Mayer-Valor R, Almadén Y, Felsenfeld A and Rodriguez M (1998)
Measurement of parathyroid in horses. Equine vet J 30: 476-481.

Heersche J, Bellows C and Aubin J (1994)
Cellular actions of parathyroid hormone on osteoblast and osteoclast differentiation. In: Bilezikian J, Marcus R and Levine M (Eds). The Parathyroids: Basic and Clinical Concepts. New York, Raven Press: 83-91.

Hiney K, Potter G, Bloomfield S and Gibbs P (1999)
Radiographic and biochemical measures of skeletal response to pretraining and race training in two-year-old racehorse. Proc 16th Equine Nutr Physiol Symp: 40-45

Ljunghall S, Akerström G, Benson L, Hetta L, Rudberg C and Wide L (1984)
Effects of epinephrine and norepinephrine on serum parathyroid hormone and calcium in normal subjects. Exp Clin Endocrinol 84: 313-318.

Zerath E, Holy X, Douce P, Guezennec C and Chatard J (1997)
Effect of endurance training on postexercise parathyroid hormone levels in elderly men. Med Sci Sports Exerc 29: 1139-1145.

Page 181   Fey K, Wenisch T and Sasse HHL

Clinic of Equine Internal Medicine,
University of Giessen, Germany

1. Aguilera TE, Pascoe JR, Tyler WS, Woliner MJ (1995)
Autologous blood instillation alters respiratory mechanics in horses. Equine Vet J 27: 46-50.

2. Beech J. Tracheobronchial Aspirates (1991)
In: Beech J (ed) Equine Respiratory Disorders. Malvern, Pennsylvania: Lea & Febiger: 41-53.

3. De-Lassence A, Fleury FJ, Escudier E, Beaune J, Bernaudin JF, Cordonnier C (1995)

Alveolar hemorrhage. Diagnostic criteria and results in 194 immunocompromised hosts. Am.J.Respir.Crit.Care Med 151: 157-63.

4. Hand WL, King TN (1983)
Effect of erythrocyte ingestion on macrophage antibacterial function. Infect.Immun 40: 917-23.

5. Kahn FW, Jones JM, England DM (1987)
Diagnosis of pulmonary hemorrhage in the immunocompromised host. Am.Rev.Respir.Dis 136: 155-60.

6. McKane SA, Canfield PJ, Rose RJ (1993)
Equine bronchoalveolar lavage cytology: survey of thoroughbred racehorses in training. Aust.Vet J 70:401-4.

7. Oehmichen M (1984)
[Blood destruction in pulmonary alveoli: signs of vitality and determination of survival time]. Z.Rechtsmed 92: 47-57.

8. Perez AJ, Losa GJ, Garcia MM, Gomez GF, Jimenez LA, de-Castro S (1992)
Hemosiderin-laden macrophages in bronchoalveolar lavage fluid. Acta Cytol 36: 26-30.

9. Whitwell KE, Greet TR (1984)
Collection and evaluation of tracheobronchial washes in the horse. Equine Vet J 16: 499-508.

Page 187   **Lopez Rivero JL[1] and Glitz F[2]**

[1]**Muscle Biology Laboratory,**
Department of Anatomy, Faculy of Veterinary Science, University of Cordoba, Cordoba, Spain.
[2] **Clinic for Horses,**
School of Veterinary Medicine, Hannover, Germany

DiMauro S and Tsujino S (1994)
Glycogenoses. In: Myology. Engel, AG and Banker, BQ (Eds). McGraw-Hill Book Co., New York: 1554-1576.

Freeston JF and Carlson GP (1991)
Muscle disorders in the horse: a retrospective study. Equine Vet J 23: 86-

90.

Jeffcott LB, Rossdale PD, Freestone J, Frank CJ, Towers-Clark PF (1982)
An assessment of wastage in Thoroughbred racing from conception to 4 yrs of age. Equine Vet J 14: 185-198.

Lindholm A and Piehl K (1974)
Fibre composition, enzyme activity and concentrations of metabolites and electrolytes in muscles of standardbred horses. Acta Physiol Scand 15: 287-309.

Snow DH and Valberg SJ (1994)
Muscle anatomy, physiology, and adaptations to exercise and training. In: The athletic horse. Hodgson DR and Rose RJ (Eds). WB Saunders, Philadelphia: 145-179.

Tinling SP, Cardinet III GH, Blythe LL, Cohen M and Vonderfecht SL (1980)
A light and electron microscopic study of sarcocysts in a horse. J Parasitol 66: 458-465.

Valberg SJ, Cardinet III GH, Carlson GP and Dimauro S (1992)
Polysaccharide storage myopathy associated with recurrent exertional rhabdomyolysis in horses. Neuuromusc Disord 2: 351-359.

Valberg SJ, Carlson GP, Cardinet III GH, Birks EK, Jones JH, Chomyn JH and Dimauro S (1994)
Skeletal muscle mitochondrial myopathy as a cause of exercise intolerance in a horse. Muscle Nerve 17: 305-312.

Valberg SJ, Macleay JM and Mickelson JR (1997)
Exertional rhabdomyolysis and polysaccharide storage myopathy in horses. Comp Cont Educ Pract Vet 19: 1077-1997.

Valentine B, Credille K, Lavoie JP, Fatone S and Cummings J (1995)
Severe polysaccharide storage myopathy in draft horses. Vet Pathol 32: 566.

Valentine B, Reynolds AJ, Ducharme NG, Hackett RP, Hintz HF, Petrone KS, Carlson MD, Barnes B and Mountan PC (1997)
Dietary Therapy of Equine Polysaccharide Storage Myopathy. Equine

Practice 19: 30-37.

Page 197   **Strand E[1], Martin GS, Haynes PF, McClure JR, Vice JD**

Strand Department of Veterinary Clinical Sciences, Louisiana State University, Baton Rouge, Louisiana and [1]Department of Equine Surgery, Norwegian Veterinary College, Oslo

Cook WR (1988)
Diagnosis and grading of hereditary recurrent laryngeal neuropathy in the horse. J Equine Vet Sci 8: 432.

Derksen FJ, Stick JA, Scott EA, et al (1986)
Effect of laryngeal hemiplegia and laryngoplasty on airway flow mechanics in exercising horses. Am J Vet Res 47:16-20.

Fleming G (1882)
Laryngismus paralytica. Vet J Ann Comp Pathol 14: 1-12.

Haynes PF (1984)
Surgery of the equine respiratory tract. In: Jennings PB (Ed) The Practice of Large Animal Surgery. WB Saunders Co, Philadelphia, USA: 388-487.

Marks D, Mackay-Smith MP, Cushing LS, Leslie JA (1970)
Use of a prosthetic device for surgical correction of laryngeal hemiplegia in horses. J Am Vet Med Assoc 157: 157-163.

Martin GS, Strand E, Kearney MT (1996)
Use of statistical models to evaluate racing performance in Thoroughbreds. J Am Vet Med Assoc 209: 1900-1906.

Martin GS, Strand E, Kearney MT (1997)
Validation of a regression model for standardizing lifetime racing performances of Thoroughbreds. J Am Vet Med Assoc 210: 1641-1645.

Raker CW (1975)
Complications related to the insertion of a suture to retract the arytenoid cartilage to correct laryngeal hemiplegia in the horse. Arch Vet Surg 4: 64-66.

Russel AP, Slone DE (1994)
Performance analysis after prosthetic laryngoplasty and bilateral ventri-culectomy for laryngeal hemiplegia in horses: 70 cases (1986-1991). J Am Vet Med Assoc 204: 1235-1241.

Page 201   Denoix JM, Audigié F, Robert C and Pourcelot P

CIRALE, Clinique Equine – U.M.R. INRA "Biomécanique du Cheval" Ecole Nationale Vétérinaire d'Alfort,
7, avenue du Général de Gaulle - 94704 Maisons-Alfort Cedex (France)
tél : 33 1 43 96 71 08 ; fax : 33 1 43 96 31 62 ; E-mail : denoix@vet-alfort.fr

Audigié F, Pourcelot P, Degueurce C, et al:
Kinematics of the equine spine: Flexion-extension movements in sound trotting horses. In Proceedings of the 5th International Conference on Equine Exercise Physiology, Utsunomiya, 1998, p 64

Audigié F:
Analyse cinématique des troubles locomoteurs de chevaux au trot. PhD Thesis, Université Paris XI - Orsay, 1999

Denoix JM:
Diagnosis of the cause of back pain in horses. In Proceedings of the Conference on Equine Sports Medicine and Science, Cordoba, 1998, pp 97-110

Denoix JM:
Spinal biomechanics and functional anatomy. Vet Clin North Am: Equine Pract 15:27-60, 1999a

Denoix JM:
Lesions of the vertebral column in poor performance horses. In Proceedings of the World Equine Veterinary Association, Paris, 1999b, pp 99-109

Denoix JM, Audigié F:
Effects of back disorders on locomotion. In Proceedings, BEVA special day meeting, 1999

Denoix JM, Robert C, Audigié F:
Neck and back motion and coordination. Vet Clin North Am: Equine Pract. In press

Jeffcott LB:
The diagnosis of diseases of the horse's back. Equine Vet J 7:69-78, 1975

Jeffcott LB, Dalin G, Drevemo S et al:
Effect of induced back pain on gait and performance of trotting horses. Equine Vet J 14:129-133, 1982

Pourcelot P, Audigié F, Degueurce C, et al:
Kinematics of the equine back: a method to study the thoracolumbar flexion-extension movements at the trot. Vet Res 29:519-525, 1998

Pourcelot P:
Développement d'un système d'analyse cinématique 3D - Application à l'étude de la symétrie locomotrice du cheval sain au trot. PhD Thesis, Université Paris XI - Orsay, 1999

Page 221   Lindholm A

Mälaren Equine Hospital,
Hälgesta 1, 193 91 Sigtuna, Sweden

Tuner J and Hode L (1999)
Low Level Laser Therapy; Clinical Practise and Scientific Background. Prima Books in Sweden AB.

Maiman TH (1960)
Stimulated optical radiation in ruby. Nature 187: 493.

Patel CKN (1960)
High-power carbon dioxide Lasers. Sci Am 219: 23.

Jako FG (1972)
Laser surgery of the vocal cords; an experimental study with the carbon dioxide laser on dogs. Laryngoscope 82: 2204.

Page 229   **McIlwraith CW**

1.Annefeld M (1985)
A new test for the standardized evaluation of changes in the ultrastructure of chondrocytes. Int J Tiss React 7: 273-289.

2.Asheim A and Lindblad G (1976)
Intra-articular treatment of arthritis in racehorses with sodium hyaluronate. Acta Vet Scand 17: 379-394.

3.Burba DJ and Collier M (1991)
In vivo kinetic study on uptake and distribution of intramuscular tritium-labeled polysulfated glycosaminoglycan in equine synovial fluid and articular cartilage. Proc Am Assoc Equine Pract 37:241-242 (abstr).

4.Burkhardt D and Ghosh P (1987)
Laboratory evaluation of anti-arthritic drugs as potential chondroprotective agents. Semin Arth Rheum 17: 3-34

5.Caron JP, Eberhart SW and Nachreiner R (1991)
Influence of polysulfated glycosaminoglycan on equine articular cartilage in explant culture. Am J Vet Res 52: 1622-1625.

6.Caron JP, Toppin DS and Block JA (1993)
Effect of polysulfated glycosaminoglycan on osteoarthritic equine articular cartilage in explant culture. Am J Vet Res 54: 1116-1121.

7.Chunekamrai S, Krook L, Lust G et al (1989)
Changes in articular cartilage after intra-articular injections of methylprednisolone acetate in horses. Am J Vet Res 50: 1733-1741.

8.Conte A, DeBernardi M, Palmieri L et al (1991)
Metabolic fate of exogenous chondroitin sulfate in man. Arnzeim-Forsch/Drug Res 41: 768-772.

9.Foland JW, McIlwraith CW, Trotter GW et al (1994)
Effect of betamethasone and exercise on equine carpal joints with osteochondral fragments. Vet Surg

10.Fraser JR, Kimpton WG, Pierscionek BK and Cahill RNP (1993)
The kinetics in normal and acutely inflamed synovial joints: Observations

with experimental arthritis in sheep. Sem Arth Rheum 22: 9-17.

11.Frisbie D, Kawcak CS, McIlwraith CW, Trotter GW and Powers BE (1995)
Unpublished data.

12.Ghosh P, Smith M and Wells C (1992)
Second-line agents in osteoarthritis. In Dixon JS, Furst DE (eds)New York, Marcel Dekker Inc: Second-line agents in the treatment of rheumatic diseases: 363.

13.Glade MJ (1990)
Polysulfated glycosaminoglycan accelerates net synthesis of collagen and glycosaminoglycans by arthritic equine cartilage tissues and chondrocytes. Am J Vet Res 51: 779-785.

14.Gustafson SB, McIlwraith CW and Jones RL (1989)
Comparison of the effect of polysulfated glycosaminoglycan, corticosteroids, and sodium hyaluronate in the potentiation of a subinfective dose of Staphylococcus aureus in the midcarpal joint of horses. Am J Vet Res 50: 2014-2017.

15.Gustafson SB, McIlwraith CW and Jones RL (1989)
Further investigations into the potentiation of infection by intra-articular injection of polysulfated glycosaminoglycan and the effect of filtration and intra-articular injection of amikacin. Am J Vet Res 50: 2018-2022.

16.Hamm D, Goldman L and Jones EW (1984)
Polysulfated glycosaminoglycan: A new intra-articular treatment for equine lameness. Vet Med 6: 811-816.

17.Hilbert BJ, Rowley G, Antonas KN et al (1985)
Changes in the synovia after the intra-articular injection of sodium hyaluronate into normal horse joints and after arthrotomy and experimental cartilage damage. Aust Vet J 62: 182-184.

18.Howard RD and McIlwraith CW (1996)
Hyaluronan and its use in the treatment of equine joint disease. In: Joint Disease in the Horse. McIlwraith CW, Trotter GW (eds), Saunders WB: 257-269.

19.Howard RD, McIlwraith CW, Trotter GW and Nyborg J (1995)
Unpublished data.

20.Kawcak CE, Frisbie DD, McIlwraith CW et al (2000)
Effects of intravenously administered sodium hyaluronate on equine carpal joints with osteochondral fragments under exercise. J Orthop Res (submitted).

21.May SA and Lees P (1996)
Nonsteroidal anti-inflammatory drugs. In: Joint Disease in the Horse. McIlwraith CW, Trotter GW (eds), Saunders WB.

22.McIlwraith CW (1996)
General pathobiology of the joint and response to injury. In: Joint Disease in the Horse. McIlwraith CW, Trotter GW (eds), Saunders WB: 40-69.

23.McIlwraith CW (1992)
The usefulness and side effects of intra-articular corticosteroids - What do we know? Proc 38th Ann Mtg Am Assoc Equine Pract: 21-30.

24.McIlwraith CW and Vachon AM (1988)
Review of pathogenesis and treatment of degenerative joint disease. Equine Vet J S6 :3-11.

25.Noack W, Fischer M, Forster K et al (1994)
Glucosamine sulfate in osteoarthritis of the knee. Osteoarth Cart 2: 51-59.

26.Rydell NV, Butler J and Balazs EA (1970)
Hyaluronic acid in synovial fluid. VI. Effect of intra-articular injection of hyaluronic acid on the clinical symptoms of arthritis in track horses. Acta Vet Scand 11: 139-155.

27.Sandy JD, Flannery CR, Neame PJ and Lohmander LS (1992)
The structure of aggrecan fragments in human synovial fluid. Evidence for the involvement in osteoarthritis of a novel proteinase which cleaves the GLU373-ALA374 bond of the interglobular domain. J Clin Invest 89: 1512-1516. ·

28.Shoemaker RS, Bertone AL, Martin GS et al (1992)
Effects of intra-articular administration of methylprednisolone acetate on normal articular cartilage and on healing of experimentally induced osteochondral defects in horses. Am J Vet Res 53 :1446-1453.

29.Smith MM and Ghosh P (1987)
The synthesis of hyaluronic acid by human synovial fibroblasts is influenced by the extracellular environment. Rheumatol Int 7: 113-122.

30.Tew WP (1982)
Demonstration by synovial fluid analysis of the efficacy in horses of an investigational drug (L-1016). J Equine Vet Sci March/April: 42-50.

31.Trotter GW (1995)
Intra-articular corticosteroids. In: Joint Disease in the Horse. McIlwraith CW, Trotter GW (eds), WB Saunders.

32.Trotter GW (1996)
Polysulfated glycosaminoglycan (AdequanR). In: Joint Disease in the Horse. McIlwraith CW, Trotter GW (eds), WB Saunders: 270-280.

33.Burba DJ and Collier M (1991)
In vivo kinetic study on uptake and distribution of intramuscular tritium-labeled polysulfated glycosaminoglycan in equine synovial fluid and articular cartilage (abstract). Proc Am Assoc Equine Pract 37: 241-242.

34.White GW, Jones EW, Hamm J et al (1994)
The efficacy of orally administered sulfated glycosaminoglycan in chemically-induced equine synovitis and degenerative joint disease. J Equine Vet Sci 14: 350-353.

35.Trotter GW, McIlwraith CW, Yovich JV et al (1991)
Effects of intra-articular administration of methylprednisolone acetate on normal equine articular cartilage. Am J Vet Res 52: 83-87.

36.Roneus B, Lindblad A, Lindholm A et al (1993)
Effects of intra-articular corticosteroid and sodium hyaluronate injections on synovial fluid production and synovial fluid content of sodium hyaluronate and proteoglycans in normal equine joints. Zentralbl Veterinarmed A 40: 10-16.

Page 245   Bathe AP, Humphrey DJ and Henson FMD

Department of Clinical Veterinary Medicine,
University of Cambridge, Madingley Road, Cambridge, England, CB3 0ES
Tel. + 44 1223 339040   Fax. + 44 1223 337672   Email: apb35@cam.ac.uk

Alwan WH, Carter SD, Bennett D and Edwards GB (1991)
Equine vet Journal 23: 44-47
Farndale RW, Buttle DJ and Barrett AJ (1986)
Biochemica et Biophysica Acta 883: 173-177.

Reid Hansen R (1996)
Equine Practice 18: 18-21.

Ronca F, Palmieri L, Panicucci P and Ronca G (1998)
Osteoarthritis and Cartilage 6 Suppl A: 14-21.

Uebelhart D, Thonar EJ-MA, Delmas PD, Chantraine A and Vignon E (1998)
Osteoarthritis and Cartilage 6 Suppl A: 39-46.

White GW (1989)
J Equine Vet Sci 9: 232-233.

White GW, Jones EW, Hamm J et al (1994)
J Equine Vet Sci 14: 350-353.

Page 253   Novales M, Lopez Rivero JL, Hernandez EM, Souza MV, Lucena R

Dpt Animal Medicine and Surgery. Hospital Clínico Veterinario, Campus de Rabanales.
Ctra. Madrid-Cádiz, km 396. 14014 Córdoba (Spain). e-mail: pv1nodum@uco.es

Alvarado AF, Marcoux M, Breton L (1989)
The incidence of osteochondrosis in a standardbred breeding farm in Quebec. Proc Am Ass Equine Practnrs 35: 293-397.

Canonici F, Serata V, Buldini A, Mascioni A (1996)
134 horses with osteochondritis dissecans of the tarso-crural joint: Clinical considerations and results following arthroscopic surgery. J Eq Vet Sci 16: 345-348.

Dik KJ, Keg PR (1990)
The efficacy of contrast to demonstrate "false thoroughpins" in five horses. Equine vet J 22: 223-225.

Firth EC, Goedegebuure SA, Dik KJ, Poulus PW (1985)
Tarsal osteomyelitis in foals. Vet Rec March: 261-266.

Hartung K, Munzer B, Keller H (1983)
Radiologic evaluation of spavin in young trotters. Vet Rad 24: 153-155.

Jeffcott LB (1997)
Osteochondrosis in horses. In Practice (Equine Practice): 64-71.

May SA (1996)
Radiological aspects of degenerative joint disease. Equine vet Educ 8: 114-120.

McDonald MH, Honnas CM and Meagher DM (1989)
Osteomyelitis of the calcaneus in horses: 28 cases. (1972-1987). J Am Vet Med Assoc 194: 1317-1322.

McIlwraith CW (1993)
Osteochondrosis dissecans of the tibiotarsal (tarsocrural) joint. Proc 39th Annu Conv Am Assoc Eq Practnr: 69-72.

Phillips TN (1986)
Unusual hock problems. Proc 32rd Annu Conv Am Assoc Eq Practnr: 663-667.

Pool RR (1996)
Pathologic manifestations of joint disease in the athletic horse. In: Joint disease in the horse. McIlwraith and Trotter (Eds). Saunders WB, Philadelphia: 87-104.

Storgaard JH, Proschowsky H, Falk-Ronne J, Willeerg P, Hesselhot M (1997)
The significance of routine radiographic findings with respect to subsequent racing performance and longevity in Standarbred trotters. Equine vet J 29: 55-59.

Verschooten F, Schramme M (1994)
Radiological examination of the tarsus. Equine vet Educ 6: 323-332.

Widmer WR, Blevins WE (1994)
Radiographic evaluation of degenerative joint disease in horses. Interpretive principles. Comp Cont Ed 16: 907-919.